D1393785

X Internet
The Executable and Extendable Internet

OTHER AUERBACH PUBLICATIONS

Agent-Based Manufacturing and Control Systems: New Agile Manufacturing Solutions for Achieving Peak Performance
Massimo Paolucci and Roberto Sacile
ISBN: 1574443364

Curing the Patch Management Headache
Felicia M. Nicastro
ISBN: 0849328543

Cyber Crime Investigator's Field Guide, Second Edition
Bruce Middleton
ISBN: 0849327687

Disassembly Modeling for Assembly, Maintenance, Reuse and Recycling
A. J. D. Lambert and Surendra M. Gupta
ISBN: 1574443348

Eaches or Pieces Order Fulfillment, Design, and Operations Handbook
David E. Mulcahy
ISBN: 0849335221

The Ethical Hack: A Framework for Business Value Penetration Testing
James S. Tiller
ISBN: 084931609X

Fundamentals of DSL Technology
Philip Golden, Herve Dedieu, and Krista Jacobsen
ISBN: 0849319137

The HIPAA Program Reference Handbook
Ross Leo
ISBN: 0849322111

Implementing the IT Balanced Scorecard: Aligning IT with Corporate Strategy
Jessica Keyes
ISBN: 0849326214

Information Security Fundamentals
Thomas R. Peltier, Justin Peltier, and John A. Blackley
ISBN: 0849319579

Information Security Management Handbook, Fifth Edition, Volume 2
Harold F. Tipton and Micki Krause
ISBN: 0849332109

Introduction to Management of Reverse Logistics and Closed Loop Supply Chain Processes
Donald F. Blumberg
ISBN: 1574443607

Maximizing ROI on Software Development
Vijay Sikka
ISBN: 0849323126

Mobile Computing Handbook
Imad Mahgoub and Mohammad Ilyas
ISBN: 0849319714

MPLS for Metropolitan Area Networks
Nam-Kee Tan
ISBN: 084932212X

Multimedia Security Handbook
Borko Furht and Darko Kirovski
ISBN: 0849327733

Network Design: Management and Technical Perspectives, Second Edition
Teresa C. Piliouras
ISBN: 0849316081

Neural Networks for Pattern Recognition in Scientific Data
Sandhya Samarasinghe
ISBN: 084933375X

Network Security Technologies, Second Edition
Kwok T. Fung
ISBN: 0849330270

Outsourcing Software Development Offshore: Making It Work
Tandy Gold
ISBN: 0849319439

Quality Management Systems: A Handbook for Product Development Organizations
Vivek Nanda
ISBN: 1574443526

A Practical Guide to Security Assessments
Sudhanshu Kairab
ISBN: 0849317061

The Real-Time Enterprise
Dimitris N. Chorafas
ISBN: 0849327776

Software Testing and Continuous Quality Improvement, Second Edition
William E. Lewis
ISBN: 0849325242

Supply Chain Architecture: A Blueprint for Networking the Flow of Material, Information, and Cash
William T. Walker
ISBN: 1574443577

The Windows Serial Port Programming Handbook
Ying Bai
ISBN: 0849322138

AUERBACH PUBLICATIONS
www.auerbach-publications.com
To Order Call: 1-800-272-7737 • Fax: 1-800-374-3401
E-mail: orders@crcpress.com

X Internet
The Executable and Extendable Internet

UNIVERSITY OF WOLVERHAMPTON
LEARNING & INFORMATION
SERVICES

ACC NO. 2418100	CLASS 823
CONTROL NO. 0849304180	004.
DATE -2. JUL 2007	SITE WV	678
		KEY

Jessica Keyes

Auerbach Publications
Taylor & Francis Group
Boca Raton   New York

Auerbach Publications is an imprint of the
Taylor & Francis Group, an informa business

Auerbach Publications
Taylor & Francis Group
6000 Broken Sound Parkway NW, Suite 300
Boca Raton, FL 33487-2742

© 2007 by Taylor & Francis Group, LLC
Auerbach is an imprint of Taylor & Francis Group, an Informa business

No claim to original U.S. Government works
Printed in Canada on acid-free paper
10 9 8 7 6 5 4 3 2 1

International Standard Book Number-10: 0-8493-0418-0 (Hardcover)
International Standard Book Number-13: 978-0-8493-0418-7 (Hardcover)

This book contains information obtained from authentic and highly regarded sources. Reprinted
material is quoted with permission, and sources are indicated. A wide variety of references are
listed. Reasonable efforts have been made to publish reliable data and information, but the author
and the publisher cannot assume responsibility for the validity of all materials or for the consequences of their use.

No part of this book may be reprinted, reproduced, transmitted, or utilized in any form by any
electronic, mechanical, or other means, now known or hereafter invented, including photocopying,
microfilming, and recording, or in any information storage or retrieval system, without written
permission from the publishers.

For permission to photocopy or use material electronically from this work, please access www.
copyright.com (http://www.copyright.com/) or contact the Copyright Clearance Center, Inc. (CCC)
222 Rosewood Drive, Danvers, MA 01923, 978-750-8400. CCC is a not-for-profit organization that
provides licenses and registration for a variety of users. For organizations that have been granted a
photocopy license by the CCC, a separate system of payment has been arranged.

Trademark Notice: Product or corporate names may be trademarks or registered trademarks, and
are used only for identification and explanation without intent to infringe.

Library of Congress Cataloging-in-Publication Data

Keyes, Jessica, 1950-
    X Internet : the executable and extendable Internet / Jessica Keyes.
        p. cm.
    Includes bibliographical references and index.
    ISBN 0-8493-0418-0 (alk. paper)
    1. Internet--Technological innovations. 2. Ambient intelligence. 3. Ubiquitous
computing. I. Title.

TK5105.875.I57.K49 2007
004.67'8--dc22   2006043082

Visit the Taylor & Francis Web site at
http://www.taylorandfrancis.com

and the Auerbach Web site at
http://www.auerbach-publications.com

Dedication

For Friends and Family

Contents

Appendices

Preface

For years, industry insiders have been whispering about a much-needed change to the paradigm of the Internet. For the most part, the Internet remains as it was commercially developed a decade or so ago — a mass of static applications, with little real intelligence or capability. Information is merely displayed, albeit in a pleasing graphical fashion, with a bit of back-end transactional processing thrown in for good measure.

In 1995, MIT's Nicholas Negroponte talked about an Internet that "pervades every aspect of our lives." The executable Internet goes a long way toward achieving this. In 2000, Forrester Research's George Colony invented the term "X Internet," which is actually composed of two components: (1) the executable Internet and (2) the extended Internet.

X Internet fundamentally alters the software and Internet landscapes by blurring the distinction between the two, both online and off, finally leading us into the era of intelligent machines.

This book defines and describes this paradigm from a strategic perspective. Written for the software engineering manager and developer who have hitherto been involved in traditional systems development, X Internet will provide a roadmap that can be used to understand the concepts, terminology, and technologies to start the planning process for building these applications. This book discusses exactly what the executable and extendable Internet is, from a practical perspective. It then delves into the legal aspects of using and creating these systems. Next, it launches into a discussion of computer–human interaction so that one can create an X user experience that is both rewarding and efficient for one's end users. This book also gets into the nitty-gritty of developing in a rich Internet environment, including graphical design, multimedia, architectures, software development techniques, tools, and information management for X-enriched systems.

X Internet: The Executable and Extendable Internet also has a rich set of appendices, including a framework for auditing X systems and various guides for using audio and video and building user interfaces.

X systems offer the organization almost limitless possibilities for building rich, interactive systems that increase productivity and dramatically enhance the user experience. Understanding these systems is critical information for the systems developer and manager.

About the Author

Jessica Keyes is president of New Art Technologies, Inc., a high-technology and management consultancy and development firm started in New York in 1989.

Keyes has given seminars for such prestigious universities as Carnegie Mellon, Boston University, University of Illinois, James Madison University, and San Francisco State University. She is a frequent keynote speaker on the topics of competitive strategy and productivity and quality. She is a former advisor for DataPro, McGraw-Hill's computer research arm, as well as a member of the Sprint Business Council. Keyes is also a founding board of directors member of the New York Software Industry Association and the Mayor of New York City's Small Business Advisory Council. She is currently a professor of computer science and management. She has been the editor for WGL's *Handbook of eBusiness* and CRC Press' *Systems Development Management* and *Information Management*.

Prior to founding New Art, Keyes was managing director of R&D for the New York Stock Exchange and has been an officer with Swiss Bank Co. and Banker's Trust, both in New York City. She holds a masters of business administration from New York University where she did her research in the area of artificial intelligence. She is currently pursuing her doctorate.

A noted columnist and correspondent with over 200 articles published, Keyes is the author of 23 books.

Chapter 1

The Strategic Internet

George Colony is the chairman of the board and CEO of Forrester Research. In 2000, he coined the term "X-Internet," which predicted the end of the Internet as we know it. Colony's idea was that the static Internet would all but disappear, to be replaced by a series of downloadable "executables" that would either replace or add to the functionality on a typical and user's clients PC.

Colony referred to the X-Internet, or "executable Internet," as a Web killer. He predicted that the design for X would emerge from pure research, academia, or open source — just as the Web itself was created. As a result of X, Colony suggested that several things would happen:

1. Web-only companies will get stuck holding the bag. Web-only software will be considered legacy code and, thus, quite outdated.
2. A new wave of X-enabled start-ups will jump into the market blowing away old web infrastructure. Colony refers to this as Internet creative destruction.
3. Peer-to-peer (P2P) networking will skyrocket. Smart executables everywhere will enable an epidemic of Napstering.
4. Companies will need to get ready for another round of change, which means enhancing the skill sets of technologists, modifying Web sites for X, and ultimately dumping Web-centric suppliers.

So, what is an example of how this would work? Suppose that you need to search through large amounts of archive text in a library ("The X Internet," n.d.). A search-specific executable is downloaded that is

1

optimized for your particular task, and the device it needs to run on, and speed that device is capable of — for example, PC, PDA, broadband, dial-up. The executable will also be able to deal with your personal preferences, such as language choice, and authors for which to search. It goes off and does the search and then stores the result somewhere. The executable will probably be smart enough to suggest improved search parameters and even access collaborative filtering data repositories that store what others have found using similar search parameters. If you no longer need the executable, it will be thrown away.

Seven years later, as I write this book, Colony's vision has not yet been fully realized. It is not unusual for research firms to extrapolate possibilities, hoping to start a trend that they can call their own. After all, the value of a research firm is its vision. The more trends that are actually realized, the more valuable the brand of the research firm.

Many disagree with Colony's vision; some even take great exception to his idea. They say that the Internet has always been and will always be extended, from the day that the first e-mail program was created as an afterthought, right up to today, with the proliferation of Java-enabled executables. An example of the latter is Smart Money's Map of the Market (http://www.smartmoney.com/marketmap/), which is a fully interactive Java applet enabling the end user to zoom into the map to focus on a particular sector or industry of interest.

The naysayers are right, of course. However, Colony can be credited with putting a label on a trend that has imperceptibly been taking place.

The use of commercial computers began with a vengeance in the 1960s. By the early 1970s, most large organizations had a massive mainframe buried somewhere in the bowels of their main offices. Back then, computer applications resided on the mainframe with user access to data primarily through paper reports. In the mid-1970s, there was a proliferation of what is referred to as "dumb terminals," similar to what we today call "thin clients," but colored in decidedly green hues and containing nothing but a visual display. Data was still stored on mainframes but end-user access programs, usually quite primitive and often nongraphical, permitted users to view reports and data right online.

When minicomputers appeared on the scene, organizations often began to port data from the mainframe to the minicomputer for departmental update and analysis. This was the beginning of two-tier architectures. In the 1980s, the first IBM-compatible personal computers began to crop up in businesses large and small. These early PCs were very limited in capacity and capability. However, in the 1980s, technological change began to accelerate at a far more rapid pace than it had ever done previously. Before our astonished eyes, the early PC quickly morphed into a very powerful, self-contained computer that was capable of functionality never before seen on such a small device. One can say that the executable Internet started then, before the idea of the public Internet was ever conceived. After all, PC programs such as Excel and Word for Windows provide client-side functionality in executable form. Is this not what Colony was envisioning?

Between the early 1980s and the mid-1990s, the capabilities of personal computers were dramatically enhanced. In fact, the advent of the PC and associated PC programs such as VisiCalc (the forerunner of Excel), Word-Perfect (the forerunner and still contender to Word for Windows), and Power Point were largely responsible for reshaping traditional business mores.

In the mid-1980s, when this author was still at the New York Stock Exchange, we migrated from having a person dedicated to creating 35-millimeter slides for presentations to doing it on our own using Microsoft PowerPoint. At the same time, we migrated from having our secretaries take dictation and type letters to using Word for Windows or WordPerfect and doing it ourselves. The world of the tech-enabled employee was thus born.

By the late 1980s, organizations were creating two- and three-tier architectures, depending on end-user requirements. It was not uncommon to find a corporate mainframe downloading data to a minicomputer for departmental analysis and end users downloading data to PCs for individual analysis. Also around this time frame, researchers and industry pundits began to predict the demise of the mainframe. The reasoning for this made sense. PCs were now cheap and powerful and mainframes were not.

In the early 1990s, services such as America Online and CompuServe were dramatically increasing in both popularity and profitability. Both business and recreational users began to use their PCs to dial into large mainframe services that contained a variety of resources such as information databases, chat rooms, message boards, etc. At the same time, large organizations were finding that even large networks of PCs were not providing the economies of scale or power required by some complex and sophisticated applications. Mainframes, it seems, were back in business. In point of fact, they had never really gone away.

In the mid-1990s, proprietary networks such as America Online and CompuServe began losing market share to this new-fangled thing called the Internet. Of course, the Internet is more than just the Web that we all know and love. In the early days, other services such as Gopher (for distributed document search and retrieval) and WAIS (the Wide Area Information Server) predominated. While these services are still available today in limited venues, they were largely overshadowed in the mid-1990s by the introduction of the World Wide Web (WWW), usually known as just the Web. The killer app back then was the Web browser. Today, the Web browser is still the killer app. However, it has been extended to the point where it can be used to do anything from reading magazines to watching last week's episode of "Lost."

So what we have here is yet another technological revolution. While the technological revolution of the early 1980s empowered the individual worker within the confines of the organization, the technological revolution of the mid-1990s empowered the worker to broaden his or her horizons outside the organization.

The executable Internet and extended Internet beyond it are indeed a technological revolution, similar to the ones we lived through in the 1980s and 1990s. However, it is less a revolution at this point than an evolution.

From X to Extended Internet

Forrester Research has posited a collection of diverse heterogeneous devices that will access the next-generation Internet, the executable Internet, called the X-Internet. The paradigm envisioned by Forrester for the X-Internet represents a vision of an executable network, as compared to a passive collection of Web pages. This re-orientation of the Internet will have wide-reaching implications for the types of devices that connect to it, and the possible future interactions among devices. In the future, the number of Internet-aware devices — devices that can connect to the Internet and speak the Internet Protocol — will increase, and their computing potential will allow them to perform intelligent tasks.

To compare the current Internet to the X-Internet, Colony (2000) uses the metaphor of someone reading a book to a friend, as compared to a full-fledged conversation. As more and more devices access the Internet, they will have sufficient memory so that programs will be loaded into the device as it negotiates access, has conversations, and executes transactions with a server or another peer device. Thus, the ultimate X-Internet will execute programs on devices, and exchange very little data.

The Forrester vision is evolutionary and starts from the Web of today, goes to the X-Internet of the near future, and then to the extended Internet. While the X-Internet will consist of intelligent executable programs that are pushed to the client device, the extended Internet will consist of smart sensors, communicating with smart devices, supported by smart services. Forrester predicts that billions of devices, that can execute real-time business transactions on sensed data, will reside on the extended Internet.

The extended Internet will help support the concept of smart sensors, smart structures, and agent-based systems. Table 1.1 compares the Web,

Table 1.1   From Web, to X Internet, to Extended Internet

	The Web	X-Internet	Extended Internet
Number of devices	Millions	Hundreds of millions	Billions
Focus	Browsers	User-focused software	Devices
Important applications	Web, instant messaging, E-commerce	Responsive experiences	Real-time business applications
Data	HTML, XML	Executables and XML	Environmental data
Model	Server centric	Peer-to-peer	Device centric
Connections	User driven	Opportunistic	Opportunistic
Time frame	1993 to 2001	2001 onward	2005 onward

Source: Forrester Research.

X-Internet, and Extended Internet along various dimensions. In an article related to the X-Internet in *The Industry Standard,* Thompson (2001) cites Forrester as claiming that by 2010, there will be 14,266 million Internet-based devices, with 13,537 million being X-Internet and extended Internet devices.

With this much intelligence and knowledge in the distributed heterogeneous network infrastructure, one can envision various types of devices, such as sensors, actuators, and controllers, organized into complex goal-driven systems that can be used for commerce, education, and man–machine interactions.

Practical X

Colony asserts that X will kill the now-ubiquitous Web browser. Many vendors are in agreement with this, or at least developing a model that mostly excludes use of the browser. Practical xi (www.practicalxi.com) is representative of this breed of vendor. Practical xi applications, written in standard programming languages and using standard Internet data protocols, can be downloaded to a client's personal computer. You might note that this methodology is not much different from the way IT (information technology) has transacted business for the past few decades — that is, an end user downloads an application program to his or her client PC.

Pre-Internet purchasers of hardware and software were given a dial-in telephone number to be able to download updates and new drivers from various vendors. Nowadays, we merely download programs, applets, and scripts from the Internet. So what has changed?

Contrary to what Colony has forecasted, the Web browser is neither dead nor will it die anytime soon. The browser is manifestly useful as the pivot around which X applications will operate. After all, one has to go somewhere to find out about business solutions, sign up for those solutions, and download whatever one needs to download for the very first time. The browser is also useful for accessing the new, rich ASP (application server provider) applications that purportedly died during the dot.crash. Practical xi offers three ways to deploy their particular software. One of them is via ASP, where one is essentially buying a software service with the data residing on the ASP's servers at their location.

The granddaddy of the modern ASP is salesforce.com. Retooled as on-demand "software as service," salesforce.com built more than just an ASP application for salespeople and marketers. The company had the vision to understand that there was also value in providing a foundation for application sharing. The AppExchange provides a way to browse, test drive, share, and install applications developed on salesforce.com's on-demand AppExchange platform. Anyone can offer their apps on the AppExchange directory. As pen is put to paper on this chapter, there are more than 60 apps available, with many of the apps being available for mobile devices. Apps run the gamut from crisis management to collaboration to e-mail marketing.

Another entry into the on-demand marketplace is Microsoft itself. Their new Office Live suite of on-demand applications puts an arsenal of business functionality in the hands of small to medium-sized business owners, as shown in Figures 1.1 and 1.2. Office Live is a set of Web-based services, but with a twist. Added to the mix, and based on Microsoft's SharePoint services, is the ability to share workspaces with clients as well as employees.

So, what we have here is a variety of alternatives to the traditional in-house client/server or mainframe-based system, among them: (1) executable download to a "smart client," (2) on-demand on your server, and (3) on-demand on an ASP's server.

Why is this important? Obviously, in an era of constrained budgets, the TCO (total cost of ownership) of these systems can be astronomical. In addition, the technical talent to support these systems might be unavailable, or far too costly to maintain.

Some would argue that browser-based ASP-driven systems do not have what it takes to be called an X system. The general consensus about the differences between these systems appears in Table 2.2.

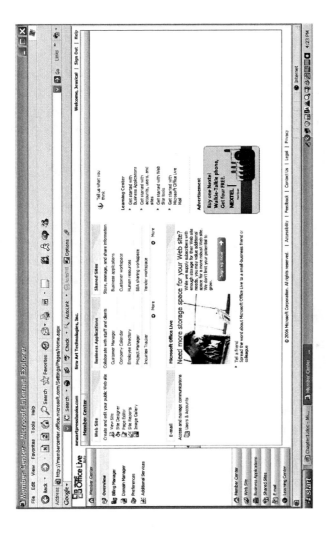

Figure 1.1 Office Live functionality. (Microsoft product screen shot reprinted with permission from Microsoft Corporation.)

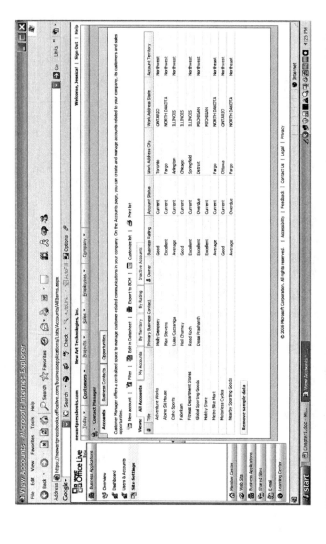

Figure 1.2 The Office Live Customer Manager. (Microsoft product screen shot(s) reprinted with permission from Microsoft Corporation.)

Table 2.2   Browser versus X (based on Practical Xi)

Capability	Browser-Applications	X-apps
Exploits local PC processing power	Display-only	Full power
Web-server requirements	Powerful/expensive	Simple/inexpensive
Application development cost	Expensive & difficult	Cost is 3–5x less
Application deployment complexity	Extensive	One-click Hyperlink
Data integration	Server-end (EAI): expensive	Client-end (desktop office apps): inexpensive
Application performance	Depends on multiple factors	Always fast
Application usability	Yahoo! & EBay look-and-feel	MS Office application look-and-feel
Offline computing	Usually no or pay extra	Yes
Complex data manipulation	No (HTML)	Yes (SQL)
Simple point-and-click	Yes	Yes
Internet/intranet capable	Yes	Yes
Bandwidth requirements	Med–High	Low (minimal)
Scalability of applications	Server dependent	Excellent
Based on standards	Yes	Yes

The fallacy behind this kind of comparison, and Colony's assertion that the browser is dead, is the simple fact that the browser is not in any way similar to the inadaptable mainframe software of yore. As mentioned above, the capability of the browser has grown by leaps and bounds during the past decade, a growth rate that will only accelerate now that there are some viable Open Source browsers (i.e., Mozilla Firefox) vying for market share.

One of the benefits of this increased richness is that the line is now blurred in the area of application usability. Many browser-based applications do sport the "look-and-feel" of Microsoft Office products. One of these is Zoho Writer, a free word processor, as shown in Figure 1.3. Google has recently incorporated the Writely (www.writely.com) free word

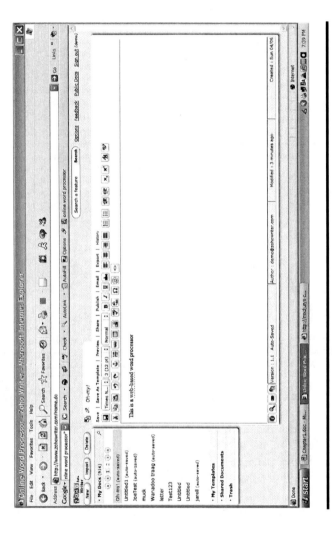

Figure 1.3 Rich user interface of ZoHo Writer.

processor, which also sports a Microsoft Word look-and-feel into its own bag of tricks.

In addition, since the advent of the Java applet, browsers have had the ability to enable download of the executables that form the foundation of X. Essentially, then, the browsers versus executable (or smart client) debate is somewhat moot. Browsers and executables have essentially converged to provide not just "smarts" anywhere, but smarts where appropriate. After all, not all functionality really needs to be downloaded to a smart client. Essentially, as Tim O'Reilly (2005) likes to say, "the value of software is proportional to the scale and dynamism of the data it helps to manage." O'Reilly said this in the context of a discussion on Web 2.0 — the Web on database-driven steroids, allowing the creation of dynamic sites such as Wikipedia and Google.

Conclusion

Software development shops are being bombarded by a barrage of new tools and techniques that they are required to understand, implement, and support. This is due to increasingly sophisticated end-user demands as well as various regulatory, legal, and competitive requirements. However, the structure of IT departments has not changed over the past few decades. Most IT shops decentralize their development efforts, while maintaining a centralized organization for network and systems administration.

Decentralized units often suffer from the "silo effect," where each unit focuses on a single set of related business problems (e.g., customer relationship management). Hence, systems are developed in isolation, which sometimes results in redundancy and always results in disconnected systems. A good example of this is the field of business intelligence (BI). BI is actually a subset of Knowledge Management (KM). However, BI is rarely well-integrated into the other aspects of KM, which also includes Content Management. Hence, it seems, many systems appear to be built in a vacuum. Web-based systems suffer from the same problem.

Unless the organization makes its living from E-commerce, development of the corporate Web site is still considered the domain of the Marketing department. Many corporate IT departments are actually divorced from the entire process, outsourcing the development of the Web site to one of the many Web design firms in the marketplace. These glitzy firms are more graphics oriented as opposed to function oriented. Today's Web sites all suffer from the same "magazine" approach to Web design. That is, the Web site looks less like a system and more like the pages of a magazine. Hence, there is an overuse of graphics and Flash — often for no reason other than the graphic designer wanted to strut his or her stuff.

Of course, there are many Web sites that necessitate being all about glitz. However, there are many more Web sites that need to offer more in the way of function as opposed to form. This is true for corporate intranets as well as the company Web site. But tying form to function is not something with which software development managers are always comfortable.

Hence, software engineering should be somewhat tweaked to incorporate all aspects of X — that is, function as well as form. The remainder of this book attempts to do that.

References

Colony, G.F. (2000). My View: X Internet. Retrieved from http://www.forrester.com/ER/Marketing/1,1503,214,FF.html, Forrester Research, 2000

O'Reilly, Tim. (2005, September 30). What is Web 2.0. O'Reilly. Retrieved April 24, 2006, from http://www.oreillynet.com/lpt/a/6228

The X Internet. (n.d.). Computer Research and Technology. Retrieved from http://www.crt.net.au/etopics/xinternet.htm

Thompson, M.J. (2001). The 'X' in What's Next, The Industry Standard, Retrieved from http://www.thestandard.com/article/0,1902,26675,00.html.

Chapter 2

The Extended Internet

Sony and Philips are co-inventors of Near Field Communication (NFC). NFC works by magnetic field induction. It operates within the globally available and unregulated RF band of 13.56 MHz. NFC specifies a way for the devices to establish a peer-to-peer (P2P) network to exchange data. After configuring the P2P network, another wireless communication technology, such as Bluetooth or Wi-Fi, can be used for longer-range communication or for transferring larger amounts of data. With one tap of a mobile device equipped with an NFC chip, a user can make purchases, access information and services, set up conference calls with colleagues, and much more. It is all done without menus, wires, or complex setups. According to Philips, touching is the clearest way to tell a device what to connect to. For example, if one touches a stadium's turnstile, it means "let me in." If one touches a band's "smart poster," it means "let me hear a sample."

In Germany, people are using NFC-enabled cell phones to buy, store, and use tickets on mass transit systems. In the Netherlands, football fans have turned in their club cards for NFC phones. They are using them to get into the stadium, to buy food and drinks, and to purchase souvenirs. In France, residents are using their phones to pay for shopping and parking, pick up tourist information, and download ringtones and bus schedules from smart posters. At the Philips Arena stadium in Atlanta, Georgia, a major NFC-based trial is allowing fans to get onto the grounds with a wave of their NFC phones. And with another wave, they can buy goods at concession stands and apparel stores just as easily.

Mobile products that incorporate NFC are committed to an architecture that supports the Extended Internet and, with its use, we get a glimpse into the future of X.

Extended Interconnectivity

There are many forces pushing us to adopt the extended Internet, which is just another way of saying interconnectivity everywhere! VoIP (Voice over Internet Protocol) is catching on in many companies, and certainly with consumers. Computer telephony integration, where information is passed seamlessly from a telephone to a customer service representative's computer is now becoming standard practice. The eXtensible Business Reporting Language (XBRL) is now making it possible to exchange data between systems on the Internet without rekeying. Broadband over power lines (BPL), a new technology approved by the FCC in 2004, may bring high-speed Internet access to any location that has access to a power grid. This means that any device plugged into the power grid has the potential for Internet connectivity.

The extended Internet will connect the physical entities in the world to the digital world of information while the executable Internet will provide the rich user experience ("Executable and extended Internets," 2004). The goal is to have vehicles, home appliances, and all other make and manner of nontrivial devices have some kind of link to the Internet.

Michelin's eTires system uses a sensor system that measures air pressure and the temperature of commercial tires. The company also uses RFID (radio frequency identification) to track the millions of tires it has in transit within its supply chain. Caterpillar's MineStar system tracks in near-time the location and status of all Caterpillar machines in a mining field, preventing costly equipment failure. Delta uses sensors to halve its maintenance costs.

OnStar is the leading provider of telematics services in the United States. Telematics is the transmission of data communications between systems and devices. OnStar's in-vehicle safety, security, and information services use Global Positioning System (GPS) satellite and cellular technology to link the vehicle and driver to the OnStar Center. The system uses front and side sensors, as well as the sensing capabilities of intelligent software. Within seconds of a moderate to severe crash, the OnStar module will send a message to the OnStar Call Center (OCC) through a cellular connection, informing the advisor that a crash has occurred. A voice connection between the advisor and the vehicle occupants is then established. The advisor then can conference in 911 dispatch or a public safety answering point (PSAP), which determines if emergency services are necessary.

The sensors can also be used to provide monthly diagnostics on components such as the engine, air bags, and brakes, deliverable to OnStar customers via e-mail.

Sensors such as the ones described above are just what Forrester's Colony was talking about when he predicted the rise of the X Internet.

The extended Internet will connect an organization's IT systems to physical products, assets, and devices (Radjou, 2004). According to research done by Forrester in 2004, most firms today do not collect in-depth data about their assets, nor do they track the location or even status of that asset. However, there are certainly regulatory and legal pressures to do so. The Container Security Initiative and Customs-Trade Partnership Against Terrorism regulations require U.S. firms that import to track inbound shipments in near-time. The FDA, which is charged with enforcing the Bioterrorism Act of 2002, is exerting pressure on the pharmaceutical companies to track such things as pallets of consumer goods. The Department of Defense has dictated that its defense contractors RFID-tag all assets. As one can see, growing pressure from regulators, customers, and competitors to link to the physical world are pushing companies to embrace the extended Internet.

Japan's Ubiquitous Network Society

Japan is on the leading edge of mobile Internet capabilities. In Japan, more non-PC devices are now connected to the Internet than are PCs. The reason for this is Japan's successful implementation and adoption of 3G. 3G is short for third-generation technology. The services associated with 3G provide the ability to transfer both voice data (a telephone call) and non-voice data (such as downloading information, exchanging e-mail, and instant messaging). Japan is currently moving very close to 4G, which will enable them to connect all kinds of objects and devices to their "truly ubiquitous network."

Japanese telecoms have introduced a variety of services, some requiring a refinement of the handsets being used by subscribers. NTT (Nippon Telegraph and Telephone) DoCoMo launched the i-mode service in 1999, which required a handset specifically geared for downloading e-mail, and accessing services such as Internet banking and ticket reservation. In 2001, DoCoMo launched the first Java-enabled handsets offering the i-appli service. This service enables the subscriber to download and run small Java applets. Some are stand-alone, such as games that can be saved in the handset. Others, such as stock quotes, require a connection to a server to provide up-to-date information.

Location-based services in Japan were introduced by NTT in the late 1990s. Ima-doko (which translates to "now where") uses technology that estimates a caller's distance from a wireless transmission tower. DoCoMo's i-area service provides weather, dining, traffic, and other information for 500 areas in Japan, based on location-service technology.

Japanese companies and researchers are investigating or using a wide variety of other extended technologies, aside from cell phones, including (Srivastava, 2004):

1. *Electronic tags.* These are currently being used as alternatives to bar codes for the purposes of physical plant distribution management. However, a study group was formed in 2003 to develop measures to promote the advanced use of electronic tags in fields such as healthcare and education.
2. *Chips.* RFID (radio frequency identification) tags are tiny chips that act as transponders (i.e., transmitters/responders). The chip continuously waits for a transceiver to send a radio signal. When a transponder receives one, it responds by transmitting a unique ID code. RFID tags are widely used to track the location of a tagged item. In Japan, this technology has also been used to great acclaim in a library. This permits the staff to locate a book even if it has been removed from the shelf. In 2003, DoCoMo tested its R-Click service, which delivers information specific to a subscriber's location using RFID tags. The prototype of R-Click has three modes. Koko Dake Click enables the user to stand in one of 10 to 20 areas (cells) in the test area. The user can click a button on his device to receive information about that area. Mite Toru Click enables the user to receive information about a product or service that is advertised on an electronic board that is showing commercials. Buratto Catch automatically e-mails area information as it detects the user moving around the test area. The system actually anticipates the user's movements and e-mails the information before the user enters it.
3. *Integrated circuit cards.* Some DoCoMo mobile phones contain IC cards that enable phone users to use their phones as tickets or cash for services such as transportation or tickets to concerts.
4. *Codes.* The 2D code developed by Japan's DENSO Corporation allows for fast reading of large amounts of text. DoCoMo has released several phones that use this technology, which uses the phone's digital camera to scan text. Japan's T-Engine Forum (http://www.t-engine.org/english/whatis.html), a nonprofit organization that is open to companies from all countries, has developed the "UC (Ubiquitous Communicator) for Business Use," a handy terminal for business use with the ucode resolution function. The newly developed UC for Business use is environmentally resistant to dust and water, and robust, which are the usual requirements

for business use. It also has a longer battery life. Ucodes are obtained by reading authorized RFID ucode tags of 13.56 MHz ISO15693 standard, as well as by using one-dimensional or two-dimensional barcode readers with CCD cameras. They can communicate in a variety of ways, including TCP/IP, VoIP, Bluetooth, infrared, etc.

Practical X

Radjou (2004) lists the extended X technologies that are practical (within the United States in the short term):

1. RFID tags are used to pinpoint product location and content. Target uses RFID to track containers containing its shipments.
2. Wi-Fi can be used by warehouse workers to track inventory on PDAs. Eastman Chemical uses Wi-Fi to let its warehouse workers track inventory on PDAs.
3. Biometrics can be used to identify employees, customers, and partners. Kroger stores use biometric payment systems.
4. Presence awareness is used to determine people's status. This technology promises real-time interactions by enabling contact using the person's choice of device. Ford uses GlobeStar Systems' ConnexALL to alert the first person available on his cell phone.

RFID

RFID, also known as Auto-ID, creates an "Internet of things" according to Schoenberger (2002). She describes a prototype of RFID at a typical Sam's Club. Microchips inside cases of Mach 3 razors and All detergent continually and silently alert wireless sensors that the goods have just arrived at the loading-dock doors. More sensors built into store shelves alert staffers when a product needs replenishment. As a shopper enters the store, scanners identify her clothing by tags embedded in her pants, shirt, and shoes. The store knows where she bought everything she is wearing. A microchip embedded in her credit card talks to the checkout reader. Payment authorization is automatic. A reader at the checkout counter automatically tallies her purchases. No shoplifting here because the reader catches everything she is carrying. As she removes a bottle of detergent, the reader on the shelf recognizes the need to restock and alerts the staff.

Low-end retailers are not the only ones succumbing to the lure of RFID. Prada, the Italian luxury goods designer, is attaching Texas Instruments chips to merchandise in its trendy SoHo, New York store. When customers hang their selections in the dressing room, the chips activate a flat-panel video screen to play clips of models wearing those items, as well as a video of designer Miuccia Prada discussing suggestions for accessories (Schoenberger, 2002).

Table 2.1 provides an extensive list of RFID applications in use today.

Of course, there are some potential problems with the use of RFID. Consumer advocates are rightly concerned about a potential loss of privacy. There is also a security issue surrounding their use. RFID systems that are used to deter car thefts and as a convenience device for the purchase of gasoline can be easily defeated with low-cost technology, according to computer scientists at The Johns Hopkins University and RSA Laboratories.

Their findings indicate that the encryption in RFID microchips in some newer car keys and wireless payment tags may not keep thieves at bay (http://rfid-analysis.org/). Using a relatively inexpensive electronic device, criminals could wirelessly probe a car key tag or payment tag in close proximity, and then use the information obtained from the probe to crack the secret cryptographic key on the tag, the scientists said. By obtaining this key, lawbreakers could more easily circumvent the auto theft prevention system in that person's car or potentially charge their own gasoline purchases to the tag owner's account.

The researchers uncovered the vulnerability while studying the Texas Instruments Registration and Identification System, a low-power, radio-frequency security system used worldwide. The researchers said that more than 150 million of these transponders are embedded in keys for newer vehicles built by at least three leading manufacturers. The transponders are also inside more than six million keychain tags used for wireless gasoline purchases. The computer security researchers discovered a way that tech-savvy thieves can get around the encryption safeguards in these systems.

Other security threats include:

1. Rogue readers introduced into the network
2. Rogue access to legitimate readers
3. Counterfeit tags
4. Rogue tags introduced to cause malicious damage or slow down the network
5. Eavesdropping or insertion of data
6. Competitive analysis of supply chain (e.g., espionage via supply chain dynamics)

Table 2.1   RFID Applications

Transportation	Manufacturing	Security	Finance	Other
Airline transponder	AGV control	Access control	Electronic cash	Animal identification
Container ID	Assembly line ID	Auto immobilizer	Automated fueling	Finish line
Global positioning	Configuration management	Baggage tag	Payphone token	Gambling token
Pallet ID	Factory automation	Boarding pass	Ski tickets	Gas cylinder ID
Parking control	Forklift positioning	EAS	University cards	Laundry tracking
Toll collection	Inventory control	Electronic keys	Food service	Loyalty programs
Traffic management	Maintenance	Fleet management	Time and attendance	Medical device ID
Truck fleet tracking	Paint shop	People locating	Document control	Membership cards
Rail car identification	Process control	Security areas		Mining
Parcel logistics	Tire manufacturing/tracking	Theft prevention		Patient ID/tracking
Vehicle movement	Brand identification	Vehicle access control		Library tracking
Passenger tracking	Supply chain management	Counterfeiting		

Despite these security threats, the rush is on to move toward RFID-enabled devices. The MIT Auto-ID Laboratory (http://autoid.mit.edu/cs/) is dedicated to creating the "Internet of Things" using RFID and wireless sensor networks. Their aim is to create a global system for tracking goods using a single numbering system called the Electronic Product Code. They are now one of a federation of six Auto-ID Laboratories around the world partnering with EPCGlobal Inc., the standards organization responsible for developing the products, systems, and standards necessary to drive this vision. The Auto-ID Laboratories have evolved from the Auto-ID Center, initially founded in 1999 to develop an open standard architecture for creating a seamless global network of physical objects. Funded in part by EPCGlobal, government, and industry, Auto-ID Laboratories are based around the world at MIT, University of Cambridge, University of Adelaide, Keio University, Fudan University, and University of St. Gallen.

Those wishing to get started and have some fun doing so are directed to the book *RFID Toys* (http://www.rfidtoys.net/index.asp) by Amal Graafstra, which will lead you through some very interesting RFID projects.

Wireless Networks

In 2002, Apple introduced Bonjour, which lets one create an instant network of computers and smart devices just by getting them connected to each other. Since its introduction, every major printer manufacturer has adopted the technology so that users can add and remove devices from networks without configuration.

Once a device is connected, the computers and devices take over by automatically broadcasting and discovering what services each is offering for the use of others. Bonjour works over today's most popular standard connection technologies, including Ethernet and AirPort (802.11). It uses the standard, ubiquitous IP networking protocol for its connections, the same protocol that runs the Internet itself. Indeed, all the technologies driving Bonjour are open and part of the standards creation process of the IETF (Internet Engineering Task Force), as is Bonjour itself.

Introduced by Sun Microsystems, Inc., the JXTA technology is a set of open, generalized peer-to-peer protocols that allows any connected device (cell phone to PDA, PC to server) on the network to communicate and collaborate. Project JXTA is an open-source effort that involved the developer community from the start (www.jxta.org). JXTA peers create a virtual, ad hoc network on top of existing networks. In a JXTA virtual network, any peer can interact with other peers, regardless of location, type of device, or operating environment. It works even when some peers and resources are located behind firewalls or are on different network transports.

JXTA technology enables developers to create innovative distributed services and applications. JXTA technology is used to create applications and services that enable people to such things as:

1. Collaborate on projects from anywhere using any connected device.
2. Share computer services, such as processor cycles or storage systems, regardless of where the systems or the users are physically located.
3. Communicate with colleagues across the world using a peer-to-peer network.
4. Share files and information to distributed locations on the network, not just to local hard drives.
5. Connect game systems so that multiple people in multiple locations can play the same game interactively.

The objectives of JXTA are:

1. Interoperability — across different peer-to-peer systems and communities
2. Platform independence — multiple and diverse languages, systems, and networks
3. Ubiquity — every device with a digital heartbeat

JXTA is based on proven technologies and standards such as HTTP, TCP/IP, and XML, and does not depend on any one programming language. Its P2P architecture is shown in Figure 2.1.

The JXTA P2P architecture is usually described as a software stack. It typically has three layers, as shown in Figure 2.1. At the bottom is the core layer that deals with peer establishment, communication management, and other utilitarian services. In the middle is a service layer that deals with high-level concepts such as indexing, searching, and file-sharing. At the top is the layer of applications. JXTA technology is designed to provide a layer on top of which services and applications are built. Sun designed this layer to be thin and small, yet providing interesting and powerful primitives for use by the services and applications. Sun envisions this layer to stay thin and small, because this is the best approach both to maintaining interoperability among competitive offerings from various P2P contributors, and to providing maximum room for innovation (and profit) by these contributors (Gong, 2001).

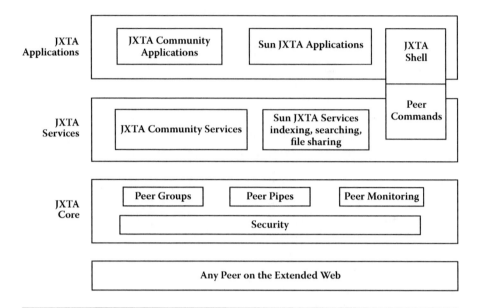

Figure 2.1   P2P Architecture.

Sensors

The Rutgers University WINLAB (http://www.winlab.rutgers.edu/pub/Index.html) is working on a multimode wireless sensor (MUSE). It is a multi-chip module that includes a sensor, RF communications circuitry, a modem, a CPU, and supporting circuits. In addition, WINLAB also developed a wireless sensor network. SOHAN (self-organizing hierarchical ad hoc network) offers significant capacity improvements over conventional ad hoc wireless networks.

The National Center for Supercomputing Applications at the University of Illinois Urbana-Champaign (http://www.ncsa.uiuc.edu/) has developed a thermal infrared (IR) wireless MEMS sensor that calibrates cameras. Micro-Electro-Mechanical Systems (MEMS) is the integration of mechanical elements, sensors, actuators, and electronics. Microelectronic integrated circuits can be thought of as the "brains" of a system, and MEMS augments this decision-making capability with "eyes" and "arms" to allow microsystems to sense and control the environment.

The MIMOSA consortium (www.mimosa-fp6.com) has developed an overall architecture specification for a mobile-device-centric, open technology platform for ambient intelligence. In the MIMOSA vision, the personal mobile phone is chosen as the trusted intelligent user interface

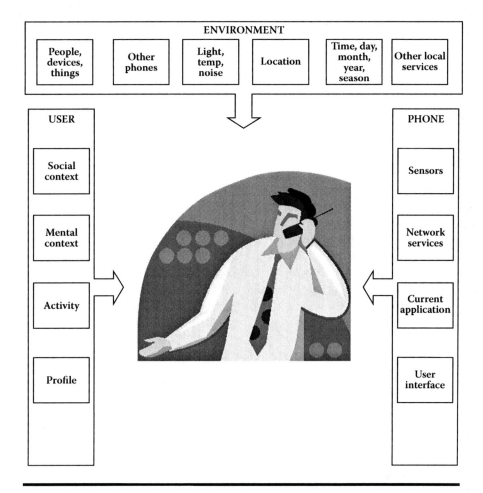

Figure 2.2 Enabling platform for ambient intelligence.

to Ambient Intelligence and a gateway between the sensors, the network of sensors, the public network, and the Internet. MIMOSA provides an open technology platform for implementing ambient intelligence in different application areas. Examples of micro- and nanosystems developments by MIMOSA include (environment domain) wireless remote-powered and autonomous sensors exploiting RFID, low-power radios exploiting RFMEMS; (user domain) microsystem-based intuitive user interfaces, MEMS-based user activity and physiological sensors, (Phone domain) MEMS-based inertial, magnetic, and audio sensors (see Figure 2.2).

Right now, the world of ubiquitous sensing, computing, and communications lacks standard software platforms. However, the University of

California at Berkeley's Tiny Operating System (TinyOS) has now become the tool of choice. TinyOS is an embedded open-source operating system. It is designed to be able to incorporate rapid innovation as well as to operate within the severe memory constraints inherent in sensor networks. TinyOS (http://www.tinyos.net/) is mostly written in C and NesC, with some Java. NesC is a component-based programming language and is an extension of the C programming language.

According to Allan (2006), wireless sensor techniques will eventually mature to permit the seamless interconnection of the physical and virtual worlds. Wireless network technologies such as WiMedia Ultra-Wideband (UWB) (http://www.wimedia.org/en/index.asp) will enable end users to download an entire television show in just one minute. Due to the extremely low emission levels, UWB systems tend to be short range. However, due to the short duration of the UWB pulses, extremely high data rates are possible, and the data rate can be readily traded for range by simply scaling the number of pulses per data bit. High data rate UWB can enable wireless monitors, the transfer of data efficiently from digital camcorders, enable wireless printing of digital pictures from a camera without the need of an intervening personal computer, and the transfer of files among cell phone handsets and other handheld devices such as personal digital audio and video players.

Conclusion

Radjou (2004) has analyzed just who will be using extended Internet systems:

1. Firms will use X to achieve functional enhancement — that is, to squeeze efficiency out of a specific function. A National Science Foundation study has shown that manufacturers can save 51 percent in asset maintenance by using X Internet-enabled predictive analytics software.
2. Firms will increase their flexibility by using the X Internet to optimize end-to-end processes such as stemming quality issues and enabling JIT store-level replenishment.
3. Firms will reinvent their business model using X-Internet. Expert asset users will become service providers. For example, half of ChevronTexaco's plant operators will be retiring over the next few years. Duke Energy, having mastered the art of asset maintenance using the X Internet, is spinning off its internal maintenance staff into an outsourced service firm.

References

Allan, R. (2006, March 30). Wireless Sensing Spawns the Connected World, *Electronic Design,* 54(7), p. 49.

Executable and extended Internets (2004, May 6). The Hindu. Retrieved fromhttp://www.hinduonnet.com/thehindu/thscrip/print.pl?file=2004050600331600.htm&date=2004/05/06/&prd=seta&

Gong, L. (2001). Project JXTA: A Technology Overview. Sun Microsystems. Retrieved from http://www.jxta.org/project/www/docs/jxtaview_01nov02.pdf

Radjou, N. (2004, January/February). The X Internet Invigorates Supply Chains. *Industrial Management,* p. 13–17.

Schoenberger, C.R. (2002, March 18). The Internet of Things. *Forbes.*

Srivastava, L. (2004). Japan's ubiquitous mobile information society. *The Journal of Policy, Regulation and Strategy for Telecommunications, Information and Media,* 6(4), p. 234.

Chapter 3

The Legal Aspects of X

Because we define X as an object, the combination of downloadable executables along with some content and functionality retrievable from a Web server, it is entirely possible that the legal issues surrounding this combined approach become a bit muddied. This chapter addresses typical legal issues surrounding a basic Web site. Then it delves into the issues surrounding those X executables.

Web Site Legal Issues

The legal issues confronting an organization creating a Web site include (1) construction of a viable privacy policy, (2) ensuring that visitors are aware of the terms and conditions of use, and (3) protection of proprietary intellectual property.

Privacy Policy

Web site visitors have every right to be concerned that their private information will be protected. The posting of a privacy policy (see Appendix J) and the knowledge that the visitor will be adhering to its strict regulations serve to comfort the user and, more important, protect organizations from lawsuits. They know you are up-to-date on all global laws and regulations. They know you are aware that if you plan to resell this data, these transactions will be under the scrutiny of governmental and consumer watchdogs. Listed below are the main points to address in such a policy.

1. What information is being collected?
2. Who is doing the collecting?
3. How will the information be used?
4. With whom can the information be shared?
5. What choices does the consumer have in the collection, use, and distribution of the information? Can they opt out? How?
6. What type of security procedures have been put in place to protect the loss, misuse, or alteration of information?
7. How can the consumer correct any inaccuracies?

It should be noted that a number of organizations have developed oversight programs to certify that a specific Web site bearing its certification seal has policies in place that make it trustworthy and reliable with regard to consumer information (e.g., TRUSTe, the AICPA, and the Better Business Bureau, "BBBOnline").

If one or more components are provided as downloadable "X" executables, then the end user needs to be reassured that the software being downloaded is not going to be used for nefarious purposes, as has been the case with spyware and adware.

In fact, X often works similarly to spyware and adware products. An end user visits a Web site and downloads a small utility for use. In the case of spyware, it has also been reported that some end users do not even actually request download of the software. The software self-downloads using a "drive-by download" technique just by virtue of the end user having visited a particular Web site. Often, the utility, such as a Web accelerator, is accompanied by additional software downloads that were not actually authorized by the end users. It is these extras that serve up the ads and track the end user's clicks for reporting back to a central "spyware" server. Once spyware and adware are resident on a computer, without the use of spyware removal software, it is difficult to figure out where the programs are stored and what they are actually doing.

Adware and spyware and executables are really no different from the executables we are discussing in this book except that, presumably, the purposes of our executables are legitimate and requested by the end users.

Because software executing on someone's PC has access to all files on that PC and also has the ability to monitor use of that PC, the privacy policy must be extended to include information specific to the use of executables:

1. What will be reviewed or altered?
2. What will be uploaded to the servers?
3. What will be downloaded to the PC?
4. How will information reviewed or uploaded be used?
5. How can the end user modify the executables' abilities to review or upload personal information?

Terms and Conditions

Written in clear, easy-to-understand language, the Web site terms and conditions (Appendix H) will detail to visitors their rights and responsibilities in relation to their interaction with the Web site and any executables downloaded from that Web site. Of prime consideration when considering these terms and conditions is the precise nature of the goods and services offered. For example, if the Web site contains bulletin boards or chat rooms, it must be clearly stipulated who owns what rights to the posted material. The terms and conditions should also provide an indemnification of the organization in case the posted material infringes a third party's rights.

Standard provisions of Web site terms and conditions should include:

1. *A limitation of liability statement.* This limits organization's responsibility for any damages in case of a legal challenge. This is particularly important in cases where executables will be downloaded. Because executables are software, the typical "shrink-wrap" licensing agreement will usually be the method of choice. These End User License Agreements (commonly referred to as EULAs) serve both as a contract and a liability disclaimer (see Appendix I). The EULA should be easily accessible right from the executables Help menu, similar to traditional software such as Microsoft's Outlook (Figure 3.1)
2. *A statement of the applicable governing law and jurisdiction.* That is, the Web site should indicate which state or country will govern a dispute and where disputes will be resolved, which is usually the country, state, and municipality in which the organization is located.
3. *A statement of the organization's proprietary rights for content.* This includes a list of all copyrights and trademarks, and should also specify ownership of the text and imagery. There should be a disclaimer that notifies users that the organization does not make any express or implied warranties regarding the currency of content on the site and does not guarantee "uptime" of the site.

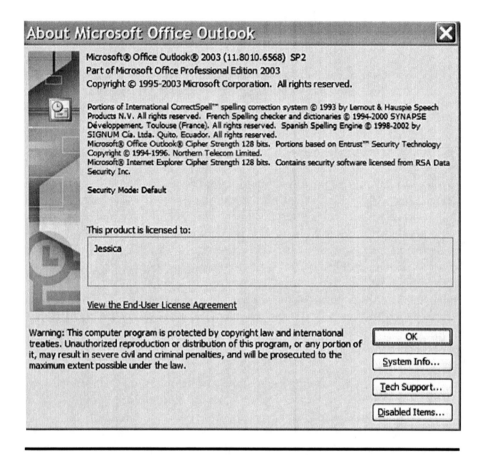

Figure 3.1 Executables will require that the EULA is prominently displayed.

False Advertising and Unfair Competition

Organizations must be cautious regarding how they laud the benefits of using their products. Statements made on Web sites and about software (i.e., the downloadable executables) are subject to Federal Trade Commission (FTC) regulations and the common laws concerning false advertising and unfair competition.

The FTC has the authority to require that an organization provide the "reasonable basis" under which it makes advertising statements. For example, the FTC might find fault with a company for making the claim that it provides the fastest possible connection at the lowest cost.

A legal dispute might also arise in situations where a Web site has linked to a third-party site in such as way as to disguise the fact that information is actually coming from this third-party site.

Organizations should also be aware that they may need to defend against an action brought under foreign laws or by foreign regulatory agencies.

Defamation

Chat rooms and bulletin boards provide ample opportunity for defamation (i.e., harming the reputation of another by making a false statement to a third person.). Interestingly, the more passive an organization is in monitoring these end-user-oriented facilities, the less likely it is that a court will hold the organization liable.

Use of Domain Names

After selecting a domain name, the organization should use the preemptive approach of registering similarly worded names, including misspellings. Google.com evidently did not do this, as typing Goggle.com (not recommended) will get you lots of annoying pop-ups that are completely unrelated to the Google.

Domain names are controlled by registrars. Registrars follow the Uniform Domain-Name Dispute-Resolution Policy (often referred to as the UDRP). Under this policy, most types of trademark-based domain-name disputes must be resolved by agreement, court action, or arbitration before a registrar will cancel, suspend, or transfer a domain name (http://www.icann.org/udrp/udrp.htm).

A dispute proceeding can only be initiated under certain circumstances: (1) the domain name at issue is identical or confusingly similar to a trademark or service mark in which the party has rights, or (2) the domain name registrant has no rights or legitimate interests in the domain name, and the registrant registered the domain name in "bad faith."

Trademarks

Trademark or service mark notices should be notably displayed wherever the marks appear. If a mark is registered with the U.S. Patent and Trademark Office (http://www.uspto.gov/), the "®" symbol should be displayed; otherwise, the "TM" or "SM" symbols should be displayed in connection with trademarks or service marks, respectively. Organizations should be vigilant in protecting their trademarks and service marks. They should be equally vigilant that they do not infringe on the marks of others. Content within an executable as well as content residing on the organization's

Web site should be audited to make sure that no trademark infringement is taking place.

Trademark infringement focuses on the question of whether two marks are likely to cause confusion with each other. Marks are considered confusing if the buying public would think that the products or services covered by one mark come from the same source or are affiliated with the goods or services covered by the previously used mark. Courts use the following factors to assess the likelihood of confusion:

1. The defendant's intent in adopting the mark
2. The relative strength of the plaintiff's mark
3. The similarity of the marks at issue
4. The similarity of the products or services covered by the mark
5. The types of purchasers or consumers and whether any actual confusion occurred
6. The advertising media use

Copyrights

A copyright is a form of protection provided to the authors of "original works of authorship," including literary, dramatic, musical, artistic, and certain other intellectual works such as software, both published and unpublished. The 1976 Copyright Act generally gives the owner of copyright the exclusive right to reproduce the copyrighted work, to prepare derivative works, to distribute copies or audio recordings of the copyrighted work, to perform the copyrighted work publicly, or to display the copyrighted work publicly.

The copyright protects the form of expression rather than the subject matter of the writing. For example, a description of a machine could be copyrighted but this would only prevent others from copying the description; it would not prevent others from writing a description of their own or from making and using the machine.

A work receives copyright protection the moment it is created and fixed in a tangible form so that it is perceptible either directly or with the aid of a machine or device. All text and imagery on a Web site and any associated executables are copyrighted to the organization the moment they are placed on the Web site and inserted into an executable. However, it is important to specify that the Web site, executable, and its works are copyrighted. This is customarily done at the bottom of each Web site page using the copyright symbol — that is, ©. In an executable, the copyright is customarily inserted in the About splash screen usually accessed through the Help menu (see Figure 3.1).

It is also important that the organization audit its Web site and associated executables to make sure that any content, data, or information is not violating anyone else's copyright. For example, an executable dynamically accesses Google and downloads research results to a client PC. Because Google's content is copyrighted to Google, you would need permission to use these materials as a result.

Patents

A patent for an invention is the grant of a property right to the inventor, issued by the United States Patent and Trademark Office (USPTO). Generally, the term of a new patent is 20 years from the date on which the application for the patent was filed in the United States or, in special cases, from the date an earlier related application was filed, subject to the payment of maintenance fees. U.S. patent grants are effective only within the United States, U.S. territories, and U.S. possessions. Under certain circumstances, patent term extensions or adjustments may be available.

The right conferred by the patent grant is, in the language of the statute and of the grant itself, "the right to exclude others from making, using, offering for sale, or selling" the invention in the United States or "importing" the invention into the United States. What is granted is not the right to make, use, offer for sale, sell, or import, but the right to exclude others from making, using, offering for sale, selling, or importing the invention. Once a patent is issued, the patentee must enforce the patent without aid of the USPTO.

There are three types of patents:

1. *Utility patents* may be granted to anyone who invents or discovers any new and useful process, machine, article of manufacture, or composition of matter, or any new and useful improvement thereof.
2. *Design patents* may be granted to anyone who invents a new, original, and ornamental design for an article of manufacture.
3. *Plant patents* may be granted to anyone who invents or discovers and asexually reproduces any distinct and new variety of plant.

In 1993, U.S. Patent 5,193,056, entitled "Data Processing System for Hub and Spoke Financial Services Configuration," was granted by the Patent Office. The USPTO held that the transformation of data, representing discrete dollar amounts, by a machine through a series of mathematical calculations into a final share price, constitutes a practical application of a mathematical algorithm, formula, or calculation because it produces a useful, concrete, and tangible result.

In 1998, in the State Street Bank Decision, the Court of Appeals affirmed this decision. This was significant because previously, "methods of doing business" had not widely been considered patentable. According to many, this is a major reason that led to a boom in software and business method patents. One example of this is Amazon.com's "one-click" patent in which a shopper's profile information, including credit card and shipping address, are stored by a business and then automatically retrieved and utilized when that user wishes to "check out" and purchase an item.

As a result of this ruling, there has been a spate of lawsuits over the use of business processes that probably should never have been patented. It seems likely that there will be many patent cases tried on the basis of X technologies.

Computer Fraud and Abuse Act

Most organizations provide their employees with PCs capable of wireless Internet access. Many companies and home users have installed wireless Internet connectivity in their offices and homes. It is not unusual for people to seek out unsecured "hot spots," as these wireless connections have come to be known. Several computer equipment manufacturers have even developed inexpensive, small hot-spot locators for this purpose. The Computer Fraud and Abuse Act (CFAA) makes punishable whoever intentionally accesses a computer without authorization. Organizations will have to develop a very clear policy warning employees against using corporate-supplied PCs in this manner (see Appendix G).

How Smarts Everywhere Design Will Engender an Epidemic of Napstering

Levy (2001) talks about the hacker ethic: (1) access to computers — and anything that might teach you something about the way the world works — should be unlimited and total; and (2) all information should be free. The second hacker ethic has become a guiding principle of the Internet, oft repeated by tech mouthpieces such as Esther Dyson. Many believe that anything stored on the Internet should be free for the taking.

Modern technology permits anyone with a PC to download and consume various forms of protected creative works, such as music, video, as well as graphic and written arts (i.e., "works"), without payment. Of course, storing copyrighted works on a server and allowing free downloads would get the owner of that server into legal trouble. Shawn Fanning and Napster found a way around this. Of course, Fanning did not actually invent peer-to-peer networks. These have long been used in academic and research settings. What Fanning did was popularize the idea for the masses by creating a file-sharing service for copyrighted music. Because Napster's form of P2P stored only the index to its collection on its server, with the music being stored on its end users' PCs, the company felt that it would win any copyright violation lawsuits that came its way. They were wrong, and shut down in order to comply with a court-ordered injunction that required Napster to stop the trading of copyrighted music, although they have since resurrected as a pay-for-service company.

What is astonishing is that so many people feel that it is permissible to download works without payment. They seem to "tune out" when asked whether they would go into a store and steal a CD. Their response is that the record companies, publishers, artists, etc., overcharge for their products, so downloading for free is a "statement" against this kind of unfairness. One should question whether these people were ever required to take ethics training (civics) in school and whether they are products of a moral upbringing.

Pegasus Originals, based in South Carolina, provides a good view into the future if P2P is allowed to run rampant in our society. The company sells patterns for needlework on its Web site. The company's owner found that another Web site was allowing people to download his artists' copyrighted works at no charge. While Pegasus itself found a way to survive, some of its artists have withdrawn altogether. It should also be noted that Pegasus' survival depends on keeping ahead of those who would break encryption algorithms and find a way to sell Pegasus' designs. All algorithms are ultimately crackable.

The Pegasus case is a bit shocking because the original target of P2P networks was only music. However, today all manner of intellectual property is being targeted, including software. It is obvious that this has ramifications for X. Because executables are in the form of .exe files, Java applets, servlets, etc., it is not much of a challenge for someone to find and copy these files for redistribution using a P2P service. Depending on the functionality or data content of your executable, security and privacy breaches could become a growing concern. For example, suppose a bank provides its customers with an executable that permits the customer to move money between his or her savings and checking accounts. If customer information is contained within the executable, and that executable is pirated, then the customer information will be pirated also. In a P2P Napstering-type environment, this customer information can be replicated and used in a matter of seconds. Appendix F addresses some of the auditing and security concerns of working in an X-enabled environment.

Conclusion

The Electronic Frontier Foundation (http://www.eff.org) suggests that lawsuits against users and distributors will have little effect on P2P traffic. The EFF recommends that copyright owners invest in business-model changes, rather than take to the courts. From developing copyright-protecting software to educating users, the industry is experimenting with making changes. Copyright holders need to acknowledge that new digital technologies have opened up new markets that …hold a potential financial windfall for everyone involved.

References

Levy, S. (2001). *Hackers: Heroes of the Computer Revolution*. New York: Penguin.

Chapter 4

Computer–Human Interaction: The Design Evaluation and Implementation of the Interface

X Internet systems are a fusion of the Web and software micro-programs. Therefore, software developers must be cognizant of "best practices" for developing both Web-based and non-Web-based systems. This chapter's purpose is to discuss some of these best practices as well as provide a set of methodologies for the development of user interfaces in both domains.

Designing the Web-Based User Interface

This author does not know why it is, but the latest generation of techno-pioneers seems to have forgotten that there is such a thing as good design. This problem manifests itself in the overuse of graphics, sloppy layouts, overuse of fonts, and general overcrowding of most of the Web pages considered "cool" by today's standards.

Thomas Wolf, in his searing attack on the art community, *The Painted Word,* decries the pseudo art of our times. Today, talent in the *avant-garde* art community is little more than some broken and bonded crockery or some politically correct, but poorly executed, canvas. Essentially, in today's market, a lack of talent appears to go a long way. The same appears to be true for the graphic arts community.

Good graphics and layout, like good art, are timeless. While Julian Schnabels (he became famous and rich in the mid-1980s for his crockery and bondo canvases) will be scarcely remembered a generation from now, Rembrandt and Picasso will live on forever.

Web pages need to be planned, not just dumped up online. Each organization will have its own unique style. That should be reflected in the organization's Web design as well — unless, of course, the organization wishes to radically alter its style. This usually happens in consumer goods companies that try to alter their image frequently to attract new and improved market share.

One must also keep in mind the target audience. Who are they? Kids? Teenagers, adults, senior citizens? Each of these groups will have a preferred style. Some market research may be in order here.

Before one even gets started, it will be worthwhile to develop a style manual.

The Style Guide

[**Note:** Appendix A (User-Interface Design Guide) and Appendix B (Web-Based System Design Guide) provide more information on this topic.]
This section demonstrates what goes into a sample style guide for a fictitious information management company. The focus of the Sample Company Web site is threefold:

1. *To build Sample Company brand awareness and image.* This is Sample Company's primary mission. While Sample Company is a global company, it might not have the brand awareness of a Reebok or a Coca-Cola. As in its traditional printed media, Sample Company is trying to build its image as *the* information management company. It wants to build awareness of that capability.
2. *To provide a rich source of information on Sample Company and its key partners.* The company wants its server to present an organized, robust view of Sample Company — its services, technologies, markets, global presence and alliances, etc. People who need to learn information about Sample Company and what the company can do should be able to find it — or find how to get

it — on the Sample Company Web site. And they should be able to find it easily, without having to slog through reams of details that are of interest only to those who work within the Sample Company walls.

3. *To serve as a proactive marketing and sales tool.* This means actively soliciting feedback from Web surfers who check into the Sample Company Web site, seeking information about themselves, their areas of interest, their needs, etc. That may involve, for instance, offering token prizes to people willing to fill out an electronic information form. By learning more about visitors, Sample Company can know more about what they are looking for and Sample Company will be able to market services and products to them.

Defining your audience is not easy when it comes to the Web. The tools for measuring specific usage of a given Web site are still primitive, although they are getting better. In reality, the audience for your Web site could be anyone who is out there surfing on the Internet and happens to bump into your site. That could be a college student, a customer, a prospective client putting out a request for proposal, someone looking for a job, or a government official. When developing your Web site, keep in mind how these different audiences might view and react to your message.

That does not mean, however, that you should develop your Web site to do all things for all people. Focus is all-important when it comes to the Web. Remember that the Internet is not a traditional "push" distribution vehicle, but rather a "pull" medium. You do not distribute a Web site to a specific set of readers the way you send out brochures to a mailing list. Your material is out there for viewing by anyone. Your job is to attract Web surfers to it. More specifically, your job is to attract the right Web surfers to it. That means focusing your material and layout on a specific audience.

Planning the Site

Consider this four-step plan:

1. *Determine exactly who your desired audience is.* It is not enough, for example, to say you that want to reach decision-makers at organizations worldwide. Are you targeting executive decision-makers? Technical decision-makers? Programmers? Are you targeting businesses or government organizations? If you are trying to reach potential employees, are you primarily interested in students coming out of college, or workers with experience?

2. *Determine the objective of your Web site.* You have seen the mission of the Sample Company above. What is your mission? To determine that, consider a few questions. What do your readers want? What do they think about Sample Company? What do you want them to think? What do you want them to know? Use whatever tools you have on hand — customer surveys, focus groups, online questionnaires — to tackle these questions. Then put down on paper the objectives of your Web site. Keep that mission statement in front of you. Pin it on your office wall. It will help keep you focused. (And do not forget to update your objectives as time goes on and your organization changes.)

3. *Tailor your Web site material to attract your targeted audience.* If you are recruiting consultants from university MBA programs, for example, you will want to showcase Sample Company service lines, service methodologies, job opportunities, training, and developmental programs. If you are selling voice messaging solutions to communications providers, you obviously need much different material with enough product detail for people to make informed buying decisions.

4. *Finally, remember to keep in mind the corporate image.* Sample Company is a $6 billion information management company doing business with some of the largest organizations in the world. Your Web site should enhance — not detract from — the larger image.

Organizing your Site

Once you have determined the audience you want the Web site to attract and the information you want to present to them, you are ready to create an organization for your material. This is a critical area in the development of your Web site. Without a highly structured, easy-to-navigate framework for your site, you will lose Web surfers right away. Your site organization must be sufficiently simple to get readers quickly to where they want to go, and yet sufficiently deep that, when they get there, they are satisfied with what they find.

The first page (i.e., "home" page) is the most critical element in your structure. It sets up the organizational scheme for your Web site. Think of your job here as creating a "view" to a rich universe of information that lies underneath your home page. What are the areas your audience is most interested in? Make them the entry points on the home page.

Do not make the common mistake of putting too many entry points on your home page. More than seven or eight entry points is probably too many. What you do not want is to put everything under the sun on your home page and immediately create the impression that not enough thought has been given to structuring and categorizing it.

Too many items on your home page is a symptom of a shallow organizational scheme. Many Web sites out there suffer from exactly this problem. Shallow Web sites typically arise due to one of two reasons: either (1) their creators have not spent enough time categorizing and structuring their material before putting it out on the Web, or (2) the site has not been adequately supervised since it was originally created and has since grown out of control like an untended bush. Either way, a shallow Web structure overwhelms viewers, turning them off before they ever become interested.

Equally important, do not create a structure that is so deep that it buries information. You will know you are in one of these Web sites when you keep hitting page after page of menus without getting to any real information. As a general rule of thumb, do not make your viewers dig down more than two or three levels without getting to the information itself.

The ideal Web site structure walks a fine balance between too shallow and too deep. You want to guide viewers down logical paths that get progressively deeper as they go. If you are marketing technology, for example, that path will go from product descriptions to feature functionality to detailed spec sheets — not the other way around.

In creating the pages underneath your home page, stay focused on maximizing ease of navigation and usability of information. A few principles to keep in mind include:

■ Every page must stand alone. Do not assume that every Web surfer will enter a given page by first going through the menu on the home page. Unlike a printed document that first presents a cover to readers, surfers on the Web can enter a site at any point from any number of other points. Include a header or footer on every page that connects to the original entry point on the home page and enough contextual information that the viewer knows where he or she is in the general scheme of things.

■ If your page includes a menu, make sure every menu item includes an adequate description of what it is all about. Nothing irritates Web surfers more than launching down a path not knowing exactly where they are going or whether it is worth their time. For example, do not (as many Web sites do) label a menu item "What's Cool." That is not enough for a viewer to know what that path is all about. Be more precise in your title as to what the Web surfer will find down that path — "Cool New Technologies to Check Out."

■ Likewise, include a short synopsis of every article included in your site. This will let viewers know whether it is something in which they are interested. Focus this synopsis on the benefits to be gained by reading the article.

Organizing Your Articles

Because of the storage power of electronic media compared to printed documents, many of us immediately want to convert lengthy brochures and other tomes into our Web site. Resist that temptation. The attention span of the typical Web surfer is measured in mouse clicks. Make your points up front and then expand on them below for anyone interested.

As a rule, avoid excessively lengthy articles unless appropriate to your audience and the information for which they are looking. Wherever possible, limit your documents to one page of text. Consider the popularity of the *USA Today* newspaper that is slid under the door of your hotel room when you are traveling. The creators of *USA Today* recognized that people today are pressed for time and desire information in short, easily digestible bites.

That does not mean everything must be written this way. Obviously, *The Wall Street Journal* is popular for its substantive articles. However, *The Wall Street Journal* is also extremely well-written, with an easy, anecdotal style that draws in the reader. Let us face it: few of us can write this well. Where longer articles are appropriate and necessary — such as an electronic "white paper" that explains a complex technical subject — include sufficient (and interesting) subheads to retain attention.

Additionally, make use of graphics, charts, photographs, and other appropriate elements to sustain interest and explain the subject about which you are writing. Nothing loses a reader more quickly than a dull page of pure text, especially on the Internet where interactivity and visual excitement are expected.

Creating Links

Finally, in organizing a Web site, pay attention to hyperlinks. These are electronic links to other online resources, either within the Sample Company server or externally to other sites on the Internet. If you are discussing the use of Oracle software technology on your platform, for example, allow the viewer to click on the word "Oracle" and launch into the portion of the Sample Company server that discusses the Sample Company relationship with Oracle and other strategic partners.

Obviously, you do not want to build so many links that readers go off and never come back, and you probably do not want to link to the page of competitors who offer products that compete with yours. Base your links on the informational value they add to your discussion. For example, if you are promoting child welfare solutions from Sample Company, you might want to link to a U.S. Government server that discusses new legislation affecting child welfare. In terms of links to other companies, build on Sample Company's strategic partnerships — Intel, Oracle, Microsoft, etc.

The effective use of hyperlinks can dramatically strengthen your own materials. Equally important, they build the impression that it is easy to do business with Sample Company.

Design and Layout

Graphics, image mapping, sound, movies, and hotlinks provide a wonderful way to show off your creativity. But before jumping into the design and layout of your Web site, consider your audience. Who do you want to impress? How can you best do that? Equally important, how can you make visiting your site a pleasurable experience? How will it help enhance the image of Sample Company?

Foremost, you must ensure that visitors to your Web site easily understand how it is organized and can quickly navigate to the information they are seeking.

Good design seeks a balance between the visual sensation that graphics offer and the text information that those graphics illustrate. Documents that are dense with text, without the visual relief of graphics, will not motivate the viewer to investigate their contents. On the other hand, pages that are heavy in graphics may take so long to download that the viewer will move on quickly, maybe never to return.

Web pages are essentially vertical. Users enter at the top and work their way down through the page. Each page should be no longer than three 640 × 480-pixel screens.

Additionally, the best Web pages usually conform to a grid. A grid is an invisible set of lines that guide the placement of graphics and text. Using a grid you can establish how major blocks of text and illustrations will appear on the page. This helps a visitor understand how the various pages on your Web site are organized, and makes it easier for the visitor to progress to the information needed. This does not mean that every page must look the same as the previous one — just that there is an organizing principle. For example, Sample Company standard dimensions are as follows:

1. Page width is no more than 600 pixels maximum
2. Home page graphic is 600 × 400 pixels maximum
3. The Sample Company logo must be included on all pages
4. Navigation graphic (optional)
5. Navigation via text links
6. Navigation links should always include a link to the Sample Company home page and to the top of your section
7. Following pages banner 600 × 250 pixels maximum

Each Web page should be designed to stand alone. At a minimum, it should identify Sample Company, provide a link to the Sample Company home page, and a link to the top of your section. It should also include a date of creation or revision, as well as links to contacts and the Sample Company statement of copyright.

A good practice is to start your page with a banner that relates to the menu that preceded it or to the contents of the page. The Sample Company logo should be part of the banner of all major pages. Because a Web surfer can jump into your site from many locations, you must let them know that they are in the Sample Company site. The banner should be followed by a head that introduces the contents of the page, unless, of course, the head is part of the banner.

Think about Navigation

Navigation aids are buttons or links that ensure that users can easily get to the information they are seeking. If you have a multi-page section, and provide a link from another section to a topic in the middle of your section, the reader should have an easy way to go to the front of the section and progress forward. Here it is a good idea to provide links for "top of section," "previous page," and "next page," as well as links back to the home page, and to other related sections. If users encounter a dead-end (i.e., a page without links), they will probably leave your site rather than back up through the pages they have already read.

Icons can be fun to create, but you should not make the reader guess what they do. Either provide navigation buttons that state exactly what they do or provide HTML links. It is best to always include HTML links, whether or not you have created graphic navigation buttons. Many users turn off graphics. Navigation buttons or links should be part of the top-of-page banner or near the top of the page. If a user arrives on a particular page and decides that it does not have the information he or she is seeking, make it easy to navigate elsewhere. It may also be appropriate to provide navigation links at the bottom of a page, particularly if the page is several screens long. The point is to make it as easy as possible on the user.

Graphics

Pictures may be "worth a 1000 words" but you must ensure that the viewer benefits from having waited for them to download. Graphics can help the Internet reader understand how to navigate through your site, aid in explaining your message, and make visiting your page a memorable experience — but be careful not to overdo them. This medium is not a multimedia CD-ROM; it is typically transmitted over relatively slow lines to the audience. Any page that takes longer than 20 seconds to download will quickly lose that audience.

Pages that use large graphic image maps as menus will tax the patience of most users. As a rule, each 1K of graphic size requires one second to download on a slow modem. Moreover, image maps, while "cool" in letting the viewer click on a point of visual interest, generally take up much more room than a simple listing of available links. Image maps should be used sparingly and kept to a minimum size — no larger than 600 × 400 pixels.

Inline graphics should be no larger than 22,500 square pixels (150 by 150). As we said, graphics can help break up a page so it is easier to read and more understandable. Still, do not include more than a total of ten individual graphics for a given page.

Color and Backgrounds

Most people who develop pages for the Web work on high-resolution monitors with graphics cards. Many if not most of our audience are using much lower resolution devices. Design your pages and select colors that will effectively present your information to most of our audience. Test your pages on lower resolution monitors and through a couple of browsers before bringing it live.

Be very careful about using backgrounds. While backgrounds can add interest if related to the graphic theme of your pages, they add to the time it takes to download. Excessively textured backgrounds and some colored backgrounds can hinder the legibility of type. Consider that 12 percent of the population is color blind. Red type on a blue background (with similar color saturation) is almost indistinguishable to most color-blind people.

Text Formatting

The HTML language is constantly being refined, as are the capabilities of the various browser packages. Again, it is very easy to get carried away with special formatting that works with one browser (like Netscape Navigator) but looks terrible when viewed by other software. So that Sample Company pages can be successfully viewed by the broadest audience, several HTML programming guidelines are presented in the technical support section of this guide. For this discussion on layout, we recommend that pages include two main heading levels: (1) the HTML H2 heading tag as a main heading for a page and (2) the H3 tag for subheads. You can set apart the body text of a page using standard HTML text formatting codes, including bold and italics. Please do not use blinking text. It is annoying to most viewers and you can get attention in numerous, more sophisticated ways.

Good Web Writing Really Counts

Writing for the screen requires very specific formatting, style and structure. This section should answer many of your questions as to what succeeds and what fails.

Be Succinct

Keep content to the point. The old adage that "less is more" definitely applies in cyber writing. The Web site is not the place for effusive, adjective-laden, abundant prose. Repetition is your enemy — reemphasize previous points but do it succinctly. If it can be said by a word with fewer syllables, say it! Use clear, easy-to-understand copy. Readers who have to run to a dictionary will run away from your site. If the information can be put in table form, do it. Short, quickly digestible paragraphs are the goal. To conclude: concise, sharp copy speeds downloads, decreases eyestrain, and ultimately nips in the bud any desire for the cyber-viewer to wander.

Aim for Scanability

Your main points should "pop." A quick scan should give all visitors a strong sense of where you will take them if future time is allotted for a more in-depth visit. Highlighting, list-making, and proper wording of the title bar will draw their eyes:

■ *The title bar.* The title bar must contain the main point of the page, and if you include your corporate name, keep it short. Department and corporate information should be placed after the title, and all corporate information dropped after the Welcome page. Clear and distinct titling (i.e., images, articles, FAQ, contact us, etc.) allows this information to be quickly found through your search facility. Make sure the titles you give to your various sections (e.g., Images, Articles, FAQs, etc.) are clearly displayed in the title bar. This is where search engines go to find just such information for the reader. Proofread carefully. Always make sure your title accurately reflects what is written on the page. If the pages that follow are sub-topics of that particular title, all should be displayed in your title bar (i.e., Search Engine: Overview; Search Engine: Simple Search; Search Engine: Advanced Search). Most importantly, be consistent — never vary the grammatical structure of your title bar.

■ *Headings and sub-headings.* Make yours meaningful and to the point — flowery, cute descriptions are definitely discouraged. The reader should grasp the gist of what is to come by just the first few words of your header. Provide two to three levels of headlines — it is your outline of the content that follows. It is what will encourage the reader to stay and get more in-depth.

■ *Highlight key words and phrases — and links.* Boldface important words and phrases, but use bolding sparingly, never more than three times in a paragraph. If chosen correctly, these highlighted facts should give the reader a strong sense of the major points to be made. Linked text should contribute to the text; it should not sound stand-alone. It should add to the content. Links should appear at the end of a sentence or paragraph.

■ *Use lists.* Bulleted or numbered lists enhance the readability of your site. If sequential points are being emphasized in a paragraph, pull them out and bullet or number them. Then arrange them in order of importance or shortest to longest (shortest coming first). Group related items together, keeping the style consistent. If you have grouped items, consider sub-heads if your list extends to the next page.

■ *Use menus that make sense.* The menus are the roadmap around your site. Ensure that each item clearly stands out from each other. Use consistent and succinct phrasing. Keep keywords at the left — as readers scan from left to right. Make headlines shout the content of the page.

Keep Paragraphs Focused, Coherent, and Unified

Each paragraph should center around one single idea. Never stray from this focus. Keep all answers sharp and tight. Make the true point stand out. Proper sentence structure demands that you proceed from the familiar to the unfamiliar — the known to the just discovered. Always keep paragraphs short. And most important, never ramble. Always be direct. State the main point at the outset.

Finally, because grabbing attention is your goal, make your first paragraph the "grabber." Let this first paragraph summarize all the points that will follow next in your text. Readers will appreciate this assist, more than likely assuring that they will proceed further down the page.

Ease of Comprehension

Edit sentences, paying particular attention to the overuse of the subordinate clause (such as those beginning with "who," "when," and "where"). One clause per sentence is recommended and it should be placed at the end of the sentence. Other clauses should either be removed (if possible) or turned into separate sentences. Short, to-the-point sentences are your ultimate goal. Ambiguity will be eliminated if you rely on active verbs, have pronouns that are clearly referenced, and use the active voice. Reduce scrolling by placing critical matter at the top of the page.

Program User Interface Design

Like many aspects of software engineering, in order to be effective, user interface design should be analyzed, planned, and implemented in a detailed and organized manner. With the demand for enhanced functionality and the implementation of increasingly complex systems, the pressure to produce user interfaces that satisfy all user requirements becomes a great challenge. Without guiding principles and a fundamental plan of attack, developers are doomed to failure. Fortunately, as computer systems have grown more complex, facilities for creating user interfaces quickly and more efficiently have also come on stream. However, tools alone do not make for a good user interface design.

User interfaces have matured rapidly over the past decade. The increasing speed and power of the PC and the growth of the Internet have fueled the development of larger, more complex applications requiring easier and more intuitive user interfaces. As application developers deliver more sophisticated and robust applications, users expect and demand better and more intuitive user interfaces to accompany those applications. Competition among application developers is fierce, and a product's user interface plays a key role in the adoption and acceptance of a product by its user community.

However, X applications are software with a difference. They are most often micro-code, more akin to Java applets than a traditional program.

Each executable is usually responsible for a single function or a small set of related functions. However, despite these limited requirements, its user interface should adhere to standard software engineering practices. The caveat to all of this is that the software developer must be fully aware of the boundaries between the micro-code and the Web site with which the micro-code might be communicating, and define a user interface that integrates both in a transparent, seamless fashion.

User Interface (UI) Design Principles

No discussion on user interface design would be complete without reference to the underlying principles that guide good user interface design. Volumes have been written on the subject. The following are pointers to a few of the lists of user interface design principles from various sources:

- IBM, "Design Basics," from the Internet:
    http://www-3.ibm.com/ibm/easy/eou_ext.nsf/Publish/6
- Tognazzini, Bruce, "Practical Real World Design, First Principles," from the Internet:
    http://www.asktog.com/basics/firstPrinciples.html
- Hobart, James, "Principles of Good GUI Design," from the Internet
    http://axp16.iie.org.mx/Monitor/v01n03/ar_ihc2.htm

While the perspectives are somewhat different, all espouse the same basic principles. These principles are reiterated here for emphasis:

- *Put the user in control.* The user is obviously the most important player in this game. The user should be able to customize the interface to suit his preferences or needs. Whenever possible, account for the user's skill level; categories such as novice, occasional user, and frequent user provide a good starting point. One example of this is a Macintosh word processing product. A set of five options enables the user to set the desired level of experience, ranging from "novice" to "power user." Choosing a level resulted in filtering menus for only those options required by a user of the selected experience. A user gaining more experience at a specific level could move to the next level when ready.
- *Be direct.* The user should be allowed to work directly with the information presented by the application. When a user performs an action, the result of the action should be immediately apparent.
- *Use appropriate metaphors.* Whenever possible, use metaphors that are familiar to the user. Metaphors help make the user more comfortable when using the software and provides for a more

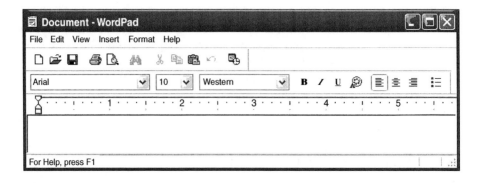

Figure 4.1 Menu order consistency.

intuitive interface. For example, a checkbook is a suitable metaphor for an application that manages a user's bank account.

- *Make the interface consistent.* Consistency in design makes it easier for the user to apply skills learned on one task to another task. Users should not have to spend time trying to remember differences in behavior among objects. Many Windows applications, for example, have the same basic pattern for menus: File and Edit are always the first two menus on the left and Help is typically the last menu on the right, as indicated in Figure 4.1. Regular users of Windows applications have come to expect these menus in this order, and therefore it does not make sense to break this paradigm.

- *Provide shortcuts.* For novice users, shortcuts may not be all that important; but as the user gains experience with the interface, inevitably he will look for faster and more efficient ways of getting his job done. Shortcuts play a key role here and are greatly appreciated by power users. This author knows one technical writer who works in Microsoft Word with both the toolbar and menu bar hidden, doing all formatting work with only shortcuts. Quite amazing!

- *Be forgiving.* The user should be allowed to change his mind and reverse an action that was previously performed. If there are circumstances where it is not possible to reverse the result of an action, provide an indication to the user up front, indicating that the action he is about to perform cannot be reversed. It is also important to make error recovery as easy as possible.

- *Provide feedback.* It is important that the user knows what task is being performed. Everyone knows how frustrating it can be when a program freezes the system while it is performing a task, with no visual indication that the task is being performed or completed. Visual queues should be used to provide user interaction and feedback that is appropriate to the task being performed.

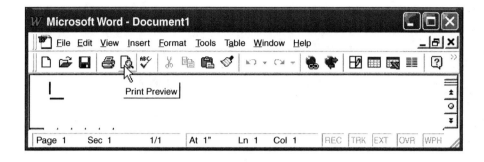

Figure 4.2   Tooltip help.

- *Make the interface aesthetically pleasing.* An important aspect of the user interface is its visual appearance. The visual elements on the screen compete for the user's attention. It is not a simple task to get the right balance so that the user's attention focuses on the right elements at the right time. Often, it is necessary to acquire the services of a graphics designer to get the right result. A professionally designed, aesthetically pleasing application is more likely to gain acceptance among users than one that lacks this characteristic.

- *Be as simple as possible.* This may sound simple but from the developer's perspective, making the user interface simple typically involves quite a bit of work. In a complex application or product, try to develop the user interface that exposes only the information necessary for the user to get the task done.

- *Provide help.* A help system is vital. Many different types of help systems are available. Embedded help is totally integrated within the application; it provides help instructions for every screen that is part of the user interface. Online help, typically accessible by choosing an item from the Help menu, is a set of topics about the product; a table of contents, index, and a search mechanism are typically provided so that the user can browse or search for a topic of interest. Context-sensitive help provides information about the current context; for example, when a specific dialog is displayed, the user can press F1 to get information about that dialog. Tooltip help displays hints; for example, when the cursor hovers over a toolbar button, help text is displayed, as shown in Figure 4.2.

The User-Interface (UI) Design Process

Principles are all well and good, but how and when do we apply them? One of the most popular UI design methodologies is one that mimics the

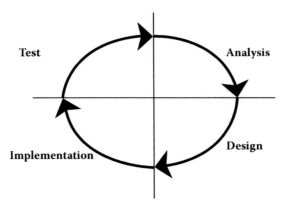

Figure 4.3   Phases of user interface design.

overall software development process. The process consists of four phases, where each phase is repeated on each iteration of the cycle. A summary of the design process is shown graphically in Figure 4.3. Each phase is described briefly below:

1. *Analysis.* This phase involves the collection of information about the user and the tasks that the user will want to perform using the application.
2. *Design.* Once the analysis has been completed and all tasks have been identified, the process of identifying the required objects and the actions to be performed can begin. User scenarios play a key role in this phase. From the scenario narrative, the designer can extract the objects (typically nouns) and the actions (typically verbs) to build a list of the required elements.
3. *Implementation.* In the implementation phase, a prototype is produced. This is typically achieved using one of the many fourth-generation languages or programming development environments that allow the rapid development of user interfaces using pre-defined libraries of components such as windows, menus, buttons, drop-down list controls, tree controls, etc.
4. *Test.* When the prototype is complete, the developer can then take the software to the customer for user interface evaluation. Users can test-drive the software and make suggestions for improvements. These improvements become part of the Analysis phase and the cycle can begin again to further refine the process. Three popular evaluation techniques are (1) expert reviews, (2) user reviews, and (3) interactive usability testing.

One aspect of good user interface design not immediately apparent from the four phases of the design cycle described above is that the design involves input from many different disciplines in addition to software development. These disciplines include visual designers, writers, human factors experts, and, of course, the user. A well-balanced team of people providing input from different perspectives is critical to the success of the user interface.

Designing Effective Input and Output

Some system analysts believe that designing input and output is the most important task in designing a system because it is the part that the end user actually sees. Although some people might disagree with this point of view, poorly designed input and output may cause an otherwise well-designed and solidly implemented system to fail. When system analysts design input and output, there are three aspects of concern:

1. The input and output data (data flow) between software components
2. The design of input and output between the software and other non-human producers and consumer of information
3. The interaction between the user and the computer

A key factor in developing the design input is the customer's requirements. This includes, but is not limited to, end-user expectations, patterns of end-user usage, security, and performance. The customer should not be the only consideration, however. All factors relevant to the design of the system should be considered, including management requirements, interface requirements, and other related processing requirements.

A variety of media and methods are used to capture and input data so that it can be used properly, including:

- Paper forms combined with data-entry screens
- Electronic forms
- Direct entry devices

Designing Paper Forms

Although the usage of computers is very common, it would be surprising to find a system that did not have at least one input or output paper form. Paper forms carry data physically. In every business or organization, there are manual transactions that might require the use of manual forms, such as order forms, sales transactions, and surveys. The data captured on these forms, therefore, must be entered into system for processing. Guidelines for designing a paper form include:

- *Select proper paper.* There are papers of different colors, grades, and weight that can be used to print a form. When selecting a paper for the form, we must consider various factors; for example, how long the company will keep it, how to fill in the form (handwritten or printed), how it will be handled (gently, roughly), and if the paper is easy and convenient to use.
- *The size of paper should be proper.* The most popular size is 8.5 × 11 inches. If you require a smaller form, try to use half of this standard size (i.e., 8.5 × 5.5 inches). For card forms, the standards start with 8 × 10 inches. It is best not to use nonstandard sizes as nonstandard sizes often have problems with regard to handling and filing and usually increase the cost of devices and papers.
- *Forms should be easy to fill out.* To make forms easy to fill out, the following techniques are used:
  - Put simple instructions or examples on the form to assist users.
  - Form flow should be designed to follow a logical sequence (i.e., left to right, top to bottom) (see Figure 4.4).

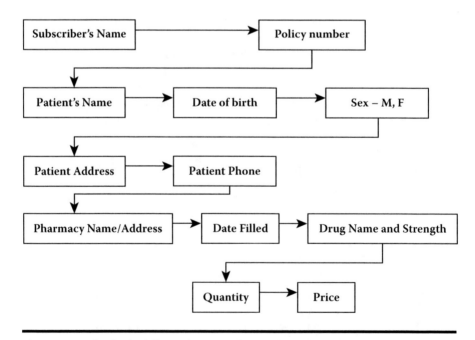

Figure 4.4 The logical flow of a prescription drug claim form.

- Group related data in the same section.
- Each section and field should have a caption that tells the user what to put in that section and field.
- Use proper spacing to make the form clearer.
- The use of lines and boxes can also help.
- There should be an alternative selections capability (e.g., the use of a checkbox).

■ *Design to meet the purpose of a form.* A systems analyst should design different forms to better reflect different process requirements even if several forms are similar to each other.

■ *Make the form attractive.* An attractive form can encourage the user to complete it. A form should be designed to look neat, and the input fields should be logically ordered. Aesthetic forms or the use of different fonts within the same form can help make it attractive.

■ *Design evaluation.* After creating a form prototype, we must give it to the user and check if it meets the user's requirements. The user can provide some suggestions, with the designer making modifications according to the user's suggestions. The evaluation cycle repeats until the users are satisfied with the form.

Designing Electronic Forms

When discussing electronic forms systems (see Figure 4.5), we turn attention from paper to screens (e.g., PDFs, etc.). Designers must design electronic forms to reflect the organization of the data source. When it is used by people (customer, clerk, etc.), it must be designed with all the captions, data-entry fields, and instructions arranged in a logical manner that will help users in completing the form. In addition, the design guidelines for the paper form can also apply to the screen form, and both have the same components.

Electronic forms have many advantages over paper and make the use of this automated capability much more efficient:

1. The ability to process calculations
2. The ability to retrieve data and populate the electronic form to reduce the number of fields that the user must fill in
3. The ability to automatically validate each field
4. The ability to coordinate processes between tasks
5. The ability to provide immediate help

In most situations, the electronic forms can replace all paper forms and substantially reduce the cost of a system. Factors that affect the cost include:

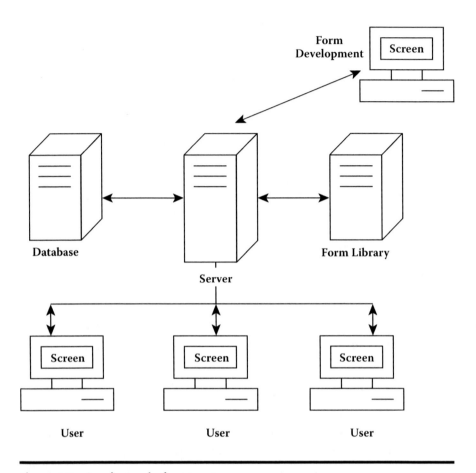

Figure 4.5 An electronic forms system.

1. Printers might run out of paper, which causes the system to pause.
2. Electronic forms can prevent many data entry errors and the end user from using the wrong form.
3. Electronic forms can be easily modified to meet new business requirements.
4. Electronic form databases efficiently manage the many forms in use in an organization.

When using electronic forms, the keyboard is the most common input device. However, there are some instances where data is not input by a user, or a keyboard is not practical. Other data entry devices include:

1. Scanner or optical character reader (OCR)
2. Point-of-sale (POS) device

3. Automatic teller machine (ATM)
4. Mouse
5. Voice recognition

Output can be produced in a variety of ways: printing, screen, audio, microform, CD-ROM, or electronic output. Each technology has a different speed, cost, and effect on the end user. When choosing an output technology, consider the following:

1. The purpose of the output
2. The person who needs the information
3. The reason the output is needed
4. The way the output will be used
5. What specific information will be included
6. How the output will be viewed: printed on paper, stored on secondary storage such as tape, CD, tape, etc. or viewed on the screen
7. How often the output is to be updated; (8) any security issues.

Usability Testing

A user interface design can benefit greatly from usability testing. While usability testing involves quite a lot of up-front investment, the results are worth the investment, especially for commercial applications that have a potentially wide audience. Usability testing involves the observance of users as they use the application to perform their required tasks. The tests are generally administered by human factors specialists and are usually performed in a special work area where the specialists are separated from the user by a one-way mirror that enables the specialists to observe the user as the tasks are performed. Users typically describe what they want to do and how they are going about it using the software. The specialists study these patterns and use the data to improve the user interface. This technique is a very effective means of detecting areas of the user interface that are misunderstood or misinterpreted. These areas can be redesigned and the tests can be performed again to check for improvement.

Conclusion

Providing a good user interface is a critical skill for application developers today. Good user interface design does not happen automatically, despite the myriad tools available to help developers create them.

A good portion of this chapter was devoted to stressing the design principles; this is not an accident. The developer must learn and apply the basic principles and follow the tried-and-true process that leads to quality user interface designs. The formula already exists; it just needs to be applied. The developer must always keep the users' interests in mind, especially when there is a conflict between satisfying a user requirement and taking an easier implementation route. The user interface should strive to delight and help the user get his job done faster and more efficiently. Developers must gain as much experience as possible when working with and being exposed to good user interface designs.

The user interface is a key component when it comes to the acceptance of an application or product — whether it be an executable or a Web site. It can mean the difference between adoption and obscurity.

Chapter 5

The X-Internet Platform

X-Internet enabled systems can be built today using the technologies that are already in place. This chapter first examines the constructs of the Internet's architecture so that we can ascertain its strengths and weaknesses. It then discusses the architectural concerns — and possibilities — of building X systems.

The Internet — A Network of Networks

The Internet is not a monolithic, uniform network; rather, it is a network of networks, owned and operated by different companies, including Internet backbone providers. Internet backbones deliver data traffic to and from their customers; often, this traffic comes from, or travels to, customers of another backbone (Kende, 2000).

End users communicate with each other using the Internet, and also access information or purchase products or services from content providers, such as the *Wall Street Journal Interactive Edition,* or E-commerce vendors, such as Amazon.com. End users access the Internet via Internet service providers (ISPs) such as America Online (AOL) or MindSpring Enterprises. Small business and residential end users generally use modems, cable-modems, and DSL to connect to their ISPs, while larger businesses and content providers generally have dedicated access to their ISPs over leased lines.

Content providers use a dedicated connection to the Internet that offers end users 24-hour access to their content. ISPs are generally connected to other ISPs through Internet backbone providers such as UUNET and

PSINet. Backbones own or lease national or international high-speed fiber-optic networks that are connected by routers, which the backbones use to deliver traffic to and from their customers. Many backbones also are vertically integrated, functioning as ISPs by selling Internet access directly to end users, as well as having ISPs as customers.

Each backbone provider essentially forms its own network that enables all connected end users and content providers to communicate with one another. End users, however, are generally not interested in communicating just with end users and content providers connected to the same backbone provider; rather, they want the ability to communicate with a wide variety of end users and content providers, regardless of backbone provider.

To provide end users with such universal connectivity, backbones must interconnect with one another to exchange traffic destined for each other's end users. It is this interconnection that makes the Internet the "network of networks" that it is today. As a result of widespread interconnection, end users currently have an implicit expectation of universal connectivity whenever they log on to the Internet, regardless of which ISP they choose. ISPs are therefore in the business of selling access to the entire Internet to their end-user customers. ISPs purchase this universal access from Internet backbones. The driving force behind the need for these firms to deliver access to the whole Internet to customers is what is known in the economics literature as *network externalities.*

Network externalities arise when the value, or utility, that a consumer derives from a product or service increases as a function of the number of other consumers of the same or compatible products or services. They are called network externalities because they generally arise for networks whose purpose it is to enable each user to communicate with other users; as a result, by definition, the more users there are, the more valuable the network.

These benefits are externalities because a user, when deciding whether to join a network (or which network to join), only takes into account the private benefits that the network will bring her, and will not consider the fact that her joining this network increases the benefit of the network for other users. This latter effect is an *externality.*

Network externalities can be direct or indirect. They are direct for networks that consumers use to communicate with one another; the more consumers who use the network, the more valuable the network is for each consumer. The phone system is a classic example of a system providing direct network externalities. The only benefit of such a system comes from access to the network of users.

Network externalities are indirect for systems that require both hardware and software to provide benefits. As more consumers buy hardware, this will lead to the production of more software compatible with this hardware, making the hardware more valuable to users. A classic example of this is the compact disc system; as more consumers purchased compact disc players, music companies increased the variety of compact discs available, making the players more valuable to their owners. These network externalities are indirect because consumers do not purchase the systems to communicate directly with others, yet they benefit indirectly from the adoption decision of other consumers.

One unique characteristic of the Internet is that it offers *both* direct and indirect network externalities. Users of applications such as e-mail and Internet telephony derive direct network externalities from the system: the more Internet users there are, the more valuable the Internet is for such communications. Users of applications such as the World Wide Web derive indirect network externalities from the system: the more Internet users there are, the more Web content will be developed, which makes the Internet even more valuable for its users. The ability to provide direct and indirect network externalities to customers provides an almost overpowering incentive for Internet backbones to cooperate with one another by interconnecting their networks.

Peering and Transit

During the early development of the Internet, there was only one backbone, and therefore interconnection between backbones was not an issue. In 1986, the National Science Foundation (NSF) funded the NSFNET, a 56-kilobit-per-second (Kbps) network created to enable long-distance access to five supercomputer centers across the country. In 1987, a partnership of Merit Network, Inc., IBM, and MCI began to manage the NSFNET, which became a T-1 network connecting 13 sites in 1988.

The issue of interconnection arose only when a number of commercial backbones came into being, and eventually supplanted the NSFNET. At the time that commercial networks began appearing, general commercial activity on the NSFNET was prohibited by an Acceptable Use Policy, thereby preventing these commercial networks from exchanging traffic with one another using the NSFNET as the backbone. This roadblock was circumvented in 1991, when a number of commercial backbone operators, including PSINet, UUNET, and CerfNET, established the Commercial Internet Exchange (CIX). CIX consisted of a router, housed in Santa Clara, California, that was set up for the purpose of interconnecting these commercial backbones and enabling them to exchange their end users' traffic. In 1993, the NSF decided to leave the management of the backbone entirely to competing, commercial backbones. To facilitate the growth of overlapping competing backbones, the NSF designed a system of geo-graphically dispersed Network Access Points (NAPs) similar to CIX, each consisting of a shared switch or local area network (LAN) used to exchange traffic. The four original NAPs were in San Francisco (operated by PacBell), Chicago (BellCore and Ameritech), New York (SprintLink), and Washington, D.C. (MFS).

Backbones could choose to interconnect with one another at any or all of these NAPs. In 1995, this network of commercial backbones and NAPs permanently replaced the NSFNET. The interconnection of commercial backbones is not subject to any industry-specific regulations. The NSF did not establish any interconnection rules at the NAPs, and interconnection between Internet backbone providers is not currently regulated by the Federal Communications Commission or any other government agency.

Instead, interconnection arrangements evolved from the informal interactions that characterized the Internet at the time the NSF was running the backbone. The commercial backbones developed a system of interconnection known as *peering*. Peering has a number of distinctive characteristics. First, peering partners only exchange traffic that originates with the customer of one backbone and terminates with the customer of the other peered backbone.

The original system of peering has evolved over time. Initially, most exchange of traffic under peering arrangements took place at the NAPs, because it was efficient for each backbone to interconnect with as many backbones as possible at the same location.

The dynamic nature of the Internet means that today's market structure and relationships likely will change. New services are continually being made available over the Internet. Many of these services, including Internet telephony and videoconferencing, are real-time applications that are sensitive to any delays in transmission. As a result, quality of service (QoS) is becoming a critical issue for backbones and ISPs.

Backbones face a number of private economic considerations in making such interconnection decisions. Any private decision by one or more backbones not to interconnect to guarantee QoS levels for new services may also have public consequences, however, because consumers of one backbone may not be able to use these new services to communicate with consumers of another backbone. This is a particularly important consideration for X-systems.

The decision to interconnect for the provision of QoS services would appear relatively similar to the one that backbones currently make when deciding whether to peer with one another. The backbones each calculate whether the benefits of interconnecting with one or more other backbones would outweigh the costs. The benefits of interconnecting to exchange traffic flow from increasing the network of customers with whom one can communicate. This helps attract new users and encourages usage from existing users. The cost comes from a competitive network externality, as defined above; one backbone's decision to interconnect with another backbone makes the other backbone more attractive to customers. The widespread interconnection available today, in the form of either peering or transit agreements, indicates that the benefits of interconnection currently outweigh any costs.

There is, however, a difference between current interconnection arrangements and new interconnection arrangements for the exchange of QoS traffic. The Internet services that interconnection enables today, such as e-mail and Web access, already are universally available, and no one backbone or ISP could differentiate itself based on its unique provision of these services. Universal connectivity, however, is a legacy of the cooperative spirit that characterized the Internet in its early days. In the commercial spirit that pervades the Internet today, backbones and ISPs can view the new services that rely on QoS as a means to differentiate themselves from their competitors. A firm that introduces these new services may be less willing to share the ability to provide these services with competitors, because such sharing may reduce the ability of the firm to charge a premium to its own customers. For example, a while back, UUNET announced a service level agreement (SLA) that guarantees, among other things, the delivery speed (latency) of customers' traffic on its network. This guarantee does not extend to traffic that leaves UUNET's network, however, which encourages customers to keep traffic on-net.

Even if backbones agree in principle to interconnect to be able to offer new services that require QoS guarantees, they may face practical difficulties in reaching a final interconnection agreement. Aside from disagreements over the terms of interconnection, it is possible that the backbones, or their ISP customers, must support compatible versions of a particular new service to be able to exchange traffic that originates with one backbone's end user and terminates with another backbone's end user. Before committing to a particular standard for this service, backbones may wish to wait for an industry-wide standard to emerge.

This presents a coordination problem that may be difficult to resolve — in particular, if any firms have developed their own proprietary standards that they wish to see adopted as the industry-wide standard. In this situation, despite the fact that backbones would be willing to interconnect to exchange QoS traffic, the end result may be the same as if they were not willing to interconnect — end users would not be able to communicate across backbones using certain services.

Another potential issue relating to interconnection for QoS services is that it may exacerbate current congestion, and therefore it may be difficult to guarantee QoS across backbones. Assuming that interconnection for QoS traffic is implemented under the current settlement-free peering system, backbones will not be paid to terminate QoS traffic. As a result, receiving backbones will have little or no economic incentive to increase capacity to terminate this traffic. QoS traffic that traverses networks may thus face congestion and would be unlikely to provide satisfactory quality. Of course, similar problems exist today with the current peering system, as described above, leading to the current congestion; but given the high data volume characterizing such services, the problem may be worsened. To provide the proper economic incentives to guarantee to customers that they can deliver QoS traffic across networks, backbones may have to implement a traffic-sensitive settlement system for such traffic.

If backbones are unable to overcome the economic, administrative, and technical hurdles to interconnect to exchange traffic flowing from new services requiring QoS, then the Internet faces the risk of balkanization. Backbones will only provide certain new services for use among their own customers. The result would be that network externalities, once taken for granted, would suddenly play a major role for consumers of Internet services. In the current environment of universal connectivity, consumers who simply want to send and receive e-mail and surf on the Web can choose any retail provider without worrying about the choices of other consumers or content providers. If the Internet balkanizes over the offering of new services, consumers would need to become aware of the choices of those with whom they wish to communicate when making their own choice of Internet provider. For example, a consumer who wishes to view real-time streaming video may need to be certain that the provider is connected to the same backbone to ensure high-quality viewing. Likewise, a business that wishes to use the Internet for videoconferencing must make sure that all relevant branches, customers, and suppliers are connected to the same backbone. Thus, any balkanization of the Internet would result in a classic example of network externalities; the specific backbone choice of each consumer would influence the choices of other consumers.

As a result of any balkanization of the Internet with respect to the provision of new services, customers wishing to communicate with a wide variety of others may end up subscribing to competing backbones, unless customers can coordinate on the choice of one backbone. This would raise the specter of the early days of telephony, when competing telephone companies refused to interconnect, resulting in many businesses and even some homes owning more than one telephone, corresponding to multiple local telephone company subscriptions.

There is some danger that a variation of this problem might be in the offing. As recently as November 2005, Vincent Cert wrote a letter to

Congress warning that the major telecoms could take actions to jeopardize the future of the Internet (Yang, 2006). Documents filed with the FCC indicated that Verizon Communications is setting aside a wide lane on its fiber-optic network for the purposes of delivering its own television service. This means that some rivals might be kicked out of the picture, all squeezing into the bandwidth that remains. Verizon contends that it needs to take such measures to earn a return on its network investments. Critics contend that no less than the future of the Internet is at stake. The Internet flourished because entrepreneurs and innovators anywhere, and any size, could reach consumers as easily as rich, large corporations. If Verizon and its peers set up "tools and express lanes," these innovators and upstarts might not be able to afford the fees.

In some cases, notably the personal computer market, more than one standard emerges. This result has nevertheless been influenced by consumer demand, as Apple is widely seen as meeting the demands of a niche market, while the IBM (Intel/Windows) standard meets the more general needs of the mass market. It is worth noting here that it has been Internet protocols and applications, such as Web browsers and the Java language, that have served to meet the demands of users of IBM and Apple's respective platforms to interact seamlessly with one another.

A final example of a standard emerging as a result of marketplace forces is the Internet itself. The protocols at the heart of the Internet, TCP/IP, only relatively recently became the dominant standard for networking, at the expense of a number of proprietary and nonproprietary standards, including SNA, DecNet, and X.25.

Although the marketplace is remarkably successful at generating compatible standards, it would be a mistake to conclude that this process is costfree for consumers or firms. Purchasers of Sony's Betamax VCRs found it impossible to rent or buy movies after the VHS standard won the standards battle, while Sony was forced to concede and begin selling its competitors' standard. The fax machine market was very slow to mature without a fixed standard, delaying the widespread adoption of a product that soon came to be regarded as almost indispensable for both consumers and firms.

IPv6

The next generation of Internet technology is called version 6, or IPv6. While the conversion to IPv6 is going to take quite some time, it is going to enable millions of devices to communicate information online through unique Internet Protocol (IP) addresses. IPv6 uses an address format of 32 numbers, compared to the current format's (IPv4) use of just 12 numbers. Technical papers on this subject say that moving from

12 numbers to 32 numbers will increase the number of possible IP addresses from 4 billion to 340 undecillion, a virtually infinite number. This is exactly what X is waiting for.

X Requirements

X systems are collaborative systems, in that parts of them might reside on the Internet, an intranet, a client — including mobile clients, with each component interacting with the others.

While current architectures certainly do enable X systems, it is worthwhile to spend a little time discussing more advanced architectures that might be available. The first of these is P2P (peer to peer), sometimes referred to as a darknet. Perhaps the best description one can offer for how this works is Shawn Fanning's testimony before the Senate Judiciary Committee in 2000 (http://judiciary.senate.gov/oldsite/1092000_sf.htm). Fanning is the inventor of Napster.

> I began designing and programming a real-time system for locating MP3 files of other users on the Internet. I designed the Napster software to find MP3s because they are the most compressed format (in consideration of bandwidth) and they were very popular at the time. The system I had in mind was unlike ordinary search engines at that time.
>
> A traditional search engine sends out "robots" to roam the Internet periodically, updating itself every hour or more to remove sites that are down or unavailable. The database created is entirely driven by what the central computer finds by "crawling" the Internet. The indexes become outdated as sites go up or down, a significant problem when looking for MP3s because most of the files were housed on people's home computers.
>
> My idea was to have users list the files they were willing to share on a computer that they all could access. That list would then be updated each time a person logged on to and off of that computer. The index computer would at all times have an up-to-date list of the files people were willing to share, and the list would be voluntarily made by the users as they logged on and off the system. A user searching the index would see all the files shared by users on the network and available to others on the network at that moment.
>
> In contrast to traditional search engines, I envisioned a system that would be affirmatively powered by the users, who would select what information they wanted to list on the index.

Then, when the user exited the application, their portion of the list (their files) would automatically drop from the index. The index was only one part of participating in the community. I also wanted users to be able to chat with each other and share information about their favorite music, so I added these functions to the application...

The Napster system I designed combined a real-time system for finding MP3s with chat rooms and instant messaging (functionality similar to IRC). The chat rooms and instant messaging are integral to creating the community experience; I imagined that they would be used similarly to how people use IRC — as a means for people to learn from each other and develop ongoing relationships. I also added a "hot list" function that enables people to see others' musical preferences by viewing the files they have chosen to share. This synergy of technologies created a platform for a community of users interested in music with different channels organized by genres of music (again, similar to IRC), and with genuine opportunity for participation, interaction, and individual involvement by the members' sharing files together.

Napster is a throwback to the original structure of the Internet. Rather than build large servers that house information, Napster relies on communication between the personal computers of the members of the Napster community. The information is distributed all across the Internet, allowing for a depth and scale of information that is virtually limitless.

Napster does not post, host, or serve MP3 files. The Napster software allows users to connect with each other, in order that they may share MP3 files stored on their individual hard drives. The number of song files available at any given time depends on the number of song files that active users choose to share from their hard drives. Users need not share any or all of their files — they can choose which ones to make available to others. MP3 files do not pass through a centralized server. The transfer is directly from computer to computer, known as "peer to peer." The "peer to peer" or decentralized nature of the technology means that the users, and only the users, determine what is shared....

I believe that the peer-to-peer technology on which Napster is based has the potential to be adopted for a many different uses. People generally speak about the ability to share other kinds of files in addition to music, and indeed, Napster has been contacted by entities such as the Human Genome Project that are interested in sharing information among specific communities of interest. But peer-to-peer, or distributed computing, also has tremendous opportunity for sharing resources or computing power, lowering information and transaction costs. Peer-to-peer could be used to create a pool of resources in aggregate to solve a range of complex problems.

Peer-to-peer also has the potential to change today's understanding of the relationship between source and site. Think how much faster and more efficient the Internet could be if instead of always connecting you to a central server every time you click on to a Web site, your computer would find the source that housed that information nearest to you — if it's already on the computer of the kid down the hall, why travel halfway around the world to retrieve it? A number of companies, from Intel on down to small start-ups, are looking at ways to develop peer-to-peer technology, and I believe that many of them will succeed. The result will be not just a better use of computing resources, but also the development of a myriad of communities and super-communities fulfilling the promise of the Internet that its founders envisioned.

P2P then, as shown in Figure 5.1, might be worthwhile to investigate as an architectural framework for X-enabled systems. In a P2P architecture, all client computers in a network act as servers and share their files with all other users on the network. Usually, only specific folders in each machine are made shareable for read access only. In an X-architecture, as shown in Figure 5.2, content as well as executables could reside on a variety of platforms (e.g., various clients, servers, etc.), all centrally indexed on the main servers. In this way, a massively large, somewhat parallel universe of knowledge, content, and functionality can be distributed quickly across one or many organizations and end users.

Another possibility is the one used by online gaming systems. Rosedale and Gamasutra (2003) created an elegant, robust architecture for their Second Life virtual world environment (www.secondlife.com). Second Life uses a distributed grid for computing and streaming its virtual game world. The developers felt that this architecture best supported a large, scalable world with an unlimited amount of user-created and editable content. They also felt that this architecture exhibits a level of performance and content complexity that exceeds any static architecture.

Shards, a term originally conceived by Ultima Online, which is another gaming company, divides an online game into a number of parallel worlds through the use of clustered servers. These have identical sets of world content but different sets of users. The advantage of this approach, referred

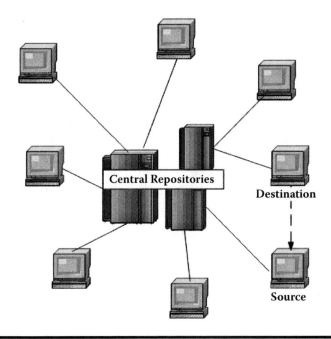

Figure 5.1   Typical P2P architecture.

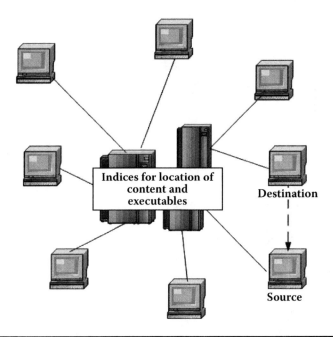

Figure 5.2   A P2X architecture.

to as shard clustering, is that it allows creators to multiply their content development efforts by reusing content across multiple sets of users. A major drawback, however, is that it separates users into separate, noninteracting worlds. This means that friends are not able to collaborate unless they are logged in to the same server. This also has the effect of creating a load-balancing problem.

Putting the entire Second Life worldscape into one world would have presented massive database challenges and would have required at least 100 CD-ROMs to store all content. This challenge was met by the use of a distributed grid approach. This approach is best used when handling a massive number of objects (i.e., an object explosion). Its purpose is to distribute the objects across a large system such that no bottlenecks are created.

Rosedale and Gamasutra (2003) built topologically tiled grids of "nearest neighbor" connected machines. These machines talk only to the four nearest neighbors, so there is no transactional scaling problem as the virtual world becomes very large. The typical bandwidth between adjacent machines is in the hundreds of kilobits per second. Therefore, it is possible that the servers can be in different co-location centers, and do not require connection via gigabit Ethernet or in the same physical cluster.

As objects move around the world, relevant information is transferred from machine to machine as they cross over the edges. Through the use of high-order prediction of the client, which is downloaded to the end user's client PC, the transitions are not visible to the end user.

Second Life's grid topology allows for a tremendously large, seamless world, with computational and storage loads spread across many machines. The Second Life viewer client is itself distributed via the Web.

As is evident, there is a wide variety of possibilities when considering the architecture for an X-system network.

Smart X Structures

The U.S. Government was responsible for the creation of the Internet. As everyone now knows, the Defense Department (DARPA) created the precursor to the modern Internet as a method for crisis and emergency management. Because crisis management is still a major focus, it should come as no surprise that the government is quite forward thinking when it comes to tracking down novel, proposed architectures that will serve to advance the state of the modern Internet. Toward that end, the Office of the Manager in the National Communications System (2002) focused on a variety of "smart X structures" (this author's term) in their discussion of network planning for 21st century intelligent systems and smart structures. This section discusses some of these structures.

Enterprise Nervous System (ENS)

Gartner has introduced the concept of the Enterprise Nervous System (ENS), in which the ENS is an intelligent network that connects people, application systems, and devices — possibly distributed at various locations, within different business units, and using diverse systems — in a real-time, proactive virtual enterprise. Although the ENS is an evolutionary step in system concepts, it is revolutionary in elevating the network to a new level, in that much more of the intelligence will reside in the network, as well as in the applications. The ENS offloads logic from the application systems by supplying higher "quality-of-service" communication, transforming messages, redirecting messages as appropriate (using logical business rules), and sometimes even tracking and controlling business processes (Schulte, 2001).

Intelligent Agent-Based Systems

Forrester's Radjou (2003) predicts the wholesale adoption of applied software agents in stages. The first stage saw software agents used to interpret environmental data. The agent-managed stage, predicted to be prevalent between 2006 and 2008, will make good use of standards such as BPEL4WS (Business Process Execution Language for Web Services) to power net-resident, Web-service infrastructure offerings. BPEL4WS, developed by vendors such as IBM, BEA, Microsoft, SAP, and Siebel (http://www-128.ibm.com/developerworks/library/specification/ws-bpel/) defines an interoperable integration model that should facilitate the expansion of automated process integration in both the intra-corporate and the business-to-business spaces. These same vendors are expected to develop tools that use notation for Agent-Based Unified Modeling Language (AUML) (http://www.auml.org/) such that business agents rather than programmers are able to design agent-based applications. Radjou predicts that by 2009, agent-optimized systems will be common, thus "paving the way for a network of systems and machines, not people."

Intelligent systems originally emerged from the artificial intelligence community. There was a great deal of interest in knowledge-based systems, which are rule-based intelligent systems (also referred to as expert systems). These systems were considered flexible because rule bases could be easily modified. However, in practice, these early systems were often monolithic rule-based systems, and as the intertwined rule base grew in size with often over 1000 interdependent rules, it often became difficult to understand and maintain. More recently, a much more flexible, distributed, and adaptable paradigm has emerged for intelligent systems, namely that of intelligent agent-based systems.

There are many definitions of agents (Milojic, 2000). The dictionary definition of agent is "one that is authorized to act for or in the place of another as a representative, emissary, or a government official." From the standards organizations, the Object Management Group (OMG) defines agents as "computer programs acting autonomously on behalf of a person or organization." The Foundation for Intelligent Physical Agents (FIPA), another standards organization, defines agents as "computational processes implementing an application's autonomous communicating functionality."

Agents vary considerably in their capabilities. While much of the early research was in artificial intelligence, the growth of the Internet has emphasized distributed computing. Java, which has many features for distributed computing, has become a popular language for programming agent-based systems. Distributed Java technologies, in particular Remote Method Invocation (RMI) and Java Intelligent Network Infrastructure (Jini), have provided the distributed application infrastructure for distributed agent-based systems implemented in Java.

An intelligent agent-based system is a highly distributed system in which agents are active concurrent objects that act on behalf of users. Agents are intermediaries between clients, which are typically user interface objects, and servers, which are typically entity objects that store persistent information. Usually, several agents participate in the problem-solving activity, communicating with each other. This leads to a more distributed and scalable environment.

Agents can be categorized in different ways, based on their mobility, their intelligence, or the roles they play in an agent-based system. One categorization is whether the agent is stationary or mobile.

Another categorization is based on the following capabilities:

- Cooperative agents communicate with other agents and their actions depend on the results of the communication.
- Proactive agents initiate actions without user prompting.
- Adaptive agents learn from past experience.

Agents can combine the above three capabilities (Case et al., 2001) as shown in Figure 5.3. Personal agents are proactive and serve individual users — they may also be adaptive. Adaptive personal agents can search for user information in background mode and are often coupled with the World Wide Web. They can refine their search strategies based on how the user reacts to previous searches. Collaborative agents are both proactive and cooperative.

Knowledge Rover Architecture

Another categorization of agents was carried out as part of the Knowledge Rover Architecture, developed in support of the Defense Advanced

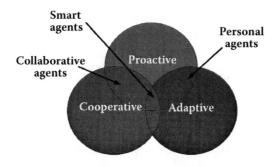

Figure 5.3   Categorization of agents.

Research Projects Agency (DARPA) Advanced Logistics Program. Knowledge rovers are cooperating intelligent agents that can be configured automatically with appropriate knowledge bases (ontologies), task-specific information, negotiation, and communication protocols for their mission into cyberspace. The different agents include:

- *Coordinator agents:* coordinate the activities of a group of agents. They are informed of significant events. A significant event can lead to the activation of new agents. For example, if the enterprise is notified of a payment request, then the coordinator agent would coordinate with other agents in implementing the payment scenario.
- *User agents:* act on behalf of a user and are responsible for assisting users in (1) browsing catalogs and information holdings such as the information repository, (2) the intelligent formulation of queries, and (3) the planning of tasks within a mission-specific scenario such as provisioning logistic support for a disaster recovery effort.
- *Real-time agents:* mission-specific, defined and configured to process incoming data and update the appropriate database or notify the appropriate users. The real-time agents are autonomous, and communicate with each other using a predefined protocol. They are responsible for monitoring the external environment, interacting with other systems, or acting on inputs from users. When an event is detected by a real-time agent, it is signaled to the relevant agents.
- *Facilitation agents:* provide intelligent dictionary and object location services. For example, a facilitation agent might accept a request from the coordinator agent to find all *external* providers of "PCs," and it might respond with the hardware manufacturers and suppliers for the region in question. Other agents such as knowledge rovers (defined below) could then arrange for the items to be requisitioned, retrieved, and paid for. A knowledge rover

could also post a request for bids, accept responses, make contracts, and provision the requested items.

- *Mediation agents:* configured to assist in the integration of information from multiple data and information sources having diverse data formats, different meanings, differing time units, and providing differing levels of information quality. Mediators (Wiederhold, 1996) are configured to accept queries from the coordinator agent, translate the queries into the query language of the appropriate database system, accept the retrieved result, integrate it with results from other sources, and return the information to the coordinator agent for presentation to the user agent.

- *Active view agents:* created to monitor real-time events from the environment or from databases, and to use these events to initiate actions that will result in the update and synchronization of objects in the data warehouse and also in local views maintained at user workstations. These agents are configured to perform very specialized monitoring tasks and have a collection of rules and actions that can be executed in response to events and conditions that occur in the environment or in the databases.

- *Information curators:* responsible for the quality of information in the information repository. They assist in evolving the data and knowledge bases associated with enterprise information resources. They work with knowledge rovers to incorporate newly discovered resources into the information repositories.

- *Knowledge rovers:* instructed to carry out specific tasks on behalf of the coordinator agent, such as to identify which vendors have a specific item on hand. This would involve obtaining information from several vendors. The knowledge rover dispatches field agents to specific sites to retrieve the relevant information. If the knowledge rover obtains similar information from more than one source, it may ask a mediator to resolve the inconsistency. The knowledge rover reports back to the coordinator agent. The rovers are also responsible for Internet resource discovery. These new information sources and their data are analyzed to determine the adequacy, quality, and reliability of retrieved information and whether it should be incorporated into the information repository.

- *Field agents:* specialized rovers that have expertise in a certain domain (e.g., pharmaceuticals) and knowledge about domain-specific information holdings at one or more sites. For example, a field agent could be tasked to monitor all aspects of a single item, say a "PC" produced by several manufactures and distributed by several vendors. The field agent negotiates with the local systems, retrieves appropriate data, and forwards it to the appropriate requesting agent.

Intelligent Integration of Information

The main problem confronting intelligent integration of information in X-systems is to access diverse data residing in multiple, autonomous, heterogeneous databases, and to integrate or fuse that data into coherent information that can be used by decision makers. To make the problem even more interesting:

- Data may be multimedia (video, images, text, and sound).
- Data sources may store data in diverse formats (flat files, network, relational- or object-oriented databases).
- Data semantics may conflict across multiple sources.
- Data may have diverse temporal and spatial granularities.
- Data that is interesting and valuable may reside outside the enterprise.
- Data may be of uncertain quality, and the reliability of the source may be questionable.

Clearly, one cannot expect to solve information integration and other large-scale system problems with a monolithic and integrated solution. Rather, the system should be composed of smaller components, with each component having the requisite knowledge to perform its tasks within the larger problem-solving framework. Thus, the use of *cooperative intelligent agents* holds promise in helping address, discuss, and understand the issues in building next-generation intelligent information systems.

Bird (1993) has proposed an agent taxonomy based on two client/server classes. They are *mobile agents* (clients) for content, communications, and messaging services, and *static agents* (servers). Bird notes that distributed intelligent systems share many of the same characteristics of multidatabase systems (Sheth and Larson, 1990), in particular, distribution, heterogeneity, and autonomy. Knowledge and data would be distributed among various experts, knowledge bases, and databases, respectively, thus making problem solving a cooperative endeavor.

There are several facets to the heterogeneity of information in systems, including:

- *Syntactic heterogeneity* refers to the myriad of knowledge representation formats (Gruber, 1993), data definition formats to represent both knowledge and data.
- *Control heterogeneity* arises from the many reasoning mechanisms for intelligent systems including induction, deduction, analogy, case-based reasoning, etc.
- *Semantic heterogeneity* arises from disagreement on the meaning, interpretation, and intended use of related knowledge and data.

Table 5.1 Three Layer Internet Information Architecture

Information Layer	Layer Service
Information Interface Layer	Users perceive the available information at this layer and may query and browse the data. This layer must support scalable organizing, browsing, and search.
Information Management Layer	Responsible for the replication, integration, distribution, and caching of information.
Information Gathering Layer	Responsible for the collecting and correlating the information from many incomplete, inconsistent, and heterogeneous repositories.

A third characteristic of intelligent systems is that of autonomy. There are several aspects to autonomy — in the control structure of an agent, in the extent to which an agent shares information with other agents, the manner in which an agent associates with other agents, and structural autonomy in the way an agent fits into an organization of agents for problem solving.

Bowman et al., (1994) describe a three-layer architecture for scalable Internet resource discovery, proposed by the Internet Research Task Group. Table 5.1 denotes the three-layer architecture that provides access to heterogeneous repositories, including those on Web servers.

The Intelligent Integration of Information Program identified a collection of services to support the following types of activities:

- *Information Interface Layer:* thesaurus services, information search services, query decomposition and semantic query optimization services, and information presentation services
- *Information Management Layer:* information integration, real-time subscription and notification services, and information mediation services (e.g., knowledge rovers, facilitators, and brokers), and federation services
- *Information Gathering Layer:* wrapper services, query execution services, and data harvesting services

Conclusion

X systems are naturally heterogeneous. Data and function must be distributable across a variety of devices. This is growing in importance as our society becomes far more mobile. For example, over 300 million camera phones were sold in 2005 alone. According to Hewlett-Packard, worldwide penetration is estimated at more than a billion. Tim Kindberg is a senior researcher at HP Labs in the United Kingdom. Kindberg and his associates imagine the camera phone operating like a computer mouse, making the camera phone easier to access mobile content. HP Labs created a camera-based code reader. Similar to scanners at the grocery store, this software enables the camera to read data-rich codes. When scanned, the codes trigger a variety of services. For example, they can open Web content, send text messages, access help lines, or download discounts. The codes themselves can be located in newspapers, magazines, signs in stores, or even on billboards.

Dedicated plug-and-play appliances are also getting some traction in this X-enabled world scene. In 2005, a niche technology called the XML acceleration appliance began to pique everyone's interest. This technology moves the load of XML processing from an application server to a dedicated plug-and-play piece of hardware (Goth, 2006). X, it seems, is going to come in a variety of flavors.

References

Bird, S.D. (1993). Toward a Taxonomy of Multi-Agent Systems, *International Journal of Man-Machine Studies, 39*, 689–704.

Bowman, C.M., Danzig, P.B., Manber, U., and Schwartz, M.F. (1994). Scalable Internet Resource Discovery: Research Problems and Approaches, *Communications of the ACM, 37*, 98–107.

Case, S. Azarmi, N. Thint, M., and Ohtani, T. (2001). Enhancing E-Communities with Agent-Based Systems, *IEEE Computer, 34*, 64–69.

Goth, G. (2006). XML: The Center of Attention Up and Down the Stack, IEEE Distributed Systems Online, 7(1).

Gruber, T. (1993). A Translation Approach to Portable Ontology Specifications, *Knowledge Acquisition, 5*, 199–220.

Kende, M. (2000, September). The Digital Handshake. Connecting Internet Backbones. Office of Plans and Policy Federal Communications Commission Working Paper No. 32. Retrieved from: http://www.fcc.gov/Bureaus/OPP/working_papers/oppwp32.pdf.

Milojic, D. (2000). Agent Systems and Applications, *IEEE Concurrency*, Vol. 8.

Office of the Manager. National Communications Systems. (2002, February). Network Planning for 21st Century Intelligent Systems and Smart Structures: Advanced Concepts in Telecommunications for National Security and Emergency Preparedness. Retrieved from: http://www.ncs.gov/library/tech_ bulletins/2002/tib_02-1.pdf

Radjou, N. (2003). Software Agents in Business: Steady Adoption Curve. Forrester Whole View TechStrategy Research.

Rosedale, P. and Gamasutra, C.O. (2003, September 18). Enabling Player-Created Online Worlds with Grid Computing. Retrieved from: http://www.cs.ubc.ca/~krasic/cpsc538a-2005/papers/rosedale.pdf

Schulte, R. (2001). Designing the Agile Enterprise. Presented at *Application Integration: Moving Toward Total Business Integration,* San Francisco, CA.

Sheth A. and Larson, J. (1990). Federated Database Systems for Managing Distributed, Heterogeneous, and Autonomous Databases, *ACM Computing Surveys,* 22, 183–236.

Wiederhold, G. (1996). Foreword to Special Issue on the Intelligent Integration of Information, *Journal of Intelligent Information Systems,* 6(2/3), 93–97.

Yang, C. (2006, February 6). Is Verizon a Network Hog?, *Business Week.*

Chapter 6

Application Development in a Rich Internet Environment

X-Internet systems use the power of the PC and the Internet to port more intelligent, rich applications to the end user. This includes a variety of multimedia technologies, many of which are unfamiliar to the typical software manager. The feasibility and planning stages of the software development life cycle (feasibility, planning, analysis, design, coding, testing) require that the development team brainstorm the applicability of software tools and techniques as part of the problem solution.

Most of the information in this chapter is old hat to graphic and Web designers. Presumably, there will be a few of these on your development team. However, it is still important that software engineers be cognizant of the functionality and requirements of these sorts of objects such that proper planning, design, and implementation techniques can be used in systems development. Therefore, this chapter provides a cursory look at some of the rich technologies that can be embedded in a Web site or executable.

Multimedia

Multimedia is the use of several different media (i.e., multiple media) to convey information: text, audio, video, graphics, animation. Use of video is sometimes referred to as Webcasting, although the more formal use of the term implies the convergence of broadcasting and the Internet. In 1999, Webcasting was used to broadcast three NetAid concerts. In 2004, Webcasting was used during the Democratic National Convention to give voters the chance to interact with and ask questions of politicians, convention delegates, and media personalities. In general, business uses of multimedia include sales automation, just-in-time training, desktop conferencing, and merchandising.

Animated GIFs, Apple QuickTime audio and video, RealPlayer audio and video, Macromedia Flash, and Shockwave are all examples of multimedia, usable on the Internet and within an executable via plug-ins available on an end user's PC. However, in the case of executables, care must be taken that the download not be so large and so lengthy that the end user exits before its completion. Chapter 8 provides further discussion on Flash.

Equipment required to create multimedia includes scanner, video camera, tape recorder, graphics and animation software, and video and audio adapters. Software that permits someone to create multimedia educational applications is referred to as authoring software. For example, Macromedia's Authorware permits the creation of rich media courseware for training. Developed to run on the Web, a CD, or across a network, a savvy Authorware developer might decide to integrate one or all three venues in one E-training application. Thus, the introduction to a particular course could be hosted on the organization's server with the separate modules hosted or executing on a network or a client PC.

Rich media is a combination of video, audio, and animation that enables interactivity.

Flash may appear in a Web page for viewing in a Web browser, or standalone Flash players may "play" them. Flash files occur most often in animations on Web pages and rich-media Web sites, and more recently Rich Internet Applications. They are also widely used in Web advertisements.

A QuickTime file functions as a multimedia container file that contains one or more tracks, each of which stores a particular type of data, such as audio, video, effects, or text. Developers can use the QuickTime software development kit to develop multimedia applications for Mac or Windows with the C programming language or with the Java programming language.

Graphics

Graphics refer to information in pictorial form. The graphics can be non-moving (static) or animated. Graphics packages typically enable the use of a wide variety of Web-compatible graphics formats (e.g., .gif, .jpg, and .png). Fractal Design's Painter and Adobe Photoshop, which are both available for Mac and Windows, are two tools of choice of graphic designers. There are many others out there that have similar functionality. Both Photoshop and Painter have a wide range of capabilities, including controlling brush size, applying special effects such as textures, cloning, tracing, extracting, layering, and text handling.

It is also possible to forego creating your own artwork and use artwork created by someone else. A royalty is the fee you pay the owner of a copyright to use copyrighted artwork such as images, animations, and photographs. Most word processors, desktop publishing software, and image processing software applications come with a wide variety of free images. There is also a wide variety of clip-art packages on the market.

The advent of digital cameras has made taking and uploading pictures to the Web rather simple. Graphics applications allow you to bring digital camera or camera phone (not recommended due to poor quality) images directly into the program via a plug-in. A plug-in is software that allows you to manipulate a specific camera or scanner within a graphics application. In some cases, these plug-ins are bundled with the application. In other cases, you will need to install plug-in software for the camera or scanner with which you are working. That software comes with the camera or scanner, which also includes instructions for installing it.

Static graphics are nonanimated pictorial representations of information (i.e., objects). They can be drawn images, computer generated, or photographic. A variety of graphics software packages is used by the graphic designer to "draw" (i.e., create) static images — for example, Photoshop, Fractal Design, and FreeHand.

The clarity of a photographic image is determined by its resolution. Digital cameras cost more, depending on the resolution of the pictures they take. For example, the standard resolution of many PC monitors is 640 × 480 pixels. Pixels are the tiny dots that make up every image, line, word of text, and anything else you see on the computer screen. The more pixels per inch of screen, the crisper the screen image will be. Whatever camera you use to capture digital images, take the pictures at the highest resolution possible. Later, when preparing your images for the Web, you can save them in Web-friendly JPEG format, which compresses your image, allowing it to load much more quickly on the Web. There are also other ways to reduce the size of an image before you upload it, including reducing the number of colors it contains, or the number of dots (pixels) per inch. You can use your graphics software (Photoshop or Picture Publisher, for example) to tweak these settings.

Both JPEG and GIF are compressed formats. This means that when you save anything in either format, the resulting file is smaller than it would be if you had saved the same image in uncompressed formats. TIFF (which use the .tif extension) is among the highest quality image formats. This format is typically used to save images that ultimately wind up in a printed publication. When paper is the final designation, there is no need to worry about the size of image files. GIF and JPEG images are smaller, in part because they support fewer colors than TIFF and other print-oriented formats do. The GIF format is excellent for compressing images that have relatively few colors or no gradations in color, while the JPEG format is best for compressing images with lots of colors. Drawings and clip-art images make great GIFs, while color photographs look best as JPEGs.

While GIF and JPEG are the two most commonly used formats on the Web, those developing executables for the Windows environment might also wind up embedding BMP (bitmapped) images into their applications. BMP files, however, are massively larger than either GIF or JPEG files.

In general, all formats of digitized images can be quite large. When you shrink the image in your graphics application, you are able to decrease its file size without compromising its quality. Most graphics software allows you to choose new dimensions for an image.

Most graphics software provides special effects capability. They include making a puzzle out of an image, creating drop shadows, making tiles, warping, and even creating psychedelic effects, as shown in Figure 6.1.

Animated GIF images are possible because of features added to the two latest versions of the CompuServe GIF file format (i.e., GIF87a and GIF89a). Both formats enable you to store multiple images within the core data stream of a single file. In addition, the GIF89a format adds several features that enhance the creation of animated GIF images, including transparency, interlacing, timing delay between frames, and the ability to animate a portion of an image.

You create animated GIFs by piecing together nearly identical images called frames, and assigning delays between the display of the frames, making the image appear to be animated, as shown in Figure 6.2. Keep in mind that the images you plan to animate must be small, because grouping a number of GIFs increases the file size fairly quickly. Designing the sequence of GIF files is called storyboarding. Storyboards are illustrations displayed in sequence for the purpose of previsualizing an animation.

Animated GIFs are created using an application or script (e.g., Adobe After Effects, Adobe Premiere, GifBuilder, Imaging Machine, or Alchemy Mindworks GIF Construction Set). The software collects individual images and compiles them into frames within a single file. When previewed, each frame displays in sequence to simulate animation. Before the series of GIFs can be animated, they must be created. This can be done using graphic imaging software. For example, a single image can be slightly

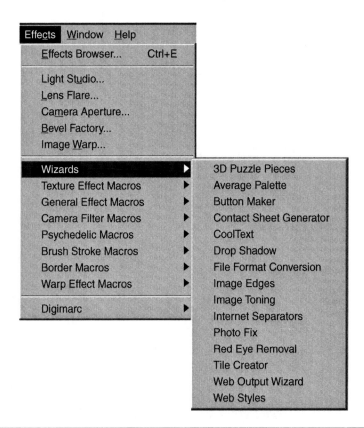

Figure 6.1   Special effects capabilities of typical graphics software.

Figure 6.2   Creating an animated GIF.

altered. When several iterations of the single image are created and combined within an animated GIF, the final image will appear as if it is moving. Figure 6.3 shows how the graphic imaging program's rotate command can be used for this purpose.

More than 390 million people have downloaded the Macromedia Shockwave plug-in. It is a mainstay on the Web and is responsible for much of the sophisticated animation seen today. Macromedia Director is the tool used to create Shockwave Web sites.

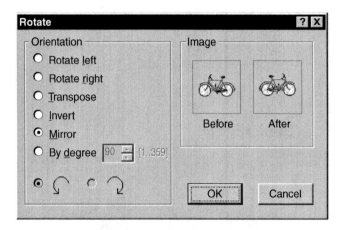

Figure 6.3   Rotating an image.

When a site uses Shockwave, it is said that the site is "shocked." Shockwave files use the .dcr extension. Macromedia Flash is a good alternative to the expense and talent demands of Shockwave. Aggressively marketed by Macromedia Flash, it is now the most widely recognized, promoted, and developed player. Flash files use the .swf extension, and 98 percent of all browsers have Flash installed. Flash files can be created using Flash as well as Macromedia Freehand.

Both Shockwave and Flash applications can be ported to the PC or to the Web. Flash also has the capability of being ported to some mobile devices, such as Sony's PSP and some mobile phones. As of this writing, Verizon Wireless just announced that it plans to allow developers to create interactive mobile content for Verizon devices. Flash Lite is the tool of choice for mobile applications.

Flash Lite is an interesting product, permitting the development of fully interactive and very rich content across a variety of mobile devices. It is worthwhile to take a quick look at the Flash Lite development process.

Creating Flash Lite content is an iterative process that involves the following steps:

1. *Identify the target devices and Flash Lite content type.* Different devices have different screen sizes, support different audio formats, and have different screen color depths, among other factors. These factors can influence the application's design or implementation. In addition, different devices support different Flash Lite content types, such as screen savers, stand-alone applications, or animated ring tones. The content type for which you are developing also determines the features that are available to your application.

2. *Create and test your application in Flash*. Flash Professional 8 includes a Flash Lite emulator that lets you test your application without having to transfer it to a device. You use the Flash Lite emulator to refine your application design and fix any problems before you test it on a mobile device.

3. *Test the application on your target device or devices*. This step is important because the emulator does not emulate all aspects of the target device, such as its processor speed, color depth, or network latency. For example, an animation that runs smoothly on the emulator might not run as quickly on the device because of its slower processor speed, or a color gradient that appears smooth in the emulator may appear banded when viewed on the actual device. After you test your application on a device, you may find that you need to refine the application's design in the Flash authoring tool.

Before starting to develop a Flash Lite application, you need to know the following:

1. *The device or devices on which the content will run (target devices)*. The Flash Lite player is installed on a variety of devices. For a list of devices that have Flash Lite installed, see the Supported Devices page on the Macromedia Web site at www.macromedia.com/mobile/supported_devices/.

2. *The Flash Lite content types that the target devices support*. Each Flash Lite installation supports one or more application modes (content types). For example, some devices use Flash Lite to enable Flash-based screen savers or animated ring tones. Other devices use Flash Lite to render Flash content that is embedded in mobile Web pages. Not all content types support all Flash Lite features.

Each Flash Lite content type, paired with a specific device, defines a specific set of Flash Lite features that are available to your application. For example, a Flash application that is running as a screen saver is not typically allowed to make network connections or download data.

Audio

Audio formats are used by different operating systems and provide varying levels of sound quality and sound compression. The latter refers to the ability to reduce the size of the sound file, an important factor in trying to increase the transmission rates for downloading. Sound formats include AIFF/AIFC, AU, MIDI, MPEG, RealAudio, SND, and WAV.

There are several types of audio — speech, music, sound effects, and narration.

Sound can be used to create atmosphere, add realism, emphasize important points, indicate progress or activity, increase interest, establish mood, cue or prompt users, and increase users' motivation.

It is possible to use a tape recorder to capture just the sound you need. You will not get professional-sounding audio, but you may be able to achieve the effects you want. Once you have recorded a sound, the next step is to use audio capture software to bring the sound you have recorded into your computer. All current Windows PCs and Macs come with simple audio software that can record sound. Microsoft includes a utility called Sound Recorder on many Windows PCs, usually under the Accessories menu. Sound Recorder lets you play and record WAV files. The Sound Recorder works the same as a conventional tape recorder. Once you have finished recording, you might notice that your WAV file includes "dead air" a few seconds at the beginning or end of the recording. Sound Recorder provides a minimal editing capability that lets you cut out parts of your WAV file. There is even some sound effect functionality.

Streaming audio enables you to play high-quality, long-form sound programs on the Web. Streaming means that when a visitor clicks on a link to an audio file, the file is not downloaded all at once and then played, as is the case with a WAV file. Instead of downloading the full sound file, site visitors who click on a link to streaming content receive the file as it plays live on the Net.

Rules for creating "good" audio include:

1. Use a good original source.
2. Set input levels correctly to use the full range of available amplitude, while avoiding clipping (i.e., high-frequency crackling noise).
3. Use high-quality equipment.
4. Select appropriate material.
5. Use the right amount of compression.
6. Understand the technical aspects of noise gating and equalization.

Streaming allows the transfer of data in a stream of packets that are interpreted as they arrive for "just-in-time" delivery of multimedia information. Non-streaming media is downloaded all at once. This technique is not effective for most large media files.

There are two main ways to implement non-streaming audio on a Web page. The one you select depends on the bandwidth available. Bandwidth is a measure of the amount of data that can be sent through a communications circuit per second.

1. Using external media – (i.e., a file external to the Web page) that is accessed by a link set up with the HTML <A> tag. Using an external media has the advantage that users can access the multimedia file only if they need to, which is good where they have a low bandwidth connection. An example is:

```
<A HREF="moody.wav">Moody Blues clip</A>
```

2. Using inline media, where the object is embedded into the Web page itself using the <EMBED> tag. Using an internal or inline media has the advantage that it works like an inline image and can be played within the page itself. The disadvantage, however, is that it takes a lot of download time. For example:

```
<EMBED SRC="moody.wav" WIDTH=145 HEIGHT=60
AUTOSTART="false">
```

Another technique for implementing sound is <BGSOUND>, which is used to play background sounds on the Web page. The syntax is: <BGSOUND SRC=URL LOOP=value> where URL is the URL or location of the sound file and the LOOP property defines how many times the sound clip will be played in the background (value is 1, 2, 3,..., or INFINITE if to be played continuously).

RealNetworks (http://www.realnetworks.com/) pioneered streaming media. The company's RealPlayer is available for PCs and Macs, and includes links to live radio feeds, Internet-only news and entertainment programming, etc. RealPlayer can stream not only audio, but also video. Apple's QuickTime is a staple on the Web as well. Microsoft's Windows Media Player has also become quite popular as a player of audio and video.

To stream RealAudio or RealVideo content (also called RealMedia), or any other streaming format, you need to buy and install software on the Web server that contains your site. If an ISP (Internet service provider) that has sold you a certain amount of disk space hosts your site, you need to check with the provider to be sure that you can stream audio and video from their server. Finally, although streaming content does not require site visitors to download large files, it does require data transfer, which may cause problems if your ISP charges by the byte.

In many cases, it is best to use your own Web server to stream audio or video content, especially if you want to do a lot of it. You can either find an ISP who will provide the hardware (fast server with lots of disk space) and resources (fast connection with a capacity for large data transfer) that you need, or run your own Internet server.

Video

Video file formats comprise the following formats: ASF, AVI, MPEG, Quick-Time, or RealVideo. The one you should use depends to a great extent on who you think your audience is and their hardware configurations.

Like streaming audio, a streaming video file begins playing right away as the file is being downloaded. RealNetworks, RealVideo, along with QuickTime and Windows Media Player, are all popular.

The sequence for creating video files includes (1) gathering source materials, (2) digitizing the source, and (3) editing nonlinearly. Computer software enables the editor to create and store a model of the video without creating the actual video. During the rendering process, the software proceeds frame by frame through the model and performs all operations necessary to create a complete frame at the desire resolution and quality.

Recommendations for video capture include:

1. Limit the amount of picture content that changes from one frame to the next frame.
2. Limit the amount of textured detail in the picture.
3. Plan for limited motion.
4. Plan for "settle time" after transitions (i.e., wait a few seconds for each "scene" to resolve).
5. Use large, clear fonts.
6. Digitize video in uncompressed format. Compression should be done at the end.

Streaming allows for the transfer of data in a stream of packets that are interpreted as they arrive for "just-in-time" delivery of multimedia information. Non-streaming media is downloaded all at once. This tech-nique is not effective for most large media files.

There are two main ways to implement nonstreaming video on a Web page. The one you select depends on the bandwidth available. Bandwidth is a measure of the amount of data that can be sent through a commu-nications circuit per second.

1. *Using external media:* that is, a file external to the Web page that is accessed by a link set up with the <A> tag. Using external media has the advantage that users can access the multimedia file only if they need to, which is good where they have a low bandwidth connection.

```
<A HREF="mymovie.avi">Moving Video</A>
```

Both Internet Explorer and Netscape can display the AVI and MOV files within the browser without plug-ins. Clicking on the hyperlink will show the clip in its own window. The user can start the clip by clicking on the control that appears with the clip, or by clicking the image. If no controls appear, the user can right-click the image.

2. *Using inline media:* that is, the object is embedded into the Web page itself using the <EMBED> tag. Using internal or inline media has the advantage that it works like an inline image and can be played within the page itself. The disadvantage, however, is that it takes a lot of download time. For example:

```
<EMBED SRC=URL WIDTH=value HEIGHT=value
AUTOSTART="startvalue">
```

where WIDTH and HEIGHT are the pixel size of the clip on the page. For example:

```
<EMBED SRC="mymovie.avi" WIDTH=200 HEIGHT=200
AUTOSTART="false">
```

While audio files or data transfers can be large, video files are much larger. It is not only the length of the video clip that increases download time, but the number of colors and frames within the clip. It is not unusual for a one-minute video to gobble up 50 MB of disk space.

Windows Movie Maker, usually found under the Accessories menu, provides a set of tools for capturing, editing, and producing videos, as shown in Figure 6.4.

One inexpensive technique for creating streaming audio or video is to use RealNetwork's RealProducer, as shown in Figure 6.5. RealProducer is powered by Helix DNA™. Helix DNA is a multi-format digital media platform developed by the Helix Community (https://helixcommunity. org/). The Helix Community is a collaborative effort among both leading technology companies and open-source developers to extend the Helix DNA. The Helix DNA itself uses an object model with over a thousand methods and interfaces. The Helix platform consists of three components:

1. Helix DNA Client: the universal playback engine supporting the decode and playback of any format and on any operating system.
2. Helix DNA Producer: the encoding engine and APIs that allow you to convert video and audio into digital media in a streamlined fashion.
3. Helix DNA Server: the core engine for digital media delivery that will enable you to build a server for any media format and any operating system you wish.

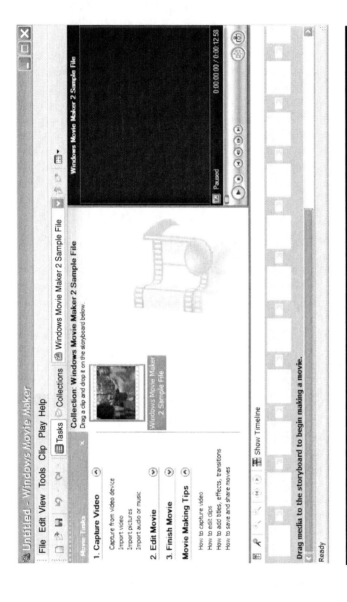

Figure 6.4   Using Windows Movie Maker.

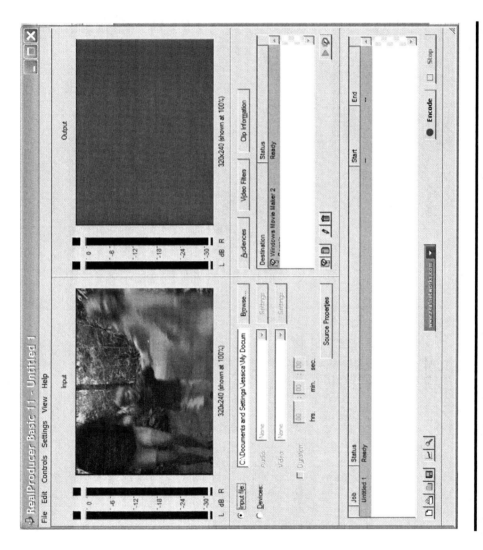

Figure 6.5   RealNetwork's RealProducer.

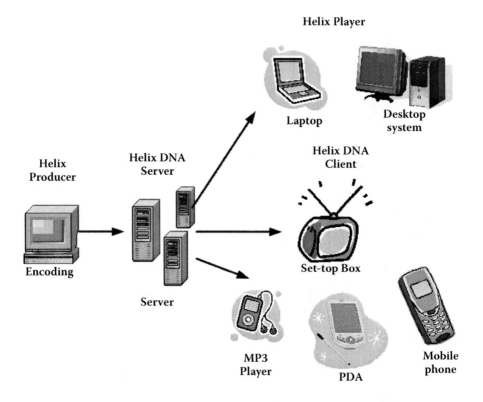

Figure 6.6   Helix DNA.

Using the Helix DNA, developers will be able to create new applications ranging from line of business applications that establish new business models to back-end applications that make digital media management and encoding more powerful and efficient. With Helix DNA, developers also will be able to create applications to support and enhance digital media playback on any IP-enabled mobile or consumer device, as shown in Figure 6.6.

Streaming video requires some kind of browser *plug-in or player* in order to play. A plug-in is software that can display file formats that your browser cannot. To play a video clip that is linked to the current page, for example, a site visitor needs to have a plug-in that can read the video format you have chosen. Some plug-ins, such as Apple's QuickTime, Real Networks' RealPlayer, or Microsoft Windows Media Player, can handle several audio and video formats.

Because streaming media works equally well from a desktop or a Web page, it provides some interesting possibilities for X development. Streaming media also works on mobile platforms, further expanding opportunities for X development. For example, according to streamingmedia.com, subscribers to RealOne for mMode, a new service combining RealNetworks' technology and expertise with AT&T Wireless service, have access to hours of content — including frequently refreshed news and business updates, entertainment, sports, and weather. In contrast with mobile streaming of canned content, mobile video messaging involves capturing, uploading, and downloading entire clips as files, and sending them to other users on PCs or mobile handsets as Multimedia Messages (MMS), similar to a photo and sound clip. Applications for mobile video messaging are expected to include mini-press interviews and newsreels, on-the-ground video reports from service technicians in the field and executives' directives to their subordinates.

Appendix C provides a good overview of audio and video production values.

Advanced Multimedia

Gaming sites are good examples of the synergy possible between X form and function. There are four main gaming platforms:

1. Personal computer games (e.g., computer games or PC games)
2. Console games (e.g., played on a computer specifically created for gaming, such as the PlayStation 2)
3. Arcade games (e.g., coin-operated games on a stand-alone device)
4. Internet games

Games can be single-player or multi-player. The four ingredients for a successful game are:

1. Game idea
2. "Playability" of the game (i.e., the game cannot be too difficult or too easy)
3. Graphics
4. Performance

Most games are developed using the C or C++ programming languages, although Delphi, Pascal, and Python, which is Open Source, are also used.

A MUD (multi-user dungeon, dimension, or sometimes domain) is a multi-player computer game that combines elements of role-playing games computer games and Internet Relay Chat. The first MUDs appeared in the 1970s. Some gaming Web sites, such as SecondLife.com and SimCity.com, are imagined, created, and owned by the players, referred to as "citizens" in these environments.

Second Life, whose architecture was discussed in Chapter 5, is a good example of the possibilities of X. Users go to the secondlife.com Web site to register, read blogs, access newsletters, and exchange currency (i.e., Second Life is a virtual world so it is natural that Second Life users use virtual money to buy and sell property). A Second Life virtual world player must be downloaded to the end user's client (e.g., PC). This player uses IP (Internet Protocol) to interact with other Second Life players, now 100,000 strong.

2D and 3D

The comparison between 2D and 3D is likened to the comparison between painting (2D or flat) and sculpture (3D and not flat). A 3D virtual representation of an object is stored in the computer for purposes of performing calculations and rendering images. The process of creating 3D computer graphics can be sequentially divided into three basic phases: (1) modeling, (2) scene layout setup, and (3) rendering

In the modeling phase, individual objects are shaped. This includes specifying color, luminosity, diffusion, shading refraction, and texturizing. There are different modeling techniques, including constructive solid geometry (i.e., describing shapes using mathematical formulas) and polygonal modeling. Rendering is the process of actually creating the image from the model.

APIs (application programmer interfaces) are used to access the hardware so that the programmer can write code for the specific hardware and graphics card, as each is different.

VRML (Virtual Reality Modeling Language) is a standard file format for representing 3D interactive vector graphics. It is a text file format where polygon objects can be specified along with the surface color, image-mapped textures, shininess, transparency, etc. VRML files are called worlds and have the file extension .wrl. The current standard is VRML97, which will soon be replaced by X3D, the ISO standard. A sample of VTML code follows:

```
#VRML V2.0 utf8
  DEF view1  viewpoint {
  position 0 0 20
  description "view1"
}
```

An avatar is an image you select or create to represent yourself to the other party in a game or chat. An avatar is a caricature, not a realistic portrayal, and can be a simple image or a bizarre fantasy figure.

Products such as Haptek's PeoplePutty (www.haptek.com) let you create your own interactive, emoting 3D characters using simple photographs and your own voice.

Putting a Haptek character in a Web page requires only two simple things: (1) a JavaScript wrapper file (HapPlayer411.js) and (2) a viewer window (VFBox). The numbers following the VFBox indicates its size (400 × 400 pixels).

```html
<HTML>
<HEAD>
<TITLE>The World's Simplest Haptek Webpage</TITLE>
</HEAD>
<BODY>
<SCRIPT SRC="http://www.haptek.com/common/
  javascript/HapPlayer411.js">
</SCRIPT>
<SCRIPT>
VFBox(400,400);
</SCRIPT>
</BODY>
</HTML>
```

The Haptek Player makes use of commands like UseMorph, UseTexture, and UseFile to change the character's shape or skin, or load a sound file or script. Adding commands is just like adding a link:

```html
<A HREF="javascript:UseFile('http://www.haptek.com/
  developers/data/sounds/about_2.ogg', 'A');">
Click to Play a Sound!</A>
```

You can make your own character using PeoplePutty, then save that character as an .htr file (an .htr file stores all the information about a character — skin, shape, emotions, etc.) and load that character in place of their default character.

```html
<SCRIPT>
AddToInitQueue("StartupCharacter();");
function StartupCharacter()
{
  UseFile('MyCharacter.htr', 'R');
}
</SCRIPT>
```

Multimedia-Enabled PDFs

Adobe Acrobat Professional provides two interactive features that you can add to an Adobe PDF document: (1) interactive buttons; and (2) movie and sound clips that can be played when they are selected or activated (Figure 6.7).

Version 7 of Adobe Acrobat Professional provides enhanced multimedia capabilities. Developers are able to create rich, interactive documents. Functionality includes adding materials, creating animations such as exploded views, editing light effects, and the ability to save as a 3D object or 2D raster/vector image. Possibilities for use of these new, improved PDFs are endless.

Picture the IRS permitting taxpayers to download data-enterable tax forms, with embedded multimedia instructions — or perhaps a short video or animation explaining the fine-points of charitable deductions.

VoiceXML

VoiceXML is a language for creating voice–user interfaces. It uses telephone-style speech recognition and DTMF (dual tone multi-frequency) touchtone (keypad entry) for input, and previously recorded audio, text-to-speech synthesis, and dictionaries for output.

When developing applications using VoiceXML, the Web's basic components and infrastructure remain the same. The main difference is that instead of using a Web browser such as Internet Explorer or Netscape, a voice browser is used. This voice browser is really a VoiceXML interpreter, which resides on a highly specialized server, with the user interface being a simple telephone.

There are many components to the VoiceXML architecture. To enable communication between the wire and wireless telephone devices and the Internet, a specialized piece of hardware/software called the VoiceXML gateway is required (Vujosevic and Laberge, 2002).

The VoiceXML gateway is basically one or more computer servers residing on the same platform and running interpreters called voice browsers. These voice browsers understand and interpret VoiceXML dialogs (or commands). The VoiceXML gateway facilitates communication between the dialogs and the Internet by controlling resources such as Automatic Speech Recognition, message recording and play, Text to Speech, DTMF tone recognition, and the PSTN network connectivity. Apart from the VoiceXML interpreter, each voice gateway includes an Automatic Speech Recognition (ASR) engine, which supports multiple languages. Also included are Text-to-Speech engine, system dictionaries, and an Internet interface (ranging from dial-up to high-speed links).

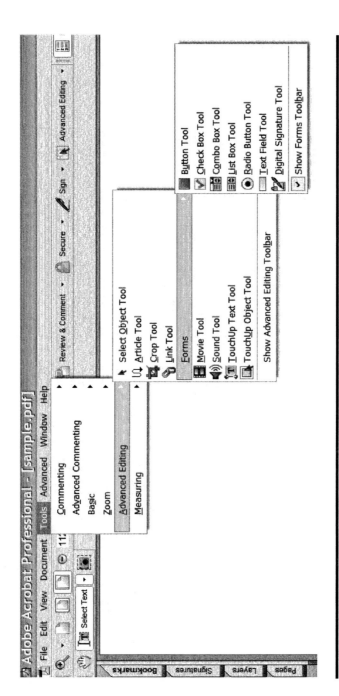

Figure 6.7 PDF multimedia capabilities.

One of the most important parts of the VoiceXML gateway is the voice browser. In a PC environment, a classic Web browser simply collects and presents data. The same idea is used on Web phones, although these are referred to as microbrowsers. It is important to note that in both cases, the browser resides on the client device (i.e., personal computer, WAP-enabled wireless device, or PDA) and the code begins its execution on the client side.

It is a completely different story for voice browsers. Voice browsers reside within the VoiceXML gateway or are built into a PSTN (public switched telephone network). These browsers allow the users to place calls from any telephone and navigate through the VoiceXML application by selecting options on voice menus and executing simple voice input commands. Navigation can also be based on end-user voice input.

Voice browser program code resides on the Web server or on the VoiceXML gateway and is therefore a server-side browser similar to active server page (ASP) code. VoiceXML developers would then maintain the code in the same fashion as they would regular HTML or ASP code.

In a VoiceXML document (or program), the user is always in a conversational state called a dialog. Each dialog determines the flow to the next dialog, all depending on which selection is chosen or which command is given. In Web programming, execution is halted when a screen is displayed. The user then enters information and clicks OK (or whatever), selects a hyperlink, or chooses a form item. In VoiceXML, instead of a screen being presented, the system tells the user a selection to make or an informational statement. Execution is then paused until the user returns a voice command. From the program's point of view, transitions to new dialogs are specified via URLs (relative or explicit). If no specific dialog is specified on the URL, the first dialog in the document is assumed. Execution is terminated when a dialog does not specify a successor, or if it has an element that explicitly exits the conversation. When programming, always guide the user by letting him or her know the next possible choices; if none exist, say so.

There are free VoiceXML gateways, such as Tellme (http://www.tellme. com), BeVocal (http://www.bevocal.com), and VoiceGenie (http://www. voicegenie.com), that take VoiceXML pages from your Web server and read them to your user. If your application needs input from the user, the gateway will interpret the incoming response and pass that response to your server in a way that your software can understand.

DHTML and XML

Dynamic HTML (DHTML) is a form of HTML used to create Web-page content that, as perceived by the viewer, appears to change each time it is viewed, without further interaction with the server. The Web-page content can use any of several technologies, including CGI (computer graphics interface) scripts.

Dynamic HTML provides Web authors with enhanced creative control so they can manipulate any page element at any time. It is also one of the easiest ways to make Web pages interactive, using open, standards-based technologies.

Dynamic HTML provides a comprehensive Document Object Model (DOM) for HTML. This model exposes all page elements as objects. These objects can easily be manipulated by changing their attributes or applying methods to them at any time. Dynamic HTML also provides full support for keyboard and mouse events on all page elements.

Support for the Document Object Model enables:

1. *Dynamic content.* Text or graphics can be added, deleted, or modified on-the-fly. For example, a Web page can display an updated headline, without refreshing the page. The text surrounding the headline reflows automatically.
2. *Dynamic styles.* Internet Explorer 4 and above fully support Cascading Style Sheets (CSS). As such, any CSS attribute, including color and font, can be updated without a server roundtrip. For example, text can change color or size when a mouse pointer passes over it. Multimedia filters and transition effects can be applied to HTML elements simply by adding the filter CSS attribute.
3. *Absolute positioning.* CSS positioning coordinates for existing page content can be updated at any time to create animated effects, without reloading the page.

Data-driven applications can be built that present, manipulate (e.g., sort, filter), and update data on the client without numerous roundtrips to the server. Using scripts, a developer can author content once, then easily reuse the content in other Web pages or applications. A scriptlet is a Web page, authored with Dynamic HTML, that can be used as a component in other Web applications.

Dynamic HTML was designed so that Web builders can use the scripting languages they already know, such as JavaScript and Visual Basic, to make their Web pages interactive. Developers can also write full-featured Web applications with controls and applets that use Dynamic HTML.

WAP (Wireless Access Protocol) is a standard for providing cellular phones, pagers, and other handheld devices with secure access to e-mail and text-based Web pages. WAP uses the Wireless Markup Language (WML), which is a streamlined version of HTML for small screen displays.

An example of WML:

```
<?xml version="1.0" encoding="UTF-8"?>
<!DOCTYPE wml PUBLIC "-//WAPFORUM//DTD WML 1.1//EN"
"http://www.wapforum.org/DTD/wml_1.1.xml">
<wml>
<head><meta http-equiv="Cache-Control" content=
"max-age=30" forua="true" /></head>
<card id="card0" title="UOP test">
<do type="prev" label="Back"><prev/></do>
<p>This is a test
</p>
</card>
</wml>
```

WAP is a "pull" model based on user requests. Some issues with mobile devices include connectivity, physical limitations of devices (e.g., CPU, memory, display, input devices, power supply), and the high percentage of sensitive (personal) information. Original content should be summarized due to limited real estate.

Content delivery can be handled by delta encoding (i.e., a way of storing or transmitting data in the form of differences [deltas] between sequential data rather than data itself), compression, or image transcoding (i.e., distillation). Newer mobile devices are able to take advantage of streaming video and audio. Verizon's V Cast service is an example.

AJAX

AJAX (or Asynchronous JavaScript and XML) is a set of technologies for developing JavaScript-based Web clients that are much more interactive than traditional Web clients. In a traditional Web client, every user action that is sent to a Web server returns an HTML page to the client. This page must be redrawn by the client and the user experiences a sluggish interface. In an AJAX application, the browser communicates asynchronously with the server and only redraws the parts of the user interface that require refreshing. The end result is a much more responsive Web client. Some examples of AJAX include Google Maps, GMail, Amazon's A9 search engine, Netflex, and the Gap. Gap.com is a particularly interesting example because the company totally redid its site recently to eliminate a "too many clicks per purchase" problem.

AJAX is not a technology in itself, but rather a term that refers to the use of a group of technologies together. AJAX uses a combination of:

1. XHTML (or HTML), CSS, for marking up and styling information
2. The DOM accessed with a client-side scripting language, to dynamically display and interact with the information presented
3. The XMLHttpRequest (XHR) object, to exchange data asynchronously with the Web server
4. XML is commonly used as the format for transferring data back from the server.

Optionally,

1. PHP or another scripting language can be used on the server.
2. SOAP can be used to dialog with the server (SOAP [Simple Object Access Protocol] is a message-based protocol based on XML for accessing services on the Web. It uses XML syntax to send text commands across the Internet using HTTP. SOAP is similar to the DCOM and CORBA distributed object systems, but is lighter weight and less programming intensive.)

Use of AJAX requires users to have JavaScript enabled in their browsers. This applies to all browsers that support AJAX except for Microsoft Internet Explorer 6 and below, which additionally require ActiveX to be enabled, as the XMLHttpRequest object is implemented with ActiveX in this browser. Internet Explorer 7, however, will implement this interface as a native JavaScript object and hence does not need ActiveX to be enabled for AJAX to work.

Figure 6.8 shows the interface for an AJAX-driven drop-down form. Freeware client and server code can be downloaded from the ClearNova Web site at http://www.clearnova.com/ajax. ClearNova is a vendor of development tools for developing rich Internet applications.

In this example, an AJAX call is made to the server to get the states and populate the select box (drop-down). The server dynamically creates JavaScript that is executed through an eval statement. The final line of the JavaScript calls the onchange event of the state drop-down, which then retrieves all the cities for that state.

The city drop-down is populated and its onchange event retrieves all the customers for a given city. When the customer changes, the server returns JavaScript that replaces all customer fields with the appropriate values. If you open the Track Changes section, you will notice that both address fields on the page are updated.

In the sample, if you add a new INPUT field that matches a column in the customer table, it will be populated for you during runtime.

The routines to retrieve the state, city, and customer drop-downs all use variations of encapsulating XMLHTTPRequests instead of using a global XMLHTTPRequest (_ajax).

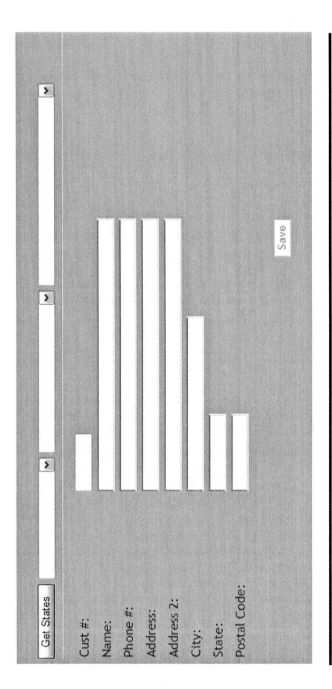

Figure 6.8 A simple AJAX example.

The Save button on the form sends the contents of the customer form back to the server. A message is shown indicating a successful save or a failure.

Sajax (Simple AJAX Toolkit) is an open source tool designed to help Web sites using the AJAX framework (http://www.modernmethod.com/sajax/index.phtml). It allows the programmer to call PHP, Perl, or Python functions from their Web pages via JavaScript without performing a browser refresh.

The key to AJAX is the XMLHTTPRequest object. This object can make its own connections to Web servers, allowing content to be downloaded and refreshed on the screen based on an event in the browser — without reloading the page.

Comet is very similar to this. It permits content refresh without reloading the page. The key difference is that Comet does not require an event to occur on the user's end. The server can push content to the client at will.

Comet uses an embedded iframe through which a connection to the server remains continuously open. In essence, a Comet application does not poll the server occasionally. Instead, the server has an open line of communication with which it can push data to the client.

Conclusion

This chapter discussed a number of "rich" technologies that might be used in an X application — for example, audio, video, animation, Flash, etc. The final section of this chapter focused on AJAX, which just might become the development methodology of choice in the X Web-based world because it is capable of providing rich user experiences using the ubiquitous browser as a client.

From the outset, this book takes the position that the Gartner definition of the "X Internet" is only half right. We will certainly see a plethora of executables being downloaded, but this will not sound a death knell for the Internet as we know it. Instead, the world of X will be a fusion of Web-based applications and downloadable executables — each capable of rich interfaces and functionality. This new, richer Internet will be very exciting indeed!

References

Vujosecic, S. and Laberge, R. (2002). VoiceXML, How to Talk to the Internet. In J. Keyes (Ed.), *The Ultimate Web Developer's Sourcebook* (pp. 267–283). New York: AMACOM.

Chapter 7

Data in an X World

For an application to be valuable, it must have the ability to process data. This is something that traditional systems do on a daily basis, and do very well. Most Web-based applications can also process data. However, the data processed by these applications is usually far more limited in scope than non-Web-based applications. For an X application to be truly valuable, it must be able to process the full cadre of data and information and knowledge resources owned by a typical organization. An X application's ability to work transparently with a server without constant browser refresh makes this form of data processing much more doable than in the past.

X applications are capable of doing far more than just processing corporate data because they are, by definition, Internet enabled. Tim Berners-Lee, who invented the World Wide Web as well as HTML, pioneered the idea of the Semantic Web. The Semantic Web is a synthesis of all corporate and external data, including results from data mining activities, hypermedia, knowledge systems, etc., which uses a common interface that makes data easily accessible by all (e.g., suppliers, customers, employees). X powered by the Semantic Web is a strategy worth pursuing. This chapter discusses the components of the Semantic Web, a component of knowledge management.

The Defined Web

The Semantic Web is sometimes called the Defined Web and is the ultimate repository of all content and knowledge on the Web, as shown in Figure

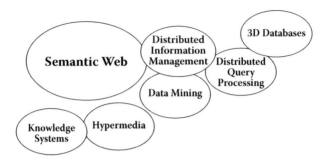

Figure 7.1   The Semantic Web.

7.1. It uses XML (eXtensible Markup Language, a formalized version of HTML) to tag information on intranets, extranets, and the Internet.

Tim Berners-Lee explains the Semantic Web as follows (Berners-Lee, Hendler, and Lassila, 2001):

> At the doctor's office, Lucy instructed her Semantic Web agent through her handheld Web browser. The agent promptly retrieved information about Mom's *prescribed treatment* from the doctor's agent, looked up several lists of *providers*, and checked for the ones *in-plan* for Mom's insurance within a *20-mile radius* of her *home* and with a *rating* of *excellent* or *very good* on trusted rating services. It then began trying to find a match between available *appointment times* (supplied by the agents of individual providers through their Web sites) and Pete's and Lucy's busy schedules.

Hewlett-Packard's Semantic Web research group frequently circulates items of interest such as news articles, software tools, and links to Web sites. They call these snippets, or information nuggets (Cayzer, 2004). Because e-mail is not the ideal medium for this type of content, they needed to find a technique for decentralized, informal knowledge management. They began a research project to create a system that was capable of aggregating, annotating, indexing, and searching a community's snippets. The required characteristics of this for this system include:

1. *Ease of use and capture.*
2. *Decentralized aggregation.* Snippets will be in a variety of locations and formats. It will be necessary to integrate them and perform some global search over the result.
3. *Distributed knowledge.* Users should be able to add value by enriching snippets at the point of use by adding ratings, annotations, etc.

4. *Flexible data model.* Snippets are polymorphic. The system should be able to handle e-mail, Web pages, documents, text fragments, images, etc.
5. *Extensible.* It should be possible to extend the snippet data schema to model the changing world.
6. *Inferencing.* It should be possible to infer new metadata from old. For example, a machine should "know" that a snippet about a particular HP Photosmart model is about a digital camera.

Some have suggested that blogs make the ideal tool for this type of content and knowledge management. However, today's blogging tools offer only three of the six capabilities cited above. Traditional blogging has many limitations, but the most important limitation is that metadata is used only for headline syndication in a blog. Metadata is not extensible; it is not linked to a risk, flexible data model; and it is not capable of supporting vocabulary mixing and inferencing.

The researchers, therefore, looked to the Semantic Web for a solution. As discussed previously, the premise of the Semantic Web is that data can be shared and reused across application, enterprise, and community boundaries — hence it is X-enabled. RSS1.0 (web.resource.org/rss/1.0) is a Semantic Web vocabulary that provides a way to express and integrate with rich information models. The Semantic Web standard Resource Description Framework (RDF) specifies a Web-scale information modeling format (www.w3.org/RDF). Using these tools they came up with a prototype (http://www.semanticblogging.org/blojsom-hp/blog/default/) for creating what they called a "Semantic Blog." The prototype has some interesting searching capabilities. For example, snippets can be searched for either through their own attributes (e.g., "I'm interested in snippets about HP.") or through the attributes of their attached blog entry (e.g., "I'm interested in snippets captured by Bob."). If one translates HP's snippets and nuggets into executables, downloadable and able to be run on a client, then one can begin to see the power of the combination of X technologies and the semantic Web.

The Semantic Web community has developed a language — the eXtensible Rule Markup Language (XRML) — to be able to process rules implicit in Web pages that cannot now be processed within XML (Lee and Sohn, 2003). Figure 7.2 provides a comparison between HTML, XM, and XRML.

XRML has three components:

1. *Rule Identification Markup Language (RIML).* The meta-knowledge expressed in RIML should identify the existence of implicit rules in the hypertexts on the Web.

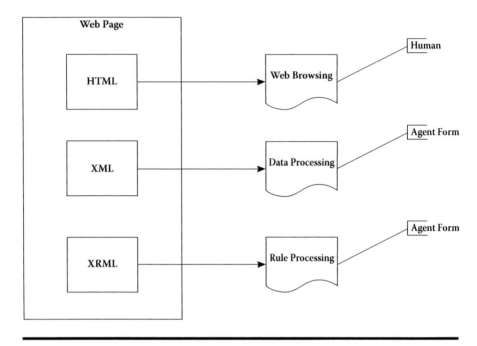

Figure 7.2   XRML and earlier technologies.

2. *Rule Structure Markup Language (RSML).* Rules in knowledge-based systems must be represented in a formal structure so they can be processed with inference engines.
3. *Rule Triggering Markup Language (RTML).* RTML defines the conditions that trigger certain rules.

XRML provides a tool to assist the convergence of knowledge-based systems (artificial intelligence) and knowledge management systems. http://xrml.kaist.ac.kr/xrml_download/XRML-Ver1.doc represents a specification for XRML language design to achieve the knowledge sharing between humans and software agents.

Semantic Standards

The Semantic Web, then, is really an add-on to the current Web in which information is given a more refined meeting, better enabling computers and people to work together. The key to the success of the Semantic Web is the development of "semantic standards." As some put it, the "software industry is building an alphabet but hasn't yet invented a common language."

This "common language" has appeared in the form of ontologies. According to Ford (2002), an ontology is an explicit specification. The term is actually borrowed from philosophy, where an ontology is a systematic account of existence.

From a Semantic Web perspective, an ontology is an explicit, formal specification of a shared conceptualization of interest. *Formal* means that the ontology should be machine readable and *shared* indicates that the ontology captures knowledge that is not private. Essentially, ontologies represent knowledge within specific domains in a machine-readable way.

Those who develop object-oriented systems will no doubt be familiar with ontologies because they are quite similar in form and structure to classes and objects. For example, an automotive ontology will have a "Car" class that is partitioned into the classes "2-Wheel Drive" and "4-Wheel Drive." Objects in an ontology can be described by assigning attributes to them. Each attribute has at least a name and a value, and is used to store information that is specific to the object to which it is attached. For example, the "Ford Explorer" object has attributes such as:

```
Name:              Ford Explorer
Number-of-doors:   4
Engine:            {4.0L, 4.6L)
Transmission:      6-speed
```

Informal ontology examples available on the Internet are Yahoo categories, which are generalized taxonomies of "things," and the Amazon.com product catalog. Ontologies are built for a wide variety of reasons (Raisinghani, 2000):

1. To share a common understanding of the structure of information among people and among software components
2. To enable reuse of domain knowledge:
   a. Avoid reinventing the wheel
   b. Introduce standards
   c. Share ontologies among different domains
3. To make domain assumptions explicit:
   a. Simple to update and extend domain knowledge
   b. Easier to understand and update legacy data
4. To separate domain knowledge from operational knowledge:
   a. Configuration based on constraints
5. To enable inferencing and reasoning on data
   Understanding interrelationships among data allows software to reason against the data to infer new information.

An ontology language is a formal language used to encode the ontology. There are a number of such languages. The World Wide Web Consortium (W3C) has standardized on OWL (Ontology Web Language) (http://www.w3.org/TR/owl-features/). OWL was developed as a follow-on to RDF. Resource Description Framework (RDF) is a W3C (World Wide Web Consortium) specification used as a general method for modeling knowledge, through a variety of syntax formats such as XML.

The RDF metadata model (http://www.w3.org/RDF/) is based on the idea of describing resources by using a subject-predicate-object expression, called a triple in RDF terminology. One way to represent the fact "The sky has the color blue" in RDF would be as a triple whose subject is "the sky," whose predicate is "has the color," and whose object is "blue." Predicates are traits or aspects about a resource and express a relationship between the subject and the object.

Ontology editors are used to create and maintain ontologies. Most tools permit the creation of a hierarchy of concepts – (e.g., a car is a sub-concept of a motor vehicle) and the ability to model relationships between these concepts (e.g., a car is driven by a person) (Sure and Studer, n.d.). Annotation tools allow for adding semantic markup to resources. Inference engines, a staple of artificial intelligence, allow for the processing of knowledge available in the Semantic Web.

Developing an ontology is similar to the creation of a typical OO (object-oriented) class diagram (Raisinghani, 2000):

1. Define terms in the domain and relations among them.
2. Concepts within the domain are objects (classes).
3. Arrange concepts in a hierarchy (sub-class/super-class).
4. Define attributes of the classes (properties) and any constraints on their values and relations.
5. Define individuals — fill in slot values (instances).
6. Object model allows for inheritance, imports, typing.

Sample ontologies can be found at SchemaWeb, a volunteer project located at http://www.schemaweb.info/schema/BrowseSchema.aspx. Chapter 10 provides a full set of references for Semantic Web toolsets.

Enterprise Information Management

The Semantic Web, then, is an excellent vehicle for X-enabled applications. Some information and processes can be Web-based, some solely client-based with both information and processes encapsulated in an executable, and some a combination of the two.

However, for these applications to work effectively, there must be an in-depth analysis of the various information sources that wrap themselves around the Semantic Web architecture. Sadly, most organizations are data driven, rather than knowledge or information driven. They are quite unaware of the real value of their own information assets and, hence, do not do a good job of managing these resources — that is, information management and knowledge management. While knowledge management is certainly practiced in many organizations, it suffers from the ever-present "silo" effect, where it is practiced by one or more decentralized business units rather than the organization as a whole. To access the nuggets of the Semantic Web, the organization will need to first embark on a strategy of effectively managing the information for the entire enterprise.

In 2002, the Nielsen Norman Group (http://www.nngroup.com, 2003) published a study on corporate intranet usability. The researchers looked at 14 separate intranets. The study emphasized the importance of effective searching by noting what happens in its absence. They observed that poor search functionality was the single greatest cause of reduced usability across the intranets studied, reducing the value of the information assets within the organization. They found that search usability accounted for an estimated 43 percent of the difference in employee productivity between the best and worst intranets. The study also found that unsuccessful search users were using inefficient alternatives or gave up altogether, bringing the ROI for the unused online assets down to zero.

The study measured user performance for 16 common tasks and found that a company with the least usable intranet would spend $3042 per employee to cover time spent on the 16 tasks, while the cost of using the most usable intranet was only $1563 per year. Extrapolating from these figures, the study concluded that the total annual cost of intranet use at various levels of usability for companies with 10,000 users would be:

- Good usability: $15.6 million annually
- Average usability: $20.7 million annually
- Poor usability: $30.4 million annually

Content can be delivered to the end user in a variety of ways — bots, search, push, browsing, and portal — all within the venue of X as well as non-X applications. This is referred to as knowledge flow. Bots, short for robots, are automated agents (i.e., software programs) that seek out information of interest and send it back to the end user by that end user's request. Push technology, or server-push as it is sometimes known, is delivery of information that is initiated by the information server rather than by the end user. The information is "pushed" from a server to an end user as a result of a programmed request initiated originally by the end user. A portal is a Web site that serves as a single gateway to information and knowledge. Each of these methodologies requires that the content be managed in some way. In the world of business, this is referred to as *enterprise information management* (EIM).

There are four major elements to EIM:

1. Correspondence management
2. Workflow management
3. Document management
4. Records management

In a modern organization, these information assets might take the form of documents, multimedia objects, corporate public relations and advertising, technical documents, images, sounds, video, databases, knowledge bases, and any combination thereof.

For the most part, these systems are automated. EIM systems should be considered strategic investments, as they will affect the conduct of business throughout every part of the organization.

Most implementers of EIM systems recommend that there be a single, clear vision of the desired end result of implementing the EIM. This vision must be understood and supported by those at the very highest levels of leadership.

There are several varieties of EIM systems that can be implemented, as shown in Figure 7.3:

1. Content management system (CMS): usually focuses on intranet-based or Internet-based corporate content, including data and knowledge bases.
2. Document management system (DMS): focuses on the storage and retrieval of work documents (e.g., forms) in their original format.

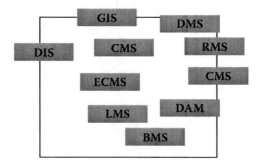

Figure 7.3 Enterprise information management system components.

3. Records management system (RMS): the management of both physical and electronic documents.
4. Digital asset management (DAM): similar to RMS but focuses on multimedia resources, such as images, audio, and video.
5. Brand management system (BMS): management of advertising and promotional materials.
6. Library management system (LMS): the administration of a (corporate) library's technical functions and services.
7. Digital imaging system (DIS): automates the creation of electronic versions of paper documents (e.g., PDF files) that are input to records management systems.
8. Learning management system (LMS): the administration of training and other learning resources. Learning content management systems (LCMS) combine content management systems with learning management systems.
9. Geographic information system (GIS): computer-based system for the capture, storage, retrieval, and analysis and display of spatial (i.e., location-referenced) data.

Enterprise content management systems (ECMS) combine all of the above within an organizational setting, in a variety of configurations.

Content Management System (CMS)

This digital content life cycle consists of six primary states:

1. Create
2. Update
3. Publish
4. Translate
5. Archive
6. Retire

each of which can take place on a variety of platforms. For example, an instance of digital content is created by one or more authors. Over time, that content might be edited. One or more individuals may provide some editorial oversight, thereby approving the content for publication. Once published, that content may be superseded by another form of content and thus retired or removed from use.

Content management is an inherently collaborative process. The process often consists of the following basic roles and responsibilities:

1. Content Author: responsible for creating and editing content.
2. Editor: responsible for tuning the content message and the style of delivery.
3. Publisher: responsible for releasing the content for consumption.
4. Administrator: responsible for managing the release of the content ultimately placing it into a repository so that it can be found and consumed.

A critical aspect of content management is the ability to manage versions of content as it evolves (i.e., version control). This is particularly important if the CMS is architected to be distributed across platforms, or certain aspects of it are pushed to the client as an X-executable.

Essentially, a content management system is a set of automated processes that can support the following features:

1. Identification of all key users and their roles
2. The ability to assign roles and responsibilities to different instances of content categories or types
3. Definition of workflow tasks often coupled with messaging so that content managers are alerted to changes in content
4. The ability to track and manage multiple versions of a single instance of content
5. The ability to publish the content to a repository to support the consumption of the content

Content management systems take the following forms:

1. A Web content management system is software for Web site management, which is often what is implicitly meant by this term
2. The work of a newspaper editorial staff organization
3. A workflow for article publication
4. A document management system
5. A single-source content management system, where content is stored in chunks, within a relational database
6. Content management systems usually focus on intranet-based or Internet-based corporate content, including data and knowledge bases.

CMSs allow end users to easily add new content in the form of articles. The articles are typically entered as plaintext, perhaps with markup to indicate where other resources (such as pictures, video, or audio) should be placed. Hence, CMSs are multimedia enabled. The system then uses rules to style the article, separating the display from the content, which has a number of advantages when trying to get many articles to conform to a consistent "look-and-feel." The system then adds the articles to a larger collection for publishing.

A popular example of this is the Wiki. A Wiki is a Web application that allows users to add content, as on an Internet forum, but also allows anyone to edit the content. The Wikipedia encyclopedia was created in this manner. Figure 7.4 shows a typical formatted page on Wikipedia. Note the "edit this page" tab at the top. Clicking on this tab obtains the display in Figure 7.5.

There are a variety of Wiki "engines," including UseMod, TWiki, MoinMoin, PmWiki, and MediaWiki. A list of some of those available can be found at http://c2.com/cgi/wiki?WikiEngines.

Wikipedia, a Wiki itself, provides the following checklist to assist in selecting Wiki software:

1. Who is developing it? A single person or a growing team?
2. Under what license is it distributed?
3. Who is using the Wiki? A good Wiki engine is likely to have a large group of existing users, and this is helpful if you need support running it.
4. Platform: should it run on a server or a local machine? Is online access needed? What OS does the machine run and is the Wiki software ported to it?
5. Features for editors: easy-to-write (and powerful) formatting rules, WYSIWYG capabilities, sectional editing, easy to roll back to earlier versions, file upload, insert image, able to write complex formulae, etc.
6. Features for readers: table of contents, search, navigation bar, access statistics, article rating, high-quality printable version.
7. User management: user personal page, personalized toolbar and preferences.
8. Groupware features: forum, gallery, message system.
9. Access controls: this is important for company intranet with security consideration.
10. Ability to import external files (HTML, Word document), export to external files (Word document, PDF).
11. Customizable interface: including main page, topbar, bottombar, sidebar; skins.
12. Multilingual support.
13. Extensibility: what third-party plug-ins exist, and what mechanisms are there for creating them?
14. Portability: are you locked into a particular package or wikitext format? Is it possible to export your text to other systems?

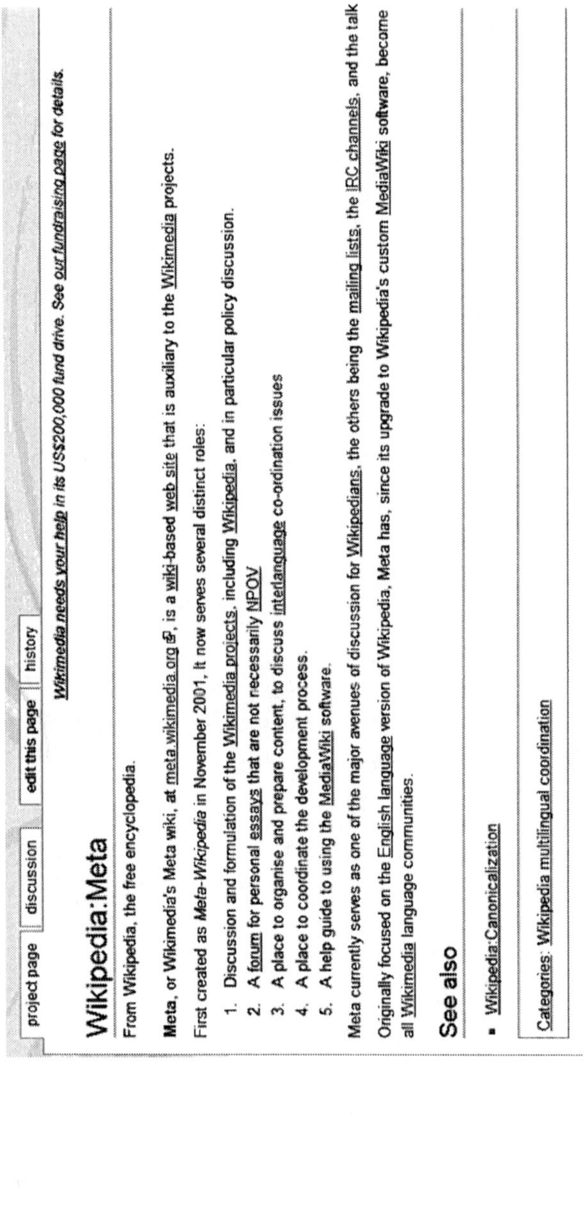

project page | discussion | **edit this page** | history

Wikimedia needs your help in its US$200,000 fund drive. See our fundraising page for details.

Wikipedia:Meta

From Wikipedia, the free encyclopedia.

Meta, or Wikimedia's Meta wiki, at meta.wikimedia.org ♂, is a wiki-based web site that is auxiliary to the Wikimedia projects.

First created as *Meta-Wikipedia* in November 2001, it now serves several distinct roles:

1. Discussion and formulation of the Wikimedia projects, including Wikipedia, and in particular policy discussion.
2. A forum for personal essays that are not necessarily NPOV
3. A place to organise and prepare content, to discuss interlanguage co-ordination issues
4. A place to coordinate the development process.
5. A help guide to using the MediaWiki software.

Meta currently serves as one of the major avenues of discussion for Wikipedians; the others being the mailing lists, the IRC channels, and the talk

Originally focused on the English language version of Wikipedia, Meta has, since its upgrade to Wikipedia's custom MediaWiki software, become all Wikimedia language communities.

See also

- Wikipedia:Canonicalization

Categories: Wikipedia multilingual coordination

Figure 7.4   Wikipedia page structure.

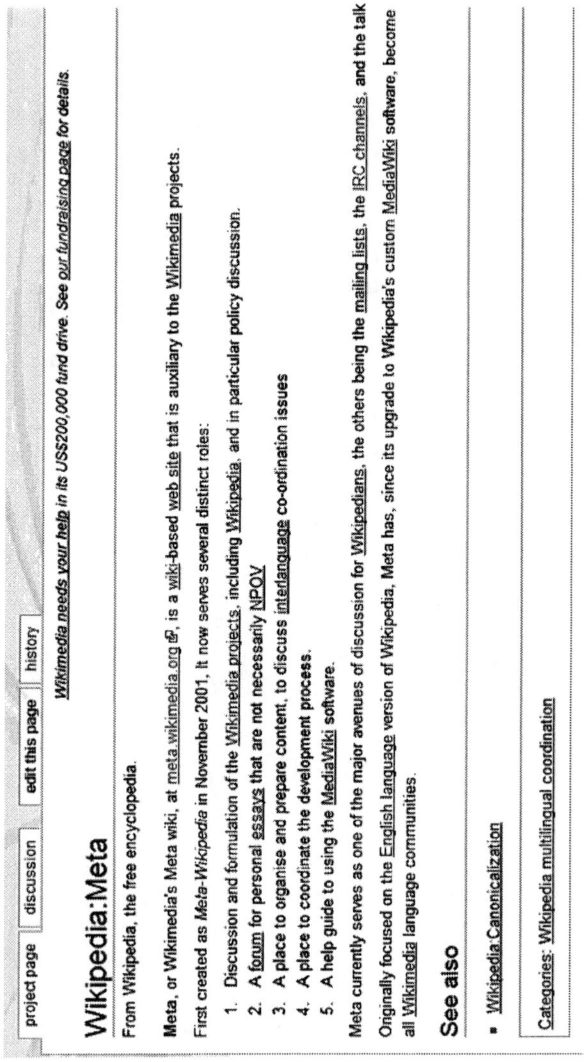

| project page | discussion | edit this page | history |

Wikimedia needs your help in its US$200,000 fund drive. See our fundraising page for details.

Wikipedia:Meta

From Wikipedia, the free encyclopedia.

Meta, or Wikimedia's Meta wiki, at meta.wikimedia.org ⮺, is a wiki-based web site that is auxiliary to the Wikimedia projects.

First created as *Meta-Wikipedia* in November 2001, it now serves several distinct roles:

1. Discussion and formulation of the Wikimedia projects, including Wikipedia, and in particular policy discussion.
2. A forum for personal essays that are not necessarily NPOV
3. A place to organise and prepare content, to discuss interlanguage co-ordination issues
4. A place to coordinate the development process.
5. A help guide to using the MediaWiki software.

Meta currently serves as one of the major avenues of discussion for Wikipedians, the others being the mailing lists, the IRC channels, and the talk pages. Originally focused on the English language version of Wikipedia, Meta has, since its upgrade to Wikipedia's custom MediaWiki software, become all Wikimedia language communities.

See also

■ Wikipedia:Canonicalization

Categories: Wikipedia multilingual coordination

Figure 7.5   Editing a Wiki.

15. Scalability: is it suitable for large numbers of pages, or is it just lightweight Wiki software? Most scalable Wiki software needs a back-end database to store pages.
16. Ease of use: is it easy to set up? Does it require php, SQL, an additional Web server? Or are you looking for something simple, like a WikiServer?

The latest "hot ticket" in the content management arena is the weblog or blog. A blog is a Web-based publication consisting primarily of periodic articles. Blogs range in scope from individual diaries to arms of political campaigns, media programs, and corporations. For example, Barack Obama, a senator from Illinois, maintains his blog at http://obama.senate.gov/blog/. Blogs range in scale from the writings of one occasional author, to the collaboration of a large community of writers. Many weblogs enable visitors to leave public comments, while others are noninteractive.

The format of weblogs varies, from simple bullet lists of hyperlinks, to article summaries or complete articles with user-provided comments and ratings. Individual weblog entries are almost always date- and time-stamped, with the newest post at the top of the page and reader comments often appearing below it. Because incoming links to specific entries are important to many weblogs, most have a way of archiving older entries and generating a static address for them; this static link is referred to as a *permalink*. The latest headlines, with hyperlinks and summaries, are frequently offered in weblogs in the RSS or Atom XML format, to be read with a feed reader or downloadable to a portable device.

RSS is a family of XML file formats for Web syndication used by news Web sites and weblogs. The abbreviation is used to refer to the following standards:

- Rich Site Summary (RSS 0.91)
- RDF Site Summary (RSS 0.9, 1.0 and 1.1)
- Really Simple Syndication (RSS 2.0)

The technology behind RSS allows you to subscribe to Web sites that have provided RSS feeds; these are typically sites that change or add content regularly. To use this technology, you need to set up some type of aggregation service. You then have to subscribe to the sites that you want to get updates on. Unlike typical subscriptions to pulp-based newspapers and magazines, your RSS subscriptions are free but they typically only give you a line or two of each article or post along with a link to the full article or post.

The RSS formats provide Web content or summaries of Web content, together with links to the full versions of the content, and other metadata.

This information is delivered as an XML file called RSS feed, webfeed, RSS stream, or RSS channel. In addition to facilitating syndication, RSS allows a Web site's frequent readers to track updates on the site using a news aggregator.

RSS news readers are small software programs that aggregate RSS feeds and display the story information. They allow you to scan headlines from hundreds of news sources in a central location.

A wide range of RSS readers can be easily downloaded from the Web. Some readers are Web based while others require you to download an executable onto your desktop or mobile device. Most are free to use. Several readers require Microsoft's .NET framework on your computer. They may be slightly more complicated to install if you do not have .NET, as they are a large install.

Google and Yahoo! both offer comprehensive lists of RSS readers. A few sample readers are offered below for the purpose of evaluation:

- Awasu — http://www.awasu.com/ (Windows)
- Bloglines — http://bloglines.com/ (All OS, browser based)
- Amphetadesk — http://www.disobey.com/amphetadesk/ (Windows)
- RSS Reader — http://www.rssreader.com/ (Windows .NET)
- NetNewsWire — http://ranchero.com/netnewswire/ (Mac OS X)

The tools for editing, organizing, and publishing weblogs are variously referred to as content management systems, publishing platforms, weblog software, and simply blogware.

Document Management Systems and Electronic Document Management Systems

Document management systems (DMSs) focus on the storage and retrieval of work documents (e.g., forms) in their original format. The key processes within the DMS are:

1. Feed: paper scanning or document importing.
2. Store: every organization has its own particular storage needs, based on data volume, accessibility requirements, archival duration, etc. Choices include magnetic (such as typical desktop hard-drives, RAID); optical (CD, DVD, WORM); magneto-optical storage technology; or a combination of these devices.
3. Indexing: tagging each document with some code for accessibility.
4. Control: one of the main advantages of an EDMS is that all documents of all types reside in the same computing environment;

yet in the context of a company's daily operations, it is quite probable that you would want for certain groups of employees to be granted access privileges to certain types of documents, while others may not.

5. Workflow: the EDMS is capable of mapping a company's organizational rules in the form of access controls to the document databases. EDMS tool suites often provide the means to model their operational procedures in the form of workflow management utilities.

6. Security.

7. Search: an efficient EDMS will allow users to search documents via pre-set indices, keywords, full-text search, even via thesaurus and synonym support. A majority of the time, filters can be applied, search criteria can be nested, and Boolean and comparison operators can be used. (We discuss this in more depth below.)

8. Access: once you have identified the documents you wish to review, the EDMS must be capable of retrieving them fast and transparently, regardless of where they are located. Documents can be distributed in multiple databases, in multiple locations. An efficient access strategy will give the end user the impression that the documents are all stored in one location, on one computer.

9. Share: collaborative capabilities prevent end users from making duplicates of the retrieved documents you have just retrieved.

The document management solution allows the user to deposit documents through multiple interfaces. Most users will access the document management system through a typical desktop configuration via a Web interface or an existing proprietary application. Access can also be obtained through imaging devices or through the organization's e-mail system, which archives e-mails as historical artifacts.

Search capabilities are typically built into the functionality of the document management system. Searches can be driven by a keyword search or through other designated parameters.

The Web content management interface depicts how documents within the document management system are published onto a Web site. Access through this Web content management interface would be independent of the access directly to a document management system, but defined accessibility and authentication would have to be established.

Originally, a document management system was a computer program (or set of programs) used to track and store images of paper documents. More recently, the term has been used to distinguish between imaging and records management systems that specialize in paper capture and records, respectively. Document management systems commonly provide check-in, check-out, storage, and retrieval of electronic documents, often in the form of word processor files and the like.

Typical systems have the user scan in the original paper document, and store the image of the document in the document management system, although increasingly, many documents are starting life as digital documents. The image is often given a name containing the date, and the user is often asked to type in additional "tags" to make finding the image easier. For example, a user scanning in an invoice might want to tag it with "hardware, CompUSA invoice, 1/1/2007."

The United States Nuclear Regulatory Commission (NRC) (www.nrc.gov) maintains a document management system for public use. The **A**gencywide **D**ocuments **A**ccess and **M**anagement **S**ystem (ADAMS) is an information system that provides access to all image and text documents that the NRC has made public since November 1, 1999, as well as bibliographic records (some with abstracts and full text) that the NRC made public before November 1999. The NRC continues to add several hundred new documents daily. ADAMS permits full-text searching and enables users to view document images, download files, and print locally. Figure 7.6 shows the ADAMS CMS interface:

Two methods for using ADAMS are available. Web-based access enables users to search ADAMS with a Web-based search engine. New

Figure 7.6   The US Nuclear Regulatory Commission ADAM CMS search interface.

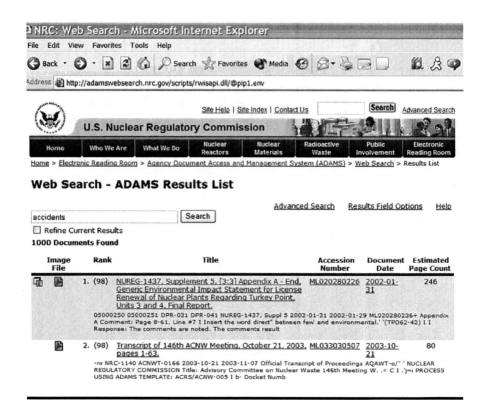

Figure 7.7 The search for accidents returns more than 1000 documents.

documents released during the day are added later that night. Most documents released before November 1999 are not available.

Citrix-based access enables users to access ADAMS using Citrix software, which must first be downloaded. Through the Citrix software, users can search for and retrieve documents using ADAMS features. This is different from browsing documents on the Internet and using a Web search engine. New documents are added throughout the day.

A search for accidents returns a list of more than 1000 documents, as shown in Figure 7.7.

ADAM and other document management systems have the look-and-feel of a typical Internet search engine. That corporate documents offer a vast opportunity has not been lost on the search engine industry. Google itself is pitching several server or client offerings, including Google Enterprise (http://www.google.com/enterprise/gsa/), Google Desktop for Enterprise (http://desktop.google.com/enterprise/index.html) and Toolbar for Enterprise (http://www.google.com/tools/toolbar/T4/enterprise/). Each of these solutions combines the power of the Internet with the power of the desktop/server — that is, an X solution. Google competitors include

Vivisimo Clustering Engine (http://vivisimo.com/html/vce), Vivisimo Content Integrator (http://vivisimo.com/html/vci) and the Metacrawler Toolbar (http://www.metacrawler.com/info.metac/tbar/).

Google, Vivisimo, and Metacrawler are three very different types of search tools. Google, which has indexed well over 4 billion Web pages (Wong, 2004), primarily returns results based on popularity using its PageRank™ technology to calculate each page's ranking and importance. Metacrawler, on the other hand, does not search Web pages directly. Instead, it searches the results of its partners' (i.e., Google, Yahoo, Ask Jeeves, About.com, and Overture) Web directories and search engine databases and tries to provide the best results. Vivisimo is also a meta-search engine. Its "chief selling proposition" is its clustering engine, which organizes the results of the search into logical clusters or groupings.

Google returns results based on importance. Vivisimo and Metacrawler are both meta-search facilities, meaning that they do not search the Internet and compile an index on their own, as does Google. Instead, they search the results of the search engine databases and Web directories of their search partners. Their goal is to improve the relevance of the search. Vivisimo refers to this as a "federated search" when the corporate repository is integrated into the search. A federated search allows users to perform multiple searches at the same time through as many diverse informational sources as needed, whether they are internal documents, intranets, partner extranets, Web sources, subscription services and databases, syndicated news feeds, or intelligence portals such as Hoover's. A user enters a search query through a single search interface that acts as an intermediary to various informational repositories. The query is sent simultaneously to all designated search sources and results are returned to the user in a single list.

Records Management Systems

Records management systems (RMSs) manage both physical and electronic documents. As of 2005, records management has increased interest among corporations due to new compliance regulations and statutes. While government, legal, and healthcare entities have a strong, historical records management discipline, general recordkeeping of corporate records has been poorly standardized and implemented. In addition, scandals such as the Enron/Andersen scandal, and more recently records-related mishaps at Morgan Stanley, have renewed interest in corporate records compliance, litigation preparedness, and issues. Statutes such as the U.S. Sarbanes-Oxley Act have created new concerns among corporate "compliance officers" that result in more standardization of records management practices within an organization.

The practice of records management involves all of the following activities:

1. Creating, approving, and enforcing records policies, including a classification system and a records retention policy
2. Developing a records storage plan, which includes the short- and long-term housing of physical records and digital information
3. Identifying existing and newly created records, classifying them, and then storing them according to standard operating procedures
4. Monitoring the access and circulation of records within and even outside an organization
5. Executing a retention policy to archive and destroy records according to operational needs, operating procedures, statues, and regulations

Trustworthy records are essential for an organization to meet its legal and internal business needs. Reliability, authenticity, integrity, and usability are the characteristics used to describe trustworthy records from a records management perspective.

Creating and maintaining trustworthy records require resources. Organizations should conduct a risk analysis to balance the level of trustworthiness of records against costs and risks.

Because companies are moving quickly to Web-based document management systems, a discussion of trustworthy records would be beneficial. Who better to provide this information than the United States National Archives (http://www.archives.gov/records-mgmt/policy/managing-web-records.html)? Billions of letters, photographs, video and audio recordings, drawings, maps, treaties, posters, and other informative materials exist that tell the stories of America's history as a nation. From the Declaration of Independence, the Constitution, and the Bill of Rights, to census records that account for every citizen — the preservation of important American documents helps illustrate what happened in the United States before and after we were born.

The National Archives and Records Administration (NARA) is America's record-keeper. NARA is the government agency that not only preserves documents and materials related to the United States, but also makes sure people can access the information.

The characteristics of trustworthy records include the following:

■ **Reliability**. A reliable Web site is one whose content can be trusted as a full and accurate representation of the transactions, activities, or facts to which it attests and therefore can be depended upon in the course of subsequent transactions or activities.

- **Authenticity.** An authentic Web site is one that is proven to be what it purports to be and to have been created by the organization with which it is identified. Web site-related records should be created by individuals who have direct knowledge of the facts or by instruments routinely used within the business to conduct the transaction.

  To demonstrate the authenticity of a Web site, organizations should implement and document policies and procedures that control the creation, transmission, receipt, and maintenance of Web site records to ensure that records creators are authorized and identified and that records are protected against unauthorized addition, deletion, and alteration (e.g., via hacking).

- **Integrity.** The integrity of a Web content record refers to it being complete and unaltered.

  Web management policies and procedures for updating and modifying Web sites should be created. The ISO (International Standards Organization) specifies that records systems should maintain audit trails or other elements sufficient to demonstrate that records were effectively protected from unauthorized alteration or destruction. The Web management policies should prescribe how changes to the Web site are to be documented.

  Another aspect of integrity is the structural integrity of a Web site's content-related records. The structure of a Web site, that is, its physical and logical format and the relationships between the pages and content elements composing the site, should remain physically or logically intact. Failure to maintain the Web site's structural integrity may impair its reliability and authenticity.

- **Usability.** A usable Web site is one that can be located, retrieved, presented, and interpreted. In retrieval and use, you should be able to directly connect the Web site to the business activity or transaction that produced it. You should be able to identify both the site and its content within the context of broader business activities and functions. The links between content, contextual, and structural Web site-related records that document organizational Web site activities should be maintained. These contextual linkages should provide an understanding of the transactions that created and used them.

What are the records management risks associated with Web sites? From a records management perspective, risk relates to (1) challenge to the trustworthiness of the records (e.g., legal challenge) that can be expected over the life of the record; and (2) unauthorized loss or destruction of records. Consequences are measured by the degree of loss that the agency or citizens would suffer if the trustworthiness of the Web site-related records could not be verified or if there was unauthorized loss or destruction.

Examples of records management-related risks associated with Web sites are mainly technical risks. Loss of information could result from:

1. An inability to document or validate transactions that occur via a Web site front end
2. An inability to reconstruct views of Web content that was created dynamically and existed only virtually for the time that they were viewed
3. Compromise of transactions
4. An inability to track Web-assisted policy development or document decisions relating to Web operations

A risk assessment should address the possible consequences of untrustworthy, lost, or unrecoverable records, including the legal risk and financial costs of losses, the likelihood that a damaging event will occur, and the costs of taking corrective actions. Organizations should have formal risk assessment procedures that may be applied to Web site operations.

The assessment factors can include *records management threats, visibility, consequences, and sensitivity.*

1. *Records management threats* relate to the likelihood of experiencing technical risks (e.g., risks of unauthorized destruction of Web site-related records, litigation risks associated with an inability to reconstruct views of Web sites at specific points in time, risks associated with inability to document web site policy decisions, etc.).
2. *Visibility* is the level of awareness of a Web site's operations.
3. *Consequences* describes the level of negative organizational, economic, or programmatic impact if Web records are untrustworthy, lost, or unrecoverable.
4. *Sensitivity* characterizes the organization's assessment of the importance of Web site operations.

The results of an assessment will support programs by providing a basis for determining what types of Web site records should be created, how they should be maintained, and how long they should be maintained. The assessment will help organizations ensure that the level of risk is tolerable and that resources are properly allocated. Assessment results can also aid in the development of Web site records schedules.

Four types of changes can occur to a Web site's content between backups:

1. Changes to the content of an individual page without changing its placement in the overall organization of the Web site
2. Wholesale replacement of an individual page (or sections of pages) without changing its placement in the overall organization of the Web site
3. Changes in location of a page (or groups of pages)
4. Combinations of changes of these first three types

Changes of the first two types (i.e., changes to content without changing the page's placement in the overall organization of the Web site) can be treated as a version-control issue. You must decide how to best keep track of the versions of content pages.

The most fundamental, nonautomated approach to tracking Web site content, particularly for relatively stable sites, is to "print and file" a recordkeeping copy in the manual recordkeeping system. Another non-automated approach to version control is to annotate changes to content pages as a comment in the HTML coding. The comment, which will not appear when the page is displayed in a browser, could indicate when the page was changed (e.g., <!--Updated by MDG on 03/02/07-->) or could reference the page that it wholesale replaced (e.g., <!--This page replaced content page Introduction_1.html on 09/10/07-->). Another manual approach would be to maintain a log file of content changes of the first two types of changes. (Keep in mind that neither of these approaches would allow you to actually reconstruct views presented at a particular time. This may be found acceptable per your risk assessment.)

Alternatively, you can use content management software (CMS) to track versions of Web content in the first two cases. CMS would also offer limited page view reconstruction capabilities-default settings for the data-bases that support most CMS software would retain only recent changes.

You can handle major changes to the site's directory structure by producing a new site map at the time of major revision. This could be accomplished in a manual or automated manner.

One tool is a type of search engine called "Web harvester." Also called a "spider" or "crawler," a harvester is a program that visits Web sites and reads their pages and other information in order to create entries for a search engine index. You can use harvester software to identify changes to Web site content and to gather content related to specific site (sub)units.

Digital Asset Management

Digital asset management (DAM) is similar to RMS but focuses on multi-media resources, such as images, audio, and video.

Digital asset management is still a new market with rapid technical evolution; hence many different types of systems will be labeled DAM systems although they are designed to address slightly different problems or were created for a specific industry. A variety of commercial systems for DAM are available, and numerous groups are trying to establish standards for DAM.DAM systems generally support functions for ingesting, managing, searching, retrieving and archiving of assets. DAM systems may also include version control and asset format conversion capabilities (i.e., dynamically downsizing a large, high-resolution image for display on a Web site). DAM systems are related to and can be considered a superset of content management systems.

DAM is a combination of workflow, software, and hardware that organizes and retrieves a company's digital assets.

There are three categories of digital asset management systems:

1. *Brand asset management systems,* with a focus on facilitation of content reuse within large organizations.
2. *Library asset management systems,* with a focus on storage and retrieval of large amounts of infrequently changing media assets, for example in video or photo archiving.
3. *Production asset management systems,* with a focus on storage, organization, and revision control of frequently changing digital assets, for example in digital media production.

From a technical perspective, DAM applications are divided into two basic categories: (1) media catalogs and (2) asset repositories (Ross, 1999).

The primary characteristic of media catalogs is the utilization of proxies, such as thumbnails, in an indexed database that can be quickly searched by keyword. The actual source files are left untouched and under control of the operating system. The benefits of media catalogs include low cost, ease of installation and administration, and scalability across multiple divisions of an enterprise.

Because media catalogs do not actually manage the content itself, anyone with system access can typically view, change, move, or delete any content element. This usually precludes such features as check-in/check-out of content, rights management, and automatic versioning (the latest version of a print, for example). Media catalogs can also become sluggish with very large catalogs, especially if distributed across multiple servers or geographic locations.

In asset repositories, the content itself is physically stored inside a secure database. This results in a host of benefits, including security levels, replication, referential integrity, and centralized data management. Also included is the comfort of full hierarchical storage management and disaster recovery.

Conclusion

As one can see, an X system is not independent of its data. In actuality, it is similar in architecture to an object-oriented system where both data and function are encapsulated (i.e., embedded) within an object. In the case of X-enabled systems, the systems architect must be mindful that there are various informational requirements and systems within an organization. The architect needs to carefully consider which information will be used, and how and where it will be embedded into the architecture.

References

Berners-Lee, T., Hendler, J., and Lassila, O. (2001, May). The Semantic Web. *Scientific American.*

Cayzer, S. (2004, December). Semantic blogging and decentralized knowledge management. *Communications of the ACM.* 47(12).

Ford, P. (2002, July 26). August 2009: How Google beat Amazon and Ebay to the Semantic Web. *FTrain.com* Retrieved fromhttp://www.ftrain.com/google_takes_all.html

Lee, J.K. and Sohn, M.M. (2003, May). The eXtensible Rule Markup Language. *Communications of the ACM.* 46(5).

Nielsen Norman Group. (2003). Simplicity and enterprise search. Retrieved from http://www.google.com/enterprise/pdf/google_simplicity_enterprise_wp.pdf.

Raisinghani, S. (2000, September 4). Ontologies and GJXDM. *Metatomix.* Retrieved from it.ojp.gov/documents/ucon/semantic.ppt

Ross, T. (1999, September). *Digital Asset Management: The Art of Archiving.* Retrieved from http://www.techexchange.com/thelibrary/DAM.html

Sure, Y. and Studer, R. (n.d.). Semantic Web Technologies for Digital Libraries. Retrieved from http://www.aifb.uni-karlsruhe.de/WBS/ysu/publications/2005_sw_for_dl.pdf

Wong, M. (2004, August 20). Company must now focus on competition, new technology. *Monterey County Herald.* Retrieved from http://www.montereyherald.com/mld/montereyherald/business/9450718.htm

Chapter 8

X-Tools: Building Executable Internet Apps

X system solutions should sport a rich client, be compatible across browsers, and can be downloaded and installed transparently to the end user. They are also compatible with the following technologies:

1. Simple Object Access Protocol (SOAP) is a lightweight, eXtensible Markup Language (XML) based protocol for exchanging information in a networked environment. The SOAP specification defines the XML message format, the bindings to HTTP, and how remote procedure calls can be represented in SOAP. Currently, the most commonly used function of SOAP is to provide a mechanism for enabling remote procedure calls through an HTTP POST.
2. Web Services Description Language (WSDL) is an XML-based format that describes the methods and parameters a given Web service accepts and the format of the response that it returns. WSDL is highly useful for developers building applications that consume Web services. Developers can expect that the creation and interpretation of WSDL are handled by development tools.
3. Universal Description, Discovery, and Integration (UDDI) is both a registry through which service providers can list their implementations and a specification for describing the service and searching the registry. Think of UDDI as the *Yellow Pages* that allow developers and businesses to locate other Web service providers.

It is also appropriate to make a note here of Remote Procedure Call (RPC) through XML (XML-RPC). XML-RPC is the forerunner to SOAP. Similar to SOAP, XML-RPC is an XML-based protocol for making remote procedure calls over HTTP. While a good portion of the industry is working on SOAP and driving it toward standards adoption, there are a growing number of XML-RPC implementations available.

In general, there are several approaches to providing an X solution. These run the gamut from language based to plug-ins. This chapter provides a sampling of a few of these. A listing of an assortment of X-enabled toolsets appears at the end of the chapter and in Chapter 10.

REBOL

Java is the most well-known language being used for Web development today. Because of its portability, the small size of its Java applets, and rich functionality, it is a natural for the tool of choice when developing X applications. However, there are other alternatives. One of them is REBOL.

REBOL is pronounced "reb-ol" (as in "rebel with a cause") and stands for "relative expression based object language." REBOL runs on a wide variety of system platforms, including both servers and clients. REBOL (http://www.rebol.com) was created by Carl Sassenrath, who is best known for bringing multitasking to personal computers with the Commodore Amiga operating system. Sassenrath has graciously permitted me to provide the information on REBOL and code samples contained within this chapter.

REBOL's take on X Internet is that it builds on the trend that local client computers are now as powerful as the back-end network servers, so more computing responsibility should be shifted to the clients. There are three advantages to this approach:

1. It improves the quality of the user experience. It makes Internet applications run at the speed of local applications. The delays inherent in the design of the Web disappear.
2. It accelerates the server. With clients doing more of the work, the server can do a lot less. That allows you to run many times more connections from the same server. How many typically? At least 10 to 50 times as many. That is like getting 10 to 50 more servers for the cost of one.
3. It makes network communication more efficient. Applications do not need to transfer user interface elements (e.g., Web pages) over the connection each time. Instead, they send just data or code that

is relevant to the actions taken by the user. This allows X Internet applications to take about 1/10th to 1/50th the bandwidth of typical web applications.

Aside from the REBOL language, the company provides an X-Internet framework. REBOL IOS lets companies dynamically connect and manage resources across the Internet, not just at their servers or within a LAN. Unlike traditional network systems, IOS connects people rather than computers so that co-workers have access to their personal workspaces (applications, information, data, and communications) anywhere they have access to the Internet.

Getting connected requires users to download a small X Internet client (500 K) and logging in. IOS restores the users' workspaces within minutes and ensures that they have the most current applications, files, and data. If they go offline, IOS continues to operate with the most recent work-spaces. When they reconnect, IOS maintains the workspaces by down-loading any changes. At all times, users access applications and data at the speed of their local computer, regardless of whether or not they are connected.

IOS was built from the ground up for the Internet. REBOL's unique dialecting capability enables information to flow automatically over man-aged, encrypted, and authenticated connections. Third-party applications can easily plug in to IOS. For example:

A leading computer hardware manufacturer is replacing its existing Web browser-based initiative with an IOS system in an effort to provide the instant response its needs to maximize the efficiency of their design engineers.

A large CRM applications provider can integrate and brand IOS modules to extend the reach of its software solutions beyond the traditional boundaries of the LAN or VPN (virtual private network).

A well-known IT solutions consultant can provide a fully integrated project management system by leveraging the hyper-efficient work-flow that distributed computing provides.

IOS applications, called reblets and built using the REBOL language, are tiny, so they download quickly and do not take much local storage space. Most IOS applications consist of both a client side and a server side, although this is transparent to users.

Reblets are REBOL applets. They are tiny X Internet applications that run on REBOL IOS and do "one thing very well." More than 40 standard reblets are prepackaged with the IOS. Figure 8.1 below shows the desktop reblet. Its function is to provide secure, synchronized file and application

Figure 8.1   The desktop reblet. The REBOL/View Desktop is a kind of specialized Internet browser.

sharing. It is intuitive and easy to use because it works like a Web page or file folder.

Reblets are extremely agile. Their small size allows them to be easily modified, customized, branded, expanded, or combined with other reblets.

Because IOS runs across Windows, Linux, UNIX, and most other systems, it is possible to integrate the entire organization. IOS also runs within a mobile environment. Unfortunately, the PalmOS is too limited in its memory architecture to allow applications such as REBOL IOS. The company has investigated the possibility several times, but they found that they need more than the 96 K of memory that applications are allotted under PalmOS. As an alternative, they recommend the Sharp Linux PDA or a Win CE PDA.

IOS can be considered peer-to-peer in the sense that you use an IOS client to communicate with other members of a group. IOS also takes advantage of server technology to allow messages and files to be stored and backed up in a safe location, even when users are not online. For example, when the user goes online, he or she will receive alerts and messages missed when the device was offline. In addition, the server model allows a greater degree of account management and user authentication that is often required in modern business environments.

REBOL Language Primer

From a programmer's perspective, it is always interesting to see how a particular language functions — particularly if you have never before heard of it. T section runs REBOL through its paces.

Here is how one codes the classic programmer's **Hello World** example:

```
print "Hello World!"
```

Or, you send it as an e-mail message to a friend:

```
send luke@rebol.com "Hello World!"
```

To run a script directly from a Web site:

```
do http://www.rebol.com/speed.r
```

That script will show how fast your computer is.
To see the script's source code:

```
print read http://www.rebol.com/speed.r
```

To save the source code to a file:

```
write %speed.r read http://www.rebol.com/speed.r
```

To run the code locally, you can type:

```
do %speed.r
```

You can save any Web page the same way:

```
write %page.html read http://www.rebol.com
```

To send a Web page to a friend through e-mail:

```
send luke@rebol.com read http://www.rebol.com
```

If you want to e-mail all the files in a directory (assuming they are all text):

```
files: load %letters/
foreach file files [send luke@rebol.com read file]
```

But, maybe you only want to send files that include the word REBOL:

```
foreach file files [
    text: read file
    if find text "REBOL" [send luke@rebol.com text]
]
```

If you want to join all those files into a single message and send it:

```
message: copy ""
foreach file files [append message read file]
send luke@rebol.com message
```

To see all your e-mail messages without removing them from your server:

```
print read pop://luke:r2d2@rebol.com
```

Of course, you might want to read them one at a time:

```
mail: open pop://luke:r2d2@rebol.com
foreach message mail [
    print message
    ask "Next? "
]
close mail
```

When you are ready to send a message to your broker which is automatically processed by her REBOL-based stock trading application:

```
send broker@sell-it-now.com [
    sell 1000 shares "Microsoft" MSFT at $50.00
]
```

The above example uses the REBOL concept of **_dialecting_** — a useful technique for sending and receiving messages over networks.

If your boss asks you to automatically e-mail several Web pages every hour:

```
pages: [
    http://www.cnet.com
    http://www.rebol.com/index.html
    http://www.news-wire.com/news/today.html
]
loop 24 [
    foreach page pages [send boss@hans.com read page]
    wait 1:00
]
```

Figure 8.2   Building a calculator with REBOL.

You need to extract and print the title of a Web page, you can parse it with:

```
page: read http://www.cnet.com
parse page [thru <title> copy title to </title>]
print title
```

REBOL is a fully fleshed-out programming language that includes structures such as scripts, series, functions, objects, file processing, and parsing. Figure 8.2 demonstrates some of this functionality. The code for the calculator appears below:

```
REBOL [
        Title: "Calculator"
        Version: 1.2.2
        Date:   17-Jun-2005 ;2-Apr-2001
        Author: ["Jeff Kreis" "Allen Kamp"
          "Carl Sassenrath"]
        Purpose: {Simple numeric calculator.}
        Needs: [1.3.0]
]

auto-clear: true
```

```
calculate: does [
     if error? try [text-box/text: form do text-box/text][
          text-box/text: "Error"
          text-box/color: red
     ]
     auto-clear: true
     show text-box
]

clear-box: does [
     clear text-box/text
     text-box/color: snow
     auto-clear: false
     show text-box
]

calculator: layout [
     style btn btn 40x24
     style kc btn red [clear-box]
     style k= btn [calculate]
     style k  btn [
          if auto-clear [clear-box]
          append text-box/text face/text
          show text-box
     ]
     origin 10 space 4
     backeffect base-effect
     text-box: field "0" 172x24 bold snow right
       feel none
     pad 4
     across
     kc "C" keycode [#"C" #"c" page-down]
     k "(" #"(" k ")" #")" k " / " #"/" return
     k "7" #"7" k "8" #"8" k "9" #"9" k " * " #"*" return
     k "4" #"4" k "5" #"5" k "6" #"6" k " - " #"-" return
     k "1" #"1" k "2" #"2" k "3" #"3" k " + " #"+" return
     k "0" #"0" k "-"      k "." #"."
     k= green "=" keycode [#"=" #"^m"] return
     key keycode [#"^(ESC)" #"^q"] [quit]
]

view center-face calculator
```

Rebsites

Any Web server can be used to publish folders and files to the REBOL/View desktop. Here are the necessary steps:

1. Create an index.r file. This is currently done with a text editor. (However, we expect to have a small REBOL application in the future that will create it for you.)
2. Upload the index.r file to a Web server. This is done with FTP, the same way that you would upload an html file to a Web server.
3. Upload any other files that are referred to from the index.r file. One can create sub-directories that also include their own index.r files.
4. Test the site by running REBOL/View and clicking on the GOTO text button in the top bar. Enter the URL for the site and see how it works.
5. Once you have it working, you can add your index.r file to the master directory in the REBOL.com/Sites folder. Click on the Add Sites icon to add your link.
6. Your Reb site will now be live. Any changes that you make to your index.r will be seen by anyone who visits your site on the Reb.

Folders are created with index files. Each index file specifies the icons, actions, attributes, and the look of a folder.

Folder index files are written as normal REBOL text files. The index files are loaded by REBOL/View and are shown on the desktop. The format of an index file is a simple dialect that describes the folder and it icons. This format is optimized to create results with very few words. It is much easier than creating an HTML file.

Index files have the following general format:

- *Header:* a normal REBOL header block, but not evaluated. This header must contain a TYPE field. (See below.)
- Folder: attributes that describe the folder and how it should appear.
- Icons: a list of icons to be displayed in the folder. Each icon can include optional information about itself.

A very simple example index file looks like:

```
REBOL [type: 'index]
file "Hello" %hello.r
file "Calendar" %calendar.r
folder "Documents" %documents.r
```

Index files must begin with a standard REBOL header to identify that they contain REBOL information. A header can contain many fields of information. However, all fields are optional, with the exception of the TYPE field. For index files, the TYPE field must be set to 'index. Here is an example of a minimal header:

```
REBOL [type: 'index
```

The index file header can be followed by a set of attributes that describe the folder and create a custom look for it. These attributes can appear in any order. Here is a sample index file that includes folder attributes:

```
REBOL [type: 'index]
summary {
    This is the home to all types of distributed
    calendars. We also host calendar servers.
}
text-color 100.0.0 0.0.100
backdrop %calendar.gif [contrast -30 luma 30]
```

There are two basic types of icons: (1) a folder and (2) a file. Both types use a similar syntax. The basic syntax for a file icon is:

```
file "name" %file.r
```

The icon will display the specified name, and it will refer to the given file. Note that the file name is preceded with a %, which tells REBOL that it is a file. The file name can also be a URL:

```
file "name" http://www.example.com/file.r
```

Similarly, the syntax for a folder is:

```
folder "name" %index.r
```

A folder icon will be displayed with the given name. The file name is that of another index file that describes the folder and its contents. The file can also be a URL:

```
folder "name" http://www.rebol.com/index.r
```

As observed from Figure 8.3, the flexibility is enormous and exciting from a developer's point of view.

Figure 8.3   Slashdot's rebsite.

Flash Remoting MX

Macromedia Flash Remoting MX (http://www.adobe.com/products/flashremoting/) provides the connection between Macromedia Flash and a Web application server, enabling the developer to integrate Flash content with applications built using Macromedia ColdFusion MX, Microsoft .NET, Java, and SOAP-based Web services. As shown in Figure 8.4, Flash apps can be ported to a wide variety of devices, making it the perfect X delivery vehicle.

Subaru Primal Quest is an expedition-length adventure race, in which four-person co-ed teams race non-stop to compete for a $250,000 prize purse, the richest in adventure racing history. Racers take part in multiple disciplines, including trail running, down-river paddling, night and day navigation, rappelling and ascending, mountain biking, and steep snow travel.

The goal was to create a data-driven site and content management system that would manage and deliver race information to teams, race administrators, fans, and syndication services over the Internet. To do this, the development team used Flash MX, Dreamweaver MX, and ColdFusion MX. They created a content management system, registration system, rich media applications, and Web services.

The biggest challenge was deciding how to deliver live race content to viewers around the world. Macromedia Flash Player provided the perfect delivery tool. The developers developed several rich media applications

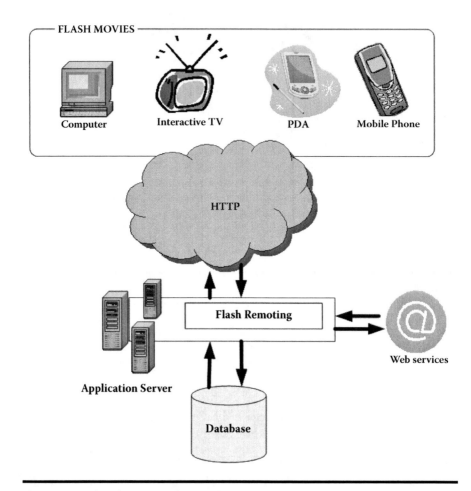

Figure 8.4   The Flash Remoting environment.

with Macromedia Flash MX to help bring the race to users' desktops via the Flash Player.

First, a Macromedia Flash MX leader board application provided live race data from all 70 teams into a compact and efficient user interface. All 70 teams and the 29 race checkpoints were available in a single-screen interface. Additionally, an interactive map application displayed the complete race map with a variety of interactive controls. Within the map, users could pan and zoom across the 400-mile race course.

The map leveraged ColdFusion MX Components (CFCs) and Macromedia Flash Remoting to provide live race data. Users were able to search for teams and checkpoints, and instantly view current race positions. The map dynamically updated as the race progressed, providing users with real-time information in a single-screen interactive interface.

Flash applications that use Flash Remoting MX resemble other client/server development platforms, including traditional HTML-based Web applications. For example, Flash applications usually appear in the context of a browser window, much like HTML pages. In addition, Flash applications can contain controls for displaying text and graphics, gathering user input, and communicating with a remote server, much like HTML.

Like a Web browser request for an HTML page, the Flash application makes a service function call to a remote service. The service function call is a client-initiated, asynchronous event. The Flash application makes a request to the remote service, and the service processes the request and returns the results. The Flash Player does not wait for the result — it handles the result when it is returned.

Because Flash Remoting MX connects two distinct and separate runtime environments, you build Flash applications with Flash Remoting MX in two programming languages, (1) ActionScript and (2) the programming language of your application server. Therefore, building Flash applications with Flash Remoting MX demands knowledge of at least two different development environments:

1. *Flash MX.* To create Flash applications that use Flash Remoting MX, you use the Flash MX authoring environment to design the user interface and write the client-side ActionScript.
2. *Application server tool.* For ColdFusion, Java, or .NET development, you typically use a text editor or an integrated development environment (IDE) that supports the associated programming languages and APIs. Macromedia Dreamweaver MX supports ColdFusion, JSP, and ASP.NET development.
3. *Java or .NET compiler.* For Java or .NET development, you need a Java or .NET compiler to create executable code.

To build a Flash application that uses Flash Remoting MX, you write ActionScript in the Flash MX authoring environment that connects to the remote service and calls a service function.

Flex

Most traditional systems developers shy away from using Flash because they find it challenging to develop in an animation-based environment. Flex appears to provide a solution to this problem.

The Flex presentation server (http://www.adobe.com/products/flex/) provides a familiar, standards-based programming framework for delivering the presentation tier of Rich Internet Applications. The goal of Flex is to allow Web application developers to quickly and easily build Rich

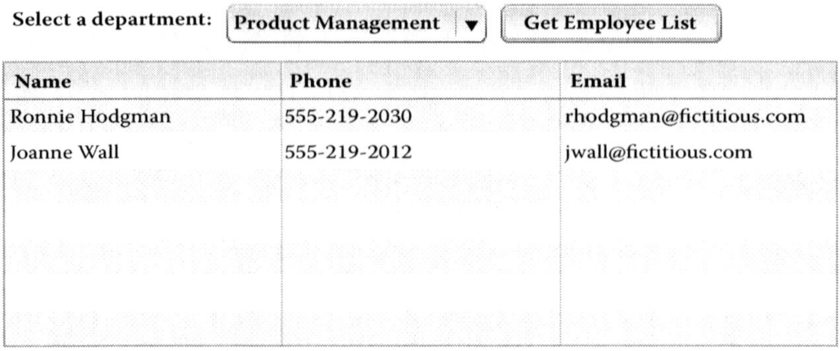

Select a department: [**Product Management** ▾] [**Get Employee List**]

Name	Phone	Email
Ronnie Hodgman	555-219-2030	rhodgman@fictitious.com
Joanne Wall	555-219-2012	jwall@fictitious.com

Figure 8.5 A simple Web services display created with Flex.

Internet Applications, otherwise known as RIAs. In a multi-tiered model, Flex applications serve as the Presentation Tier.

Flex utilizes an XML-based language (MXML) for defining Rich Internet Application front ends and an object-oriented, ECMAScript-based language (ActionScript 2.0) for scripting front-end logic. The MXML code for creating the display in Figure 8.5 follows:

```
</mx:WebService>

  <mx:HBox>

    <mx:Label text="Select a department:"/>

    <mx:ComboBox id="dept" width="150">
      <mx:dataProvider>
        <mx:Array>
          <mx:Object label="Engineering" data=
          "ENG"/>
          <mx:Object label="Product Management"
          data="PM"/>
          <mx:Object label="Marketing" data="MKT"/>
        </mx:Array>
      </mx:dataProvider>
    </mx:ComboBox>

  <mx:Button label="Get Employee List" click=
    "employeeWS.getList.send()"/>

    </mx:HBox>
```

```
<mx:DataGrid dataProvider="{employeeWS.getList.
  result}" width="100%">
  <mx:columns>
    <mx:Array>
      <mx:DataGridColumn columnName="name"
        headerText="Name"/>
      <mx:DataGridColumn columnName="phone"
        headerText="Phone"/>
      <mx:DataGridColumn columnName="email"
        headerText="Email"/>
    </mx:Array>
  </mx:columns>
</mx:DataGrid>

</mx:Application>
```

Flex provides an object-oriented development approach, so you can assemble applications with components.

New and Improved HTML: Nexaweb

A Nexaweb-based application (http://www.nexaweb.com) is created and delivered just like a normal Web application, except for one main difference: typical Web applications use HTML for the user interface (UI) while Nexaweb applications use XML for the UI. Nexaweb applications are just like other J2EE applications, composed of JSP, Servlets, EJB, JDBC/ODBC, and other similar coding structures. Nexaweb applications can be administrated using any standard J2EE application management tools.

The Nexaweb Client is an XML rendering and communications engine with a small footprint. The Nexaweb Client is implemented in Java, based on JDK 1.1, and is compatible with the Personal Java Specification (which evolved into J2ME). Although the footprint is extremely small (~150 kb), the Nexaweb Client supports user interface functionality that is comparable to Windows MFC and Java/Swing/JFC. The Nexaweb Client communicates with the Nexaweb Server and retrieves the application's user interface description via XUL/SVG and renders it accordingly.

The user interface functionality built into the Nexaweb Client processes most UI operations locally. Functionality includes rendering, table sorting, etc. In addition, customized code can be transported and run solely on the client. Using Nexaweb, businesses can build Internet applications that look and function like Windows applications, as shown in Figure 8.6. Most enterprise-level applications require complex functionality such as nonlinear workflows, drag-and-drop, and a rich user interface — none of

Figure 8.6 Nexaweb enables rich UI functionality when developing an application.

which today's Web standards can adequately support. The Nexaweb platform allows developers to deliver familiar desktop metaphors in their Web-based applications, along with whatever multimedia functionality is deemed appropriate. Today our customers are delivering visually and functionally rich applications.

Curl

Curl started life as a research project at MIT's Laboratory for Computer Science, under the direction of Professor Steve Ward (http://www.cag.lcs.mit.edu/curl/).

Curl provides a rich set of formatting operations similar to those implemented by HTML tags. Unlike HTML, the Curl formatter can be extended by users to provide additional functionality, from simple macros (e.g., to provide a convenient way to switch to a particular font, size, and color) to direct control over the positioning of sub-components (e.g., as in a TeX-like equation formatter). Using a toolkit of interactive components, Curl makes it easy to build simple interactive Web pages. One can view interactive objects such as buttons or editable fields as extensions to the basic formatting operations provided.

Other components of an interactive document may require more sophisticated mechanisms than are provided by the interface toolkit. These components can also be developed using Curl because, at its heart, Curl is really an object-oriented programming language. Curl expressions embedded in the Web document are securely compiled to native code by the built-in, on-the-fly compiler and then executed without the need for any kind of interpreter. Curl provides many of the features of a modern object-oriented programming language: multiple inheritance, extensible syntax, a strong type system that includes a dynamic "any" type, safe execution through encapsulation of user code, and extensive checking performed both at compile and runtime.

According to Professor Ward, Curl is intended to be a *gentle slope system*, accessible to content creators at all skill levels ranging from authors new to the Web to experienced programmers. By using a simple, uniform language syntax and semantics, Curl avoids the discontinuities experienced by current Web users who have to juggle HTML, JavaScript, Java, Perl, etc. to create today's exciting sites.

Cambridge-based Curl Corporation (http://www.curl.com) has commercialized MIT's project. Curl applications execute on the Surge™ Runtime Environment, a fast, stable client platform. It includes a just-in-time compiler executing on-the-fly; a multimedia engine enabling integration of text, graphics, animation, audio, and end-user input; an advanced GUI system for creation of interfaces either standardized or highly customized; an XML parser for direct interpretation of data from any database; and standard HTTP networking for connectivity with any Web-based back end.

The runtime operates within a strict security model that ensures system administrators have sole control over security features. The Curl Client/Web Platform is completed with the Surge Lab™ Integrated Development Environment (IDE), a set of development tools, including a visual layout editor, a robust source editor, full debugging capability, and extensive language documentation. The IDE, and in particular its visual layout editor, enables easy use of our extendible programming language, which encompasses all the capabilities of the full spectrum of languages deployed on the Web today. Curl therefore supports programming at all levels: It enables both the easy formatting and layout associated with mark-up languages such as HTML and the event-driven interactivity and simple dynamic content found in scripting languages such as JavaScript; but because it is also a fully robust object-oriented language, like Java or C++, Curl can be used to build applications with complex business logic, rich graphics, full interactivity, networking, and XML-driven dynamic data presentation. Purpose-built for Web applications, Curl source code is extremely compact, as shown below:

```
curl 3.0 applet}
{let container = {HBox}}
{for i:int = 1 to 4 do
  {container.add
     {bold World}
   }
}
Hello {value container}!
```

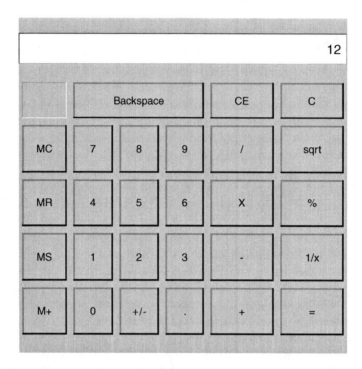

Figure 8.7 Using Curl to create a calculator.

Because Curl applications are compiled on the client, they are delivered over the network as source code rather than in expanded bytecode or binary form. Curl application downloads are therefore considerably smaller than comparable Java applets or ActiveX controls.

A Curl-based application works as follows. Upon an initial request from a user, the back-end server will send down the app and, optionally, its associated data in a compact file that can be an order of magnitude smaller than a comparable HTML-based application. From that point, the full power of the application is literally in the hands of the user; it runs on the user's local machine, not the server. It will request additional data from the network only as needed.

The server is freed from much of the processing it typically does because the application offloads all of the presentation work and appropriate business logic tasks onto the client. Graphics, for example, instead of being sent down as large files from the server, are generated on the client. The network is freed of the constant back-and-forth requests and sending down of fresh Web pages that are typical today. The huge savings in both server power and network bandwidth make Curl-based applications enormously scalable. The object-oriented power of the language also means that any Curl-based app is completely extensible. The runtime environment includes more than 4000 APIs that programmers can use out-of-the-box; developers can build their own features on top, with no limits. Figure 8.7 demonstrates a calculator developed using the Curl language. The rather lengthy code for the calculator can be downloaded from http://www.curl.com/developers/samples/utilities/calculator/calculator.zip.

X Products

Company:	Altio
Product:	AltioLive Platform http://www.integrasp.com/products_overview.htm
Description:	A framework for the development of rich clients that execute as applets within a Web browser

Company:	Bindows
Product:	Bindows http://www.bindows.net/
Description:	Code in JavaScript and access the Bindows API to create AJAX applications

Company:	Canoo
Product:	ULC (Ultra Light Client) http://www.canoo.com/ulc/
Description:	A display processor (presentation engine) for the client

Company:	Curl Corporation
Product:	Curl Content Language (Surge) http://www.curl.com
Description:	A browser plug-in that runs applets written in the Curl language

Company:	DreamFactory
Product:	DreamFactory http://www.dreamfactory.com/
Description:	XML-based application development

Company:	Droplets
Product:	Droplets User Interface Server http://www.droplets.com/
Description:	A presentation server similar to Remote AWT

Company:	IBM (Alphaworks)
Product:	BML (Bean Markup Language) http://www.alphaworks.ibm.com/formula/bml
Description:	An XML-based language customized for the JavaBean component model

Company:	Isomorphic Software
Product:	SmartClient http://www.isomorphic.com/
Description:	DHTML/AJAX technology provider for rich-client, zero-install Web applications

Company:	Adobe
Product:	Flash Remoting FX and Flex http://www.adobe.com
Description:	Animation and multimedia programming language

Company:	Microsoft
Product:	.Net Framework http://www.microsoft.com/net/default.mspx
Description:	The Microsoft XML Web services platform
Company:	Mozilla
Product:	XPToolkit http://www.mozilla.org/xpfe/xptoolkit/index.html
Description:	Makes UIs as easy to build as Web pages, and we will make applications easier to write and to customize along the way

Company:	NexusEdge
Product:	Facado http://www.nexusedge.com/
Description:	Java applet-based rich client framework

Company:	Nexaweb
Product:	Nexaweb http://www.nexaweb.com
Description:	XUL and SVG rendered using a thin java applet; rich applications developed using servlets and jsp; applet is written under the Personal Java Spec

Company:	NextApp
Product:	Echo http://www.nextapp.com/platform/echo1/echo/
Description:	A framework for developing object-oriented, event-driven Web applications; JavaScript API

Company:	NorPath
Product:	Norpath Elements http://www.norpath.com/
Description:	Rich media authoring

Company:	Orbeon
Product:	Orbeon PresentationServer http://www.orbeon.com/
Description:	Create XHTML, XSLT, and XForms

Company:	Sun Microsystems
Product:	Java (JVM) http://java.sun.com/
Description:	Platform with rich client capability (Swing GUI)
Notes:	Sun's Java JVM is a key player in the X arena

Company:	XWT.org
Product:	XWT (XML Windowing Toolkit) http://www.xwt.org/
Description:	Java-based interpreter for a new XML language

Conclusion

This chapter discussed several programming tools that can be used to implement the X strategy. Like any software development project, developing an X system for the first time will take careful planning. This should include an analysis of the tools available.

References

Picard, E. (2002, June 10). Flash flood rising. ClickZ Network. Retrieved fromhttp://www.clickz.com/experts/ad/ad_tech/article.php/1355361

Chapter 9

Extreme Programming Concepts for X-Development

Extreme programming (XP) is a software methodology developed by Kent Beck (1999) to help software developers design and build a system more efficiently and successfully. Extreme programming is a disciplined and well-planned approach to software development. What makes XP so popular is that it is one of the first lightweight methodologies. A lightweight methodology has only a few rules and practices or ones that are easy to follow. XP does not require any additional paperwork, and programmers do not have to go through tons of methods. Extreme programming stresses customer satisfaction and can be used when the customer is not certain of his requirements or when new technology is to be introduced. The XP methodology, therefore, is perfect to use when implementing X systems. Because X is likely new to your organization, XP is a natural fit.

The Rules of Extreme Programming

X systems, by definition, must be extremely reactive to the end user. Karat (1998) espouses a "User's Bill of Rights":

1. The user is always right. If there is a problem with the use of the system, the system is the problem, not the user.
2. The user has the right to easily install and uninstall software and hardware systems without negative consequences.
3. The user has the right to a system that performs exactly as promised.
4. The user has the right to easy-to-use instructions (user guides, online or contextual help, error messages) for understanding and utilizing a system to achieve desired goals and recover efficiently and gracefully from problem situations.
5. The user has the right to be in control of the system and to be able to get the system to respond to a request for attention.
6. The user has the right to a system that provides clear, understandable, and accurate information regarding the task it is performing and the progress toward completion.
7. The user has the right to be clearly informed about all system requirements for successfully using software or hardware.
8. The user has the right to know the limits of the system's capabilities.
9. The user has the right to communicate with the technology provider and receive a thoughtful and helpful response when raising concerns.
10. The user should be the master of software and hardware technology, not vice versa. Products should be natural and intuitive to use.

In my research for past books on software engineering, I have found that many organizations do not practice formal software engineering methodologies. This accounts for many of the project failures discussed in the Standish Group's periodic "Chaos Reports." A recent report does find some progress, however. Project success rates have increased to just over a third (or 34 percent) of all projects. Of course, this means that 66 percent of the projects are "challenged" or downright failures (http://www. standishgroup.com/press/article.php?id=2). One of the reasons for an increase in success rates is the deployment of rapid development methodologies such as XP.

XP applies four rules in developing the software project:

1. *Communication.* The programmer must communicate with customers and elicit their requirements — thus the emphasis on customer satisfaction. The programmers also must communicate with fellow workers — thus the emphasis on teamwork.
2. *Simplicity.* The design is maintained as simply as possible. This lends itself very nicely to X applications, where executables are usually single-function.
3. *Feedback.* The software is tested from its early stages, feedback is obtained, and changes are made. This is a cyclical process.
4. *Courage.* The programmers can make changes even at last stages and implement new technologies as and when introducing them.

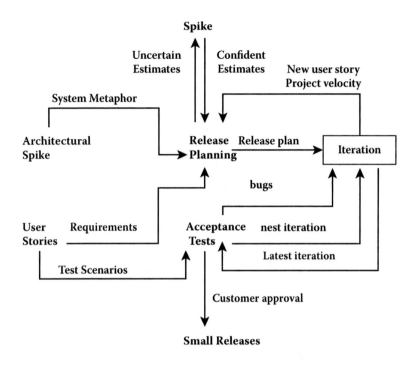

Figure 9.1   The extreme programming (XP) process of software development.

Extreme programming is a process of project development, as shown in Figure 9.1. Customer requirements are obtained in the form of user stories. The programmers select the user stories to be implemented first with help of customers. A plan is released that indicates how many user stories can be implemented in a single iteration, thus starting iterative development. The user stories are broken down into programming tasks and assigned to programmers. The time required to complete these tasks is estimated first. These initial estimates are referred to as uncertain estimates. Using feedback, the estimates can be adjusted and made more certain.

Once these programming tasks have been implemented, they are sent for acceptance testing. If the programming tasks produce an error or indicate a bug, they are sent back to be recoded in the next iteration. Once the programming tasks are approved by the customer, a small release of the tasks is made to check functionality.

The components of XP include user stories, release planning, iteration, development, CRC cards, system metaphor, collective code ownership, unit test, acceptance test, project velocity, small releases, simple design, coding standard, refactoring, pair programming, continuous integration, 40-hour work week, and on-site customer.

User stories. User stories are written by the customer and describe the requirements of a system. The customer need not specify his requirements using any particular format or technical language. The end user merely writes these in his own words. Aside from describing what the system must be, the user stories are used to calculate the time estimates for release planning. Detailed information is obtained from the customer by the developer at the time of the implementation of the user stories. The time estimate is usually in the form of ideal development time — defined as how long it would take to implement the story in code if there were no distractions, no other assignments, and you knew exactly what to do. Typically, each story will get one to three weeks. The user stories are also used to produce test scenarios for the acceptance testing by the customer as well as to verify if the user stories have been implemented correctly.

Release planning. Release planning produces a release plan that is followed during the development of the system. Release planning is also called the "planning game." During release planning, a meeting is set up with the customers and the development team.

During this meeting, customers and developers set up a set of rules to which all agree. A schedule is then prepared.

A development team is selected to calculate each user story in terms of ideal programming weeks, which is how long it would take to implement that story if you had absolutely nothing else to do.

Release planning is guided by four values:

1. Scope: how much needs to be done.
2. Resources: how many people are available.
3. Time: when the project or release will be done.
4. Quality: how good the software will be and how well tested it will be.

Candidate systems for XP are those that are reusable, testable, and have good business values.

Iteration. At the beginning of every iteration, an iteration planning meeting is held, at which the user stories implemented during that iteration are chosen. The user stories are selected by the customer. The selected user stories are broken down into discrete programming tasks during the planning session. The programming tasks are specified in the programmer's language.

The number of selected user stories or the programming tasks increases or decreases the project velocity. Each programming task is estimated based on ideal programming days, which are the number of days it would take to program a task if you had no distractions or interruptions.

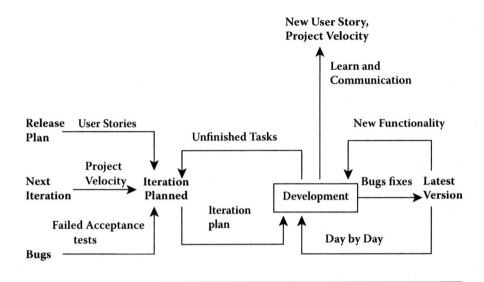

Figure 9.2 The iterative nature of XP.

After these programming tasks have been developed, they are tested. If bugs are found, the offending programming tasks are added back into to the release plan to be handled by the next iteration.

During each iteration (see Figure 9.2), the plan is checked to detect duplicate programming tasks. If duplicate programming tasks are found, they are removed or consolidated. If a single iteration has too much to do, several user stories are dropped. If the iteration has too little to do, a few user stories are added.

Development. During the development phase, stand-up meetings are held every morning to discuss the problems being faced during the development effort, to devise a solution to these problems, and, perhaps most important, to promote focus.

No individual programmer owns his or her code. Instead, the code is collectively owned and collaboratively worked on. The focus of development is on small, manageable releases that can be thoroughly tested.

CRC cards. CRC is an acronym for Class, Responsibilities, and Collaboration. CRC cards (Figure 9.3) contain information about the class, responsibilities, and collaboration for designing the system as a team. CRC cards allow all members of the project team to contribute to the project; this will provide a number of good ideas that can then be incorporated in the design.

Each CRC card is used to represent an object. The class name of the object can be written on top of the CRC card. The responsibilities of the class are written on the left side of the card. And the collaborating classes

CRC Card

Class Name: MotionSensor (subclass of Sensor)	
Class Type: device, aggregate, concurrent	
Class Characteristics: tangible	
Responsibilities:	**Collaborations:**
registerEvent(sensorEvent) – registers a SensorEvent object to observe. Inherited from Sensor.	SensorEvent
isActive( )– report whether or not the sensor is still active. Inherited from Sensor.	None
reset( )– report the sensor (isActive=false)	None

Figure 9.3   CRC card.

are written to the right of each of the responsibilities. A CRC session consists of a person simulating the system by speaking about the relationships between the objects and the process. In this way, weaknesses and problems are easily discerned. The various design alternatives can be explored quickly by simulating the design being proposed.

System metaphor. Classes, objects, and methods coded by the programmer can be reused. Instead of writing the code for a class, object, or method that already exists, it is important to name the objects in a standardized manner, which enables other programmers to seek and reuse these objects. Thus, a common system or common system description is used by all programmers.

Collective code ownership: Collective code ownership is a contribution of the programmers to the project in the form of ideas to any segment of the project. Any programmer can add or change code, fix bugs, or refactor — that is, reuse the code. The entire team is responsible for the system's architecture. It is difficult to believe that an entire team can have authority over the entire project, but it is actually possible. Each developer creates unit tests for his or her code as the code is being developed. Code is released into a source code repository after being thoroughly tested.

Unit test. Unit tests are written by the programmer before coding starts. Writing the unit tests first gives the programmer a better understanding of the requirements specified by the customer. In addition, writing unit tests prior to coding helps the programmer write the code much easier and faster.

Acceptance Test. Functional tests have been renamed within the XP methodology to acceptance tests, to indicate that the system is accepted by the customer. The customer specifies the test scenarios during the specification of the user stories. Each user story will have one or more acceptance tests. The acceptance tests are the expectation of the customer for the system. These acceptance test are black box system tests, which enable the programmer to derive sets of input conditions that will fully exercise all functional requirements for a program. The user tests and reviews the results of the acceptance tests and determines the priorities of the test failures. The team schedules time to fix the failed test for every iteration.

Project velocity. The project velocity is used to measure how much work is being completed on the project. Project velocity is obtained by adding up the estimates of the user stories completed during the iteration. It can also be obtained by adding up the estimates for the tasks during the iteration. If the project velocity shows significant variations, a release planning meeting is conducted and a new plan is released. Project velocity is a measure of accuracy. How accurately are we able to produce results on time? How well are we able to make estimates?

Small releases. The development team makes small releases of the iterative versions of the system to the customer. It is very essential to get customer feedback on time instead of waiting until the last moment, which results in making changes at the last minute as well.

Simple Design. Keep the design as simple as possible. A complex design is difficult to understand when changes are to be made in the future.

Coding standard. Programmers follow a specific set of standard rules in writing code. This helps in communication among teams and enables a programmer to easily understand the code written by any other programmer.

Refactoring. Refactoring is the art of removing any duplicate code — that is, the reuse of code that is already present. This helps in keeping the system design simple. Refactoring also saves a lot of time and increases the quality of the system.

Pair programming. Pair programming specifies that a pair of programmers work collaboratively on a task. This helps in assessing the code as it is written. Pair programming increases software quality and takes the same time to deliver the system as a single programmer working on a single machine.

Continuous integration. Coding is done by dividing big projects into small, manageable programming tasks. After coding, the discrete programming tasks are joined together. However, each of these programming tasks is tested individually for bugs. During the integration of the programming tasks, it is quite possible that new bugs will surface. Therefore, after every integration, the integrated code is retested for bugs.

Changes can be made at the request of the customer. All changes made to the code are integrated at least daily. The tests are then run both before and after the changes. The code is not released if any bugs are found.

40-Hour work week. Each programmer works only 40 hours per week. This helps the productivity of the project in the long term. No programmer is overloaded with work and no overtime is allowed. Overtime usually exhausts the programmer, and chances are he or she will make mistakes.

On-site customer. A single customer or a group of customers is available at all times for the programmers. This helps in resolving the ambiguities that developers encounter during the development of the project, in setting priorities, and in providing live scenarios.

Conclusion

Extreme programming can be stated as follows: a fast and a highly organized process for the development of a software system, particularly those as dynamic as X applications. XP emphasizes communication, which is essential in encouraging new ideas.

Because pair programming is stressed in this method, the fear of losing any programmer in the middle of the project and the risk associated with programmers is substantially decreased. Theoretically, XP reduces the competition among programmers — insisting that they all work as single team.

Extreme programming can be used where the requirements change rapidly and the customer is not fully sure of the requirements, which is typical in early X development efforts. Because feedback is integral to this process, the end product will be developed according to customer requirements.

References

Beck, Kent (1999). *Extreme Programming Explained.* Boston: Addison-Wesley.
Karat, C-M. (1998, December). Guaranteeing rights for the user. *Communications of the ACM,* 41(12).

Chapter 10

Resources

AJAX

Article on AJAX by the developer of the idea:
  http://www.adaptivepath.com/publications/essays/archives/
  000385.php
Community Portal — AJAX community portal:
  http://www.ajaxresources.com/
Getting starting with AJAX — Oracle Web site:
  http://www.oracle.com/technology/tech/java/ajax.html
AJAXwith:
  http://www.ajaxwith.com/
AJAX Magazine:
  http://ajax.phpmagazine.net/
Deitel AJAX resource center:
  http://www.deitel.com/ajax/AJAX_resourcecenter.html
W3 AJAX tutorial:
  http://www.w3schools.com/ajax/default.asp
AJAX tutorials:
  http://codinginparadise.org/projects/tutorials/
AJAX in ASP.NET:
  http://www.developerfusion.co.uk/show/4704/
AJAX examples:
  http://www.clearnova.com/ajax/
AJAX and PHP:
  http://giraffenecks.com/tutorials/index.php?ID=14

Nexaweb — a framework for building AJAX applications:
http://www.nexaweb.com

Ruby on Rails — an open source Web application framework written in Ruby that closely follows the Model-View-Controller (MVC) architecture: http://rubyinstaller.rubyforge.org/wiki/wiki.pl

DoJo — AJAX toolkit:
http://dojotoolkit.org

GLM — AJAX toolkit:
http://sourceforge.net/projects/glm-ajax

DWR — AJAX toolkit:
http://getahead.ltd.uk/dwr

Cascading Style Sheets

Browser Chart — Which browser software (Internet Explorer or Netscape) will accept your style sheet commands? Use this chart from Webmonkey.com to find out:
http://www.webmonkey.com/reference/browser_chart/

CSSShark Answers FAQs — This site answers some of those frequently asked questions regarding CSS. The site also explains some of the basics of CSS, provides tips and tricks, offers a tutorial concerning positioning with CSS (CSS-P, Web design without tables), and gives links to other related sites:
http://www.mako4css.com/

Cascading Style Sheet Summary — this summary is published as part of the *Web Publishing Curriculum Resources* from the University of Oregon:
http://libweb.uoregon.edu/it/webpub/css-chart.html

Cascading Style Sheet Tutorial:
http://wdvl.internet.com/Authoring/Style/Sheets/

Comprehensive Guide to Style Sheets:
http://www.htmlhelp.com/reference/css/

Common Graphical Interface Scripts — CGI

CGI City — Perl and CGI resources:
http://www.icthus.net/CGI-City/

CGI: Common Gateway Interface — specifications, documentation, and other CGI related information provided by the World Wide Web Consortium (W3C):
http://www.w3.org/CGI/

CGIDir.com — scripts, tutorials, and more:
  http://www.cgidir.com/
CGI Made Really Easy — a quick tutorial:
  http://www.jmarshall.com/easy/cgi/
CGI Programming FAQ:
  http://www.htmlhelp.com/faq/cgifaq.html
CGI Resource Index — containing over 1400 CGI scripts this site has
  programs and scripts for AppleScript, C and C++, Perl, Tcl, Unix Shell,
  and Visual Basic.
Common Gateway Interface — introduction to CGI, documentation, and
  examples:
  http://cgi.resourceindex.com/
HotScripts.com — site has more than 25,000 scripts available for ASP, CGI,
  Perl, PHP, Java, XML, etc.:
  http://www.hotscripts.com/CGI_and_Perl/index.html
Scriptsearch — "the world's largest CGI library," this site has in excess of
  5000 CGI scripts available. Indexed in 12 languages, this site has scripts
  for AppleScript, Java, Perl, and C/C++. The database is searchable by
  keyword and language:
  http://scriptsearch.internet.com/

Common Object Request Broker Architecture (CORBA)

CORBA FAQ:
  http://www.omg.org/gettingstarted/corbafaq.htm
Introduction to CORBA — a short course from Sun.com:
  http://java.sun.com/developer/onlineTraining/corba/
Object Management Group (OMG) — OMG is a coalition of 11 companies
  formed to develop standards and specifications for the development
  and use of CORBA/IIOP, object services, internet facilities, and domain
  interfaces:
  http://www.omg.org/corba/
Overview of CORBA:
  http://www.cs.wustl.edu/~schmidt/corba-overview.html

Curl/Surge Software Platform

Curl Technology — Curl Corporation is the developer of the Curl
  programming language:
  http://www.curl.com/

CurlUnit 1.0:
   http://curlunit.sourceforge.net/
CurlUnit Cookbook:
   http://curlunit.sourceforge.net/doc/cookbook/cookbook.html
MIT Curl Research Project:
   http://www.cag.lcs.mit.edu/curl/
Surge Software Platform v. 1.2:
   http://www.curl.com/products/rte.php
Taking Curl for a Whirl — A *Wired News* article:
   http://www.wired.com/news/technology/0,1282,48818,00.html

Flash

FlashKit:
   http://www.flashkit.com/index.shtml
Macromedia Flash documentation:
   http://www.adobe.com/support/documentation/en/flash/
Flash MX tutorials:
   http://www.flash-mx.com/flash/index.cfm
Flash Lite:
   http://www.adobe.com/devnet/devices/flashlite.html
Macromedia Flex:
   http://www.adobe.com/products/flex/
Flash Central:
   http://www.flashcentral.com/Tech/Resources/Flash.htm

Graphics

Absolute Background Textures Archive — with more than 2400 textures available, this site is billed as "the largest collection of free background textures on the Internet."
   http://www.grsites.com/textures/
Clip Art Index:
   http://www.kidsdomain.com/clip/
Cool Archive — free vault of more than 6000 fonts, icons, GIF animations, bars, bullets, etc.:
   http://www.coolarchive.com/
Creating Graphics for the Web — this site is updated every two weeks:
   http://www.widearea.co.uk/designer/
Design Tech — Design resources for beginners:
   http://www.angelfire.com/biz/DesignTech/index.html

Ender's Realm Graphics — containing more than 340 page backgrounds, 380 bullets, 130 buttons, 510 icons, and 350 lines, this site offers a wealth of graphics and ideas for Web page designers:
http://www.ender-design.com/rg/

Open GL — this site contains information for OpenGL software, which is used to create 2D and 3D graphics:
http://www.opengl.org/

PC Webopedia: Graphic Standards:
http://webopedia.internet.com/Graphics/Graphics_Standards/

Scream Design — thousands of images available for downloading:
http://screamdesign.daz3d.com/free.html

Using Web Color — An four-page article from Project Cool that covers color theory, color wheels, and the use of color on the Web:
http://www.devx.com/projectcool/Article/19956

HTML/DHTML

BigNoseBird — scripts, html tag reference, tutorials, Webmaster tips and much more can be found on this site:
http://bignosebird.com/

CSS Pointers Group — this site contains tips, links to CSS standards, tutorials, demos, bug reports, and browser support information:
http://css.nu/pointers/index.html

HTML Help — tips, FAQ's, tools, and additional links to other sites are included:
http://www.htmlhelp.com/

HTML Code Tutorial — The Idocs Guide to HTML— this site contains sections on links, Java applets, fonts, images, scripts, style sheets, and tables.:
http://www.htmlcodetutorial.com/

HTML Writer's Guild — home page of the international organization of Web page authors and Internet publishing professionals:
http://www.hwg.org/

Meta Tag Tutorial:
http://www.htmlcenter.com/tutorials/tutorials.cfm/114/HTML/

RGB Color Chart — a useful chart that gives hexadecimal and RGB values:
http://www.htmlcenter.com/tutorials/tutorials.cfm/89/General/

Simply the Best— SimplyTheBest.com has a broad variety of categories ranging from back-end development to DHTML. In fact, its listing of ready-to-go DHTML/Java Menu scripts are the best on the Net:
http://www.simplythebest.net/info/dhtml_menus.html

Web Design From Scratch:
http://www.webdesignfromscratch.com/current-style.cfm

Web Developer's Virtual Library: Color:
   http://www.wdvl.com/Graphics/Colour/
Web Publishing Curriculum Resources — this University of Oregon based
   site includes workshops on Web mechanics, page creation, and
   publishing practices:
   http://libweb.uoregon.edu/it/webpub/
WWW Consortium HTML Page:
   http://www.w3.org/MarkUp/
Web Design Resource — a collection of tutorials on various aspects of
   HTML:
   http://www.pageresource.com/html/index.html

Java/JavaScript/J2ee/J2me

Changes in Swing for JDK1.3:
   http://java.sun.com/j2se/1.3/docs/guide/swing/SwingChanges.html
DEV.X - Development Exchange - Java Zone:
   http://www.devx.com/Java/Door/6972
Developer.com – Java — produced by Developer.com, this site claims to
   be the largest repository of Java scripts:
   http://www.developer.com/java/
Hibernate.org — Hibernate is a new facet of Java programming that allows
   for persistent classes. The Hibernate Query Language is an extension
   of SQL:
   http://www.hibernate.org/
Java.sun.com: The Source for Java Developers:
   http://java.sun.com/
HotScripts.com — this site has more 25,000 scripts available for ASP, CGI,
   Perl, PHP, Java, XML, etc.:
   http://www.hotscripts.com/
HotSyte:
   http://www.serve.com/hotsyte/
Introduction to Programming Using Java — an online textbook created
   by a professor of computer science at Hobart and William Smith
   Colleges:
   http://math.hws.edu/javanotes/index.html
J2EE Resources:
   http://www.jdance.com/j2ee.shtm
J2ME Archive:
   http://www.billday.com/j2me/

Java 2 Platform Enterprise Edition (J2EE):
  http://java.sun.com/javaee/index.jsp
Java 2 Platform Micro Edition (J2ME) — Get the latest information on
  J2me from the source — Sun Microsystems.
Java 2 Platform Micro Edition, Wireless Tookit:
  http://java.sun.com/products/sjwtoolkit/
Javabeans — Sun's Javabean site direct:
  http://java.sun.com/products/javabeans/index.jsp
Javafile — more than 600 free Java and JavaScript files to download:
  http://www.javafile.com/
Java Lobby:
  http://www.javalobby.org/
Javanumerics:
  http://math.nist.gov/javanumerics/
JavaPowered.com — Java Applets, tips, tricks, articles, games, and
  previews are all available at this site:
  http://www.perfectscripts.com/detailed/javapowered.com.html
JavaScript.com — If it concerns JavaScript, then it can be found on this
  site that has "all things java":
  http://www.javascript.com/
JavaScript Source — A "cut-and-paste" resource for Java scripts. JavaScript
  Source contains buttons, cookies, forms, and much more. Each script
  has a working demonstration:
  http://javascript.internet.com/
Java Security – FAQ:
  http://java.sun.com/sfaq/
Java Security Web Site:
  http://www.cigital.com/javasecurity/
JBoss.org — JBoss is an Open Source, standards-compliant, Enterprise
  JavaBeans application server implemented in pure Java. This site
  contains the sourcecode and documentation:
  http://labs.jboss.com/portal/index.html?ctrl:id=page.default.default
Operations Research: Java Objects — offers 500+ Java classes for
  developing operations research, scientific and engineering applications:
  http://opsresearch.com/OR-Objects/
Programmer's Heaven:
  http://www.programmersheaven.com/zone13/index.htm
Swing Timers:
  http://java.sun.com/products/jfc/tsc/articles/timer/
Tutorial:
   http://www.javacoffeebreak.com/java101/java101.html

Object-Oriented Programming (OOP)

Bibliographies on Object-Oriented Programming and Systems:
http://liinwww.ira.uka.de/bibliography/Object/
Interactive Web Tutorial for Object-Oriented Programming:
http://homepages.north.londonmet.ac.uk/~chalkp/proj/ootutor/index.html
Introduction to PHP Classes:
(OOP):
http://www.phpfreaks.com/tutorials/48/0.php
Just What Is OO Programming (Flash orientation):
http://www.debreuil.com/docs/ch01_Intro.htm
Object Oriented Programming Concepts:
http://java.sun.com/docs/books/tutorial/java/concepts/
Object Oriented Programming Tutorial:
http://www.aonaware.com/OOP1.htm

PERL (Practical Extraction and Report Language)

Comprehensive Perl Archive Network (CPAN) — a central distribution point for everything related to Perl (including source code):
http://www.perl.com/CPAN/
Introduction to Perl (University of Missouri-Columbia):
http://www.cclabs.missouri.edu/things/instruction/perl/perlcourse.html
PERL Resources:
http://www.utexas.edu/cc/unix/perl/
Perl Tutorial: Start:
http://www.comp.leeds.ac.uk/Perl/
Programmer's Heaven:
http://www.programmersheaven.com/zone27/index.htm
Site for People Learning Perl — there are several sources on this site of value to anyone learning or needing a refresher on Perl. The Online Library section contains four full-text books on Perl:
http://learn.perl.org/
WWW Perl.com — O'Reilly and Associates, Inc Perl site:
http://www.perl.com/

PHP

HotScripts.com — this site has more than 25,000 scripts available for ASP, CGI, Perl, PHP, Java, XML, etc.:
http://www.hotscripts.com/

PHP Architect: the magazine for PHP professionals:
   http://www.phparch.com/
PHP Functions List:
   http://www.php.net/quickref.php
PHP Manual:
   http://www.zend.com/manual/
PHP.net — an official source for information related to PHP:
   http://www.php.net/
PHP.net FAQ:
   http://us2.php.net/FAQ.php
PHP Resource Index — includes scripts, documentation, functions, and
   classes:
   http://php.resourceindex.com/
Planet PHP — a weblog of PHP discussions:
   http://www.planet-php.net/

Python/Jython

Jython FAQ:
   http://www.jython.org/cgi-bin/faqw.py?req=index
Jython.org Home Page:
   http://www.jython.org/
Python FAQ:
   http://www.python.org/doc/faq/
Python.org Home Page:
   http://www.python.org/
The What, Why, Who, and Where of Python:
   http://www.networkcomputing.com/unixworld/tutorial/005/005.html

Relative Expression-Based Object Language (REBOL)

Rebol Cookbook of Code Examples:
   http://www.rebol.net/cookbook/
Rebol Miscellaneous Scripts Archive — site maintained by TUCOWS:
   http://html.dekooi.nl/programmer/scriptarchives/rebolmisc.html
Rebol.org Script Library:
   http://www.rebol.org/
Rebol Technologies — Amiga operating system architect Carl Sassenrath
   has developed a cross-platform scripting language called REBOL.
   Intended for Internet programming, Rebol contains very easy-to-use
   networking capabilities. Available for downloading in binary form:
   http://www.rebol.com/

Semantic Web

Altova's SemanticWorks — Visual RDF/OWL editor:
http://www.altova.com/products/semanticworks/rdf_owl_editor.html

IODT, — IBM Integrated Ontology Development Toolkit, a toolkit for ontology development. It includes ODM-based RDF/OWL programming APIs, Eclipse-based OWL editor, and a high-performance OWL repository:
http://www.alphaworks.ibm.com/tech/semanticstk

Tucana Technologies Inc. — a scalable RDF triple store that includes some OWL inferencing and is adding more:
http://tucana.es.northropgrumman.com/

AIFB SEmantic PortAL — the Institute AIFB Web site of the University of Karlsruhe provides annotated pages that contain dynamically generated machine processable content in form of OWL annotations:
http://www.aifb.uni-karlsruhe.de/about.html

The AKT Portal — at the University of Southampton, is largely based on ontologies, and is now using OWL:
http://www.aktors.org/akt/

The MINDSWAP project Web site — uses OWL to generate all the Web pages and "custom home pages" for members of the research group, as well as for doing photo markup:
http://www.mindswap.org/

KAON2 — a reasoner for OWL extended with the DL-safe subset of SWRL; it also provides an OWL API:
http://kaon2.semanticweb.org/

SWI-Prolog Semantic Web Library — contains *owl.pl*, an OWL reasoning package:
http://www.swi-prolog.org/packages/semweb.html

F-OWL — an f-logic based Owl tool from UMBC:
http://fowl.sourceforge.net/

E-wallet — an E-commerce and mobile computing tool based on a rule-based OWL reasoner:
http://mycampus.sadehlab.cs.cmu.edu/tests/

DAML Ontology Library — organizes hundreds of ontologies in a variety of different ways (keyword, organization, submission date, etc.):
http://www.daml.org/ontologies/

Swoogle — a search engine for Semantic Web documents, including OWL ontologies, built by the University of Maryland Baltimore County under funding from the National Science Foundation:
http://swoogle.umbc.edu/

OntoBroker — a semantic inference engine:
http://www.ontoprise.de/e1171/index_eng.html

Protégé — free Stanford University ontology editor:
  http://protege.stanford.edu/
KAON — open-source ontology management infrastructure:
  http://kaon.semanticweb.org/
KIMA — a knowledge and information management infrastructure:
  http://www.ontotext.com/kim/

Software Engineering

Extreme Programming: A Gentle Introduction — Extreme programming
  (XP) is a methodology of software development that maximizes
  programming efficiency. This site offers a very thorough overview of
  the techniques involved in XP, and specific rules and guidelines are
  set forth to help individuals or businesses implement the XP process:
  http://www.extremeprogramming.org/
IBM Research — includes a searchable database:
  http://www.research.ibm.com/
IBM Almaden Research Center — Almaden Research Center conducts
  research in the areas of computer science software, computer science
  storage systems, science and technology, services research, and
  WebFountain:
  http://www.almaden.ibm.com/almaden/
PlanetPDF — This Australian site (BinaryThing.com) is a useful resource
  for everything PDF. Resources include news, tools, plug-ins, articles,
  developer tips, and papers:
  http://www.planetpdf.com/

Tutorials

Cascading Style Sheet Tutorial:
  http://wdvl.internet.com/Authoring/Style/Sheets/
CSS Pointers Group — a good resource for Cascading Style Sheet
  beginners. This site contains tips, links to CSS standards, tutorials,
  demos, bug reports, and browser support information:
  http://css.nu/pointers/index.html
CSSShark Answers FAQs — for users interested in learning more about
  Cascading Style Sheets, this informative and well-constructed site
  answers some of those frequently asked questions regarding CSS. The
  site also explains some of the basics of CSS, provides tips and tricks,
  offers a tutorial concerning positioning with CSS (CSS-P, Web design
  without tables), and gives links to other related sites:
  http://www.mako4css.com/

Dynamic Duo DHTML Tutorial:
   http://www.internetadsales.com/modules/wfsection/article.php?articlei
   d=1973
HTML Code Tutorial — contains sections on links, Java applets, fonts,
   images, scripts, style sheets, and tables.:
   http://www.htmlcodetutorial.com/
Java Tutorial — David Reilly, a recent graduate of Bond University,
   Australia, has written several tutorials for the Web:
   http://www.javacoffeebreak.com/java101/java101.html
A Look at XML — a basic tutorial on XML from Developer.com:
   http://www.webdeveloper.com/xml/xml_a_look_at_xml.html
Meta Tags - Tutorial:
   http://searchenginewatch.com/webmasters/article.php/2167931
PHP/MySQL Tutorial:
   http://www.webmonkey.com//programming/php/tutorials/tutorial4.ht
   ml
Working with XML — a good tutorial on XML and Java by Eric Armstrong:
   http://java.sun.com/webservices/jaxp/dist/1.1/docs/tutorial/index.html
XML Tutorial by Microsoft:
   http://msdn.microsoft.com/library/default.asp?url=/library/en-
   us/csref/html/vcwlkXMLDocumentationTutorial.asp

Unified Modeling Language (UML)

Unified Modeling Language Resource Center — site contains tutorials,
   reading lists, links, documentation, tools, etc.:
   http://www-306.ibm.com/software/rational/uml/
UML 1.5 Specification:
   http://www.omg.org/technology/documents/formal/uml.htm
UML Bibliography:
   http://www.db.informatik.uni-bremen.de/umlbib/home.html
UML Tutorial:
   http://pigseye.kennesaw.edu/~dbraun/csis4650/A&D/UML_tutorial/

WAP/WML

Building the Intelligent Wireless Web — this site is the home page of "a
   software research laboratory specializing in developing Web Services
   capable of running over Semantic Web Architecture":
   http://www.web-iq.com/

WAP Forum:
    http://www.openmobilealliance.org/tech/affiliates/wap/wapindex.html
Wireless Developer's Network:
    http://www.wirelessdevnet.com/
Wireless In A Nutshell:
    http://www.wirelessinanutshell.com/wap/

World Wide Web Accessibility

Designing More Usable Web Sites:
    http://trace.wisc.edu/world/web/
Introducing Web Accessibility:
    http://www.ddj.com/184412400
IBM Accessibility Center:
    http://www-306.ibm.com/able/guidelines/web/accessweb.html

XML (eXtensible Markup Language)

Cover Pages — online resource for markup language technologies:
    http://xml.coverpages.org/xml.html
ebXML – Enabling a Global Electronic Market — designed to allow
    businesses of any size in any geographic location to conduct business
    over the Internet, ebXML (Electronic Business eXtensible Markup
    Language) is an XML-styled language sponsored by the United Nations
    Centre for Trade Facilitation and Electronic Business (UN/CEFACT) and
    OASIS (nonprofit international consortium):
    http://www.ebxml.org/specs/
eXtensible Markup Language (XML) – Standards — get the latest standards
    data from the source — the W3C:
    http://www.w3.org/XML/
Extensive Stylesheet Language (XSL) – W3C:
    http://www.w3.org/TR/xsl/
IBM Developers Portal: XML Zone — XML Zone contains a good selection
    of pointers to XML tools and source code, annotated pointers to
    educational and reference resources, an XML e-mail newsletter, and
    more:
    http://www-128.ibm.com/developerworks/xml/
An Introduction to ebXML:
    http://www.webservicesarchitect.com/content/articles/irani02.asp
Introduction to RSS:
    http://www.webreference.com/authoring/languages/xml/rss/intro/

A Look at XML — a basic tutorial on XML from Developer.com:
http://www.webdeveloper.com/xml/xml_a_look_at_xml.html
Microsoft MSXML:
http://msdn.microsoft.com/xml/default.aspx
Perfect XML — sample book chapters from numerous books can be viewed, covering a wide range of XML topics. There are also links to XML editors, conversion tools, and many other software resources:
http://www.perfectxml.com/
RDF Rich Site Summary (RSS):
http://www.oasis-open.org/cover/rss.html
RDF Rich Site Summary (RSS) 1.0 Specification:
http://web.resource.org/rss/1.0/spec
RSS Headline Syndication:
http://asprss.com/FAQ.asp
Using WSDL in SOAP Applications:
http://www-128.ibm.com/developerworks/webservices/library/ws-soap/?dwzone=ws
Voice eXtensible Markup Language;
http://www.voicexml.com/
World Wide Web Consortium:
WSDL — Web Services Description Language:
http://www.w3.org/TR/wsdl
XPath Specification:
http://www.w3.org/TR/xpath
XSLT Site:
http://www.w3.org/Style/XSL/
Working with XML — A tutorial on XML and Java:
http://java.sun.com/webservices/jaxp/dist/1.1/docs/tutorial/index.html
XML.org, The XML Industry Portal:
http://www.xml.org/
XHTML, The eXtensible HyperText Markup Language version 2.0 — to bridge the gap between XML and HTML, the World Wide Web Consortium (W3C) has developed and written an XHTML standard:
http://www.w3.org/TR/xhtml2/
XML Cover Pages — a bibliography of resources related to SGML and XML:
http://www.oasis-open.org/cover/biblio.html
XML From the Inside Out — XML is the next big Web language. This site has recent technology developments, definitions, white papers, news, and developer notes:
http://www.xml.com/
X-VRML Language — developed in Poland, X-VRML integrates XML with virtual reality standards:
http://xvrml.kti.ae.poznan.pl/

X Frameworks

AltioLive Platform — a framework for the development of rich clients that execute as applets within a Web browser:
http://www.integrasp.com/products_overview.htm

Bindows — code in JavaScript and access the Bindows API to create AJAX applications:
http://www.bindows.net/

ULC (Ultra Light Client) — a display processor (presentation engine) for the client:
http://www.canoo.com/ulc/

DreamFactory — XML-based application development:
http://www.dreamfactory.com/

Droplets User Interface Server — a presentation server similar to Remote AWT:
http://www.droplets.com/

BML (Bean Markup Language) — an XML-based language customized for the JavaBean component:
http://www.alphaworks.ibm.com/formula/bml

SmartClient — DHTML/AJAX technology provider for rich-client, zero-install Web applications:
http://www.isomorphic.com/

Net Framework — the Microsoft XML Web services platform:
http://www.microsoft.com/net/default.mspx

XPToolkit — make UIs as easy to build as Web pages, and we will make applications easier to write and to customize along the way:
http://www.mozilla.org/xpfe/xptoolkit/index.html

Facado — Java -based rich client framework:
http://www.nexusedge.com/

Echo — a framework for developing object-oriented, event-driven Web applications. JavaScript API:
http://www.nextapp.com/platform/echo1/echo/

Norpath Elements — rich media authoring:
http://www.norpath.com/

Orbeon PresentationServer — create XHTML, XSLT, and Xforms:
http://www.orbeon.com/

Java (JVM) — platform with rich client capability (Swing GUI):
http://java.sun.com/

XWT (XML Windowing Toolkit) — Java-based interpreter for a new XML language:
http://www.xwt.org/

VoiceXML Gateways

Tellme:
    http://studio.tellme.com/
VoiceGenie:
    http://developer.voicegenie.com/
Voxeo:
    http://www.voxeo.com/
BeVocal Café:
    http://cafe.bevocal.com/
HeyAnita Freespeech:
    http://freespeech.heyanita.com/

Related links:

VoiceXML Forum:
    http://www.voicexml.org/
Voice articles at developer.com:
    http://www.developer.com/voice/
Specifications and news from the Web Consortium,
    http://www.w3.org/Voice/. Notably, interesting specs at press time
    include:
    Voice Extensible Markup Language (VoiceXML) Specification Version 2.0:
        http://www.w3.org/TR/voicexml20/
    Speech Recognition Grammar Specification Version 1.0:
        http://www.w3.org/TR/grammar-spec/
Source code and case studies from an earlier version of the article,
    "VoiceXML: Letting People Talk to Your HTTP Server through the
    Telephone," available at http://eveandersson.com/arsdigita/asj/vxml

Appendix A

User-Interface
Design Guide

1.0 Introduction: How to Use the Guidelines

The guidelines on user-interface design found in this document are necessarily generic. They are meant to apply across a wide range of applications. To do so, they must be worded at a relatively high level. The guidelines are a starting point for the development of an application-specific style guide. They do not, in themselves, represent a style guide that can be handed to developers with any expectation that a consistent, usable interface will emerge.

What each project needs to do is select the guidelines that are meaningful in the context of the user interface to be developed. Next, each guideline must be developed further, until a clear, specific design rule is defined. The full set of design rules then makes up the project's style guide.

1.1 Developing a Style Guide

The process involved in developing a style guide includes the following steps:

- *Identify relevant guidelines.* From the overall set of guidelines, select those that pertain to the application under development.
- *Narrow down the subset of pertinent guidelines.* The subset of guidelines selected in the first step may include some that conflict. The choice of which guidelines to retain can be based on relative importance or impact, given constraints of time and budget.

■ *Develop design rules from the guidelines.* A process of translation is required to move from high-level guidelines to specific design rules. One guideline may require a whole set of design rules. If a guideline states that displays should be formatted consistently, for example, a set of design rules are needed to specify the location of such display features as menu titles, icon labels, dialog boxes, and error messages. Design rules take the guidelines down to a concrete, highly specific level.

Because a particular guideline can be translated in numerous ways, translation requires designers to define interface components, application components, and constraints that must be met.

■ *Document and distribute the design rules.* Each member of the design and development team needs unambiguous guidance on the rules to be followed. The goal of collecting the design rules in a style guide is to encourage consistency in the "look and feel" of the application.

■ *Allow for reasonable exceptions.* Because the design rules are applied during design, some rules may turn out to be in conflict with others or may simply be inapplicable due to design constraints. In such cases, the group can agree to make exceptions, record and distribute the rationale for any exceptions, and perhaps revise the rules in question.

Occasionally, a conflict may arise between guidelines. Sometimes the development team can decide which guideline to accept simply by considering whether one or the other is more appropriate for the application. When the answer is not clear, however, the team can use a more formal decision-making process, according to the following steps:

1. Identify the attributes of user performance that may be affected by the conflicting guidelines (e.g., color discrimination, target detection, speed of response).
2. Weight the importance of those attributes for overall system performance. These weightings are likely to vary from project to project.
3. Rate the conflicting guidelines for their expected effect on each performance outcome. The rating scale should have at least three alternatives (e.g., high (1), moderate (2), low (3)) but should always have an odd number of alternatives so that a mid-point is defined.
4. Multiply ratings by weights and sum the products. Select the guideline with the higher total.

1.2 From Guidelines to Design Rules

Several examples follow to illustrate the transition from guideline to design rule:

- *Guideline example for buttons.* When the same buttons are used for different windows, consistently place them in the same location and keep related buttons together.
  - *Transition questions.* Which buttons are involved? Are there any related buttons? Where should these buttons be placed in this application?
  - *Sample design rule.* Place "window-level" buttons at the bottom of the window.
- *Guideline example for labels.* Label each data field to inform users of entries to be made. Keep labels close to associated data fields; separate them by at least one space. For more clarity, employ additional cues in a field label or in the field itself.
  - *Transition questions.* How can we aid users in knowing where the label ends and the entry field begins? How many spaces should there be between the label and the data?
  - *Sample design rule.* Use three-dimensional (3D) shading to delineate a data field.
- *Guideline example for graphical aids.* Provide graphical or textual aids to assist users in maintaining their orientation within the underlying menu structure.
  - *Transition questions.* Will a graphical or textual aid benefit our users? If the aid is to be graphical, what should it include? Should the aid be displayed continuously, or not?
  - *Sample design rule.* At user request, display a small schematic of the entire menu structure. Use the schematic provided by the menu project manager. As the user proceeds through the menu structure, highlight the path taken in yellow.

Design rules should be specific enough that different developers will produce exactly the same features when applying them. For this reason, they should be pretested to ensure that developers will agree on their interpretation. There should be little room for a variety of interpretations.

2.0 User-Centered Design Principles and Guidelines

User productivity can be enhanced by providing consistent and comprehensible displays, flexibility to change or structure a system, informative feedback, error tolerance, and reduced demands on short-term memory — all of which give the user a sense of competence, mastery, and control over the system.

The following principles are offered as general guidance in designing a user interface. These principles represent a condensation of the many general principles articulated in the literature on user-interface design.

2.1 Maintain Consistency in Look and Feel

Consistent visual appearance and consistent response to user input are required throughout the user interface. Interface characteristics should be uniform and familiar, with consistent sequences of actions in similar situations. Terminology must be used consistently to avoid confusing the user. A user interface becomes intuitive by consistently meeting users' expectations.

2.1.1 Consistent Interface Characteristics

Allow the user to build up expectations and predict system actions based on the system's performance of other actions.

2.1.1.1   Permit the user to take the general knowledge and skills learned in one system and transfer them to another like it, without requiring extensive learning and training exercises.

Positive transfer may be based on any or all of the following:
- Analogy with manual methods (e.g., a file cabinet for a collection of files)
- Experience with similar systems
- Previous experience in life or culture (e.g., red = danger)
- Experience with this system's consistent "look and feel"

2.1.1.2   Maintain consistency in the following design areas:

Display:	System Control:
Icon design and meaning	Command terminology
Title field location	Command meanings
Menu bar location	Editing procedures
Message location	Function keys
Cursor shape and function	Command keys
Cursor home position	Abbreviations
Field delimiters	Mnemonics
Color meanings	Acronyms
Data entry prompt	Alarms and warnings
Labeling terminology	Visual coding

2.1.1.3   Occasional departures from consistency may be necessary to support user task performance or convenience. If such departures are necessary, try to minimize the extent of inconsistency with the remainder of the user interface.

2.2   Provide Shortcuts and Flexibility

The experienced user needs the means to go directly to specific locations in the user interface (UI) structure. The UI should be sufficiently flexible to accommodate different user styles of performing tasks.

2.2.1   Number of Interactions

Limit the number of interactions a frequent user must perform. Based on their knowledge, skill, and experience, users should have the flexibility to change or structure a system to suit their particular requirements.

2.2.2   Self-Pacing

Ensure that the user controls the pacing of inputs.

2.2.3   Keyboard Commands

Provide keyboard commands for use by more experienced users, as alternatives to cursor pointing and selection.

2.2.4   Loading on User Memory

To support job performance, mnemonics, codes, special or long sequences, and detailed instructions should be kept to a minimum. For example, use a one-letter mnemonic such as F for File and O for Format.

2.2.5   Log-On/Off

Support ease of logging on and logging off by:

■ Providing the user the means to log on and log off by a single action
■ Prior to accepting log-off, informing the user if there are pending actions
■ For automatic log-off, providing an audible signal prior to log off
■ Permitting the user to save the contents of the task document before log-off

2.3 Present Informative Feedback

Learning and user confidence result from feedback. Feedback informs the user when processing is in progress or when the system has completed a request. Feedback also indicates user selection of a displayed element, such as a menu option.

2.3.1 Automatic Validation

For data processing, provide automatic validation to check for entries of correct content and format. If incorrect data is entered, a message should be generated requesting a revised entry.

2.3.2 Temporary Deferral

For the user who wants to defer a required data item, provide a special symbol to be entered by the user, indicating that the item has been temporarily omitted and not ignored. Upon a request to process entries that include deferred data items, inform the user of the omissions and permit immediate entry of missing items, or allow for further deferral.

2.3.3 Clarity and Brevity

Present information in a manner that is understandable and concise.

2.3.3.1   When displaying text for user guidance, use simple and clear wording.
2.3.3.2   Begin sentences with the main topic. Keep sentences short and simple.
2.3.3.3   Use distinct words. Avoid contractions or combined forms.

2.3.4 Rules of Message Composition

2.3.4.1   Use affirmative rather than negative command statements.
2.3.4.2   Use active voice rather than passive voice.
2.3.4.3   Phrase a sequence of events in corresponding word order.
2.3.4.4   Display a series of related items in a list, not continuous text (Table A.1).
2.3.4.5   Base the level of detail on the user's knowledge and experience. Examples of messages for inexperienced users are illustrated in the Better column of Table A.2.

Table A.1   List of Related Items

Not Good	Better
Create a new log-on by entering a user ID, entering your full name, entering the organization code, and pressing the Save button.	To Create A New Log-on: ■ Enter a user ID ■ Enter the organization code ■ Press the Save button

Table A.2   Examples of Messages for the Novice

Not Good	Better
Position the cursor on Save and click	Click on the Save button
Date:	Date mm/dd/yy: _ _/_ _/_ _
Press UP/DOWN arrows to move up or down	To move up: Press UP arrow To move down: Press DOWN arrow
Pressing ESC will cause you to exit	To exit, press the ESC button

2.3.5 Message Location

Provide a consistent location for messages, such as a designated line at the bottom of the screen or a window.

2.3.5.1   Make the message distinct from other displayed information using techniques such as highlighting, reverse video, or different fonts.
2.3.5.2   Display messages in mixed-case.

2.4   Design for Recovery from Error

When an error occurs, tell the user what the error is and how to correct it.

2.4.1 Undo Function

When possible, permit easy reversal of actions. It benefits the user to know that an error can be "undone."

2.4.1.1   Provide an undo command that immediately enables the user to reverse the previous control, entry, change, or delete action.
2.4.1.2   Make an undo action reversible. A second undo action should reinstate whatever was just undone.

2.4.2 Meaningful Error Messages

2.4.2.1   Present error messages that state the nature of the error and provide possible solutions. The messages should be brief and worded in terms of the task.

2.4.2.2   Enable the user to inquire about the error in more detail or request additional information on the operation in progress.

2.4.3 Backup Function

Make it possible to back up in a transaction sequence to correct errors and make changes.

2.4.4 Minor Deviations

Accept minor deviations. Under some circumstances, there are acceptable deviations, such as equating "exit" with off, log-off, quit, or bye.

2.5   Reduce Memory Demands

Human capacity for information processing has its limitations. Short-term memory provides a limited mental "scratchpad" for information processing and problem solving. Too many facts and decisions may overload short-term memory.

2.5.1 Length and Complexity

Do not require the user to remember lengthy lists of codes and complex command strings.

2.5.2 Amount of Input Activity

Require fewer input activities to increase user productivity.

2.5.3 Selection through Recognition

Provide selections from a list of choices. This eliminates memorization, structures decision-making, and does away with typographical errors. Selecting from a pull-down menu is an example of recognition, which places little demand on short-term memory, as compared to unaided recall of command strings.

2.6 Design for Task Relevance

Present information that pertains to the user's task. Any arrangement of items on the screen (in menus, lists, tables, etc.) should reflect task requirements.

2.6.1 Task-Related Capabilities

Use system capabilities to support the user's task performance. For example, use color, highlighting techniques, and graphics only to enhance user task accomplishment.

2.6.1.1   Make the design focus on the task, not on what the user must do with the hardware and software to accomplish the task.
2.6.1.2   Use dialog techniques that reflect the user's view and conception of what needs to be done.

2.6.2 Familiar Terms

Use terminology that is familiar to the user. Abbreviations, icons, mnemonics, codes, and acronyms should stem from specific job-related terminology or a known logic. Avoid the technical language of designers and programmers.

2.7 Aid Orientation and Navigation

Provide orientation aids and instructions to help users maintain a sense of where they are in the system, what they can do, and how they can get out.

2.7.1 Descriptive Title

Include a descriptive title placed in a consistent location on each screen, window, and menu.

2.7.1.1   Provide a clear, distinctive, and short title that reflects the content and purpose of the screen. Avoid words such as FORM and SCREEN and connecting words like "of" in the title.
2.7.1.2   Center the title on the screen.
2.7.1.3   Display the screen title in capital letters or mixed case.

2.7.2 Numbering System

Use a numbering scheme to identify the currently displayed page and the total number of pages in a multi-page display (e.g., 2 of 20).

2.7.2.1   Locate screen identifiers consistently, preferably to the right of the screen title.

2.7.3 System Map

When appropriate, provide a "system map" to show users where they are in the system.

2.7.4 Anticipation of User Action

Anticipate possible user actions. In preparation for possible user actions, provide the user with the following:

- A uniform starting point for control entries
- Available transaction options
- Task-relevant menus and consistently located control options
- Editable fields that are distinct from non-editable fields
- Default values, displayed automatically in the appropriate data fields
- User-interrupt, continue, and abort functions
- A simple means of navigating between windows

2.7.5 Exiting

Provide the user with a means to log off by a single action (e.g., menu option, command input).

2.7.5.1   Inform the user of any pending actions that will be lost upon log-off.
2.7.5.2   Permit the user to exit a file without saving changes, but require a confirmation to exit without saving changes.
2.7.5.3   Give the user a means to stop interacting with any type of file by a single exiting action (e.g., menu option, command input).

2.8   Provide Online Help

Provide users with online help that can be entered whenever needed. Tailor help to the task context and requirements. Presenting the entire user's manual in response to a help query will only frustrate the user. Effective help can serve as a data-protection resource.

2.8.1 *Multi-Level Help*

Provide multi-level help, beginning with summary information and providing more detailed explanations on request.

2.8.2 *Access to Help*

Permit the user to enter help at any point.

2.8.3 *Request for Help*

Use a simple, standard action for the user to request help.

2.8.4 *Help Browser*

Permit the user to browse help topics.

2.8.5 *Context-Sensitive Help*

Tailor available help to task context and requirements. (See Section 8 for further details).

2.8.6 *Automatic Help*

Activate the help function automatically (or offer help) when the user is making repeated errors.

2.8.7 *Return to Task*

Provide an easy means of returning to the task after accessing help.

2.9 Maintain a User-Centered Perspective

Focusing on user requirements is the key to maintaining a user-centered perspective. Every element of the design should be traceable to user requirements. From this perspective it is counterproductive to introduce "bells and whistles" just because it is technically possible to implement them. Capabilities not needed by the user will remain unused or, worse, may result in confusion.

2.9.1 User in Control

Keep the user in charge. A system that gives users a sense of control and responds to their actions builds trust and acceptance.

2.9.2 Decision Assistants

Design any required decision aids as assistants to (not replacements for) the user's flexible decision-making capabilities.

3.0 Guidelines for Basic User-Interface Components

Basic components of alphanumeric user interfaces include such elements as text fields, tables, and lists. Graphical user interfaces add lines, shapes, pushbuttons, icons, and dialog boxes. Both types of user interfaces incorporate one or more cursors, and labeling is important in both. The key design challenge is to select and integrate all user interface (UI) components into a seamless whole.

3.1 Cursors

Cursors enable the user to move the focus of input or attention within a display. Cursor control should provide fast movement and accurate placement.

A placeholding cursor should be easy to see and should not interfere with detection of any adjacent symbol or character. A second, pointing cursor should be visually distinct from the placeholding cursor.

3.1.1 Placeholding Cursor

On the screen, a cursor is typically positioned for a quick and easy start of the keying process. The placeholding cursor is a mark on the display, indicating the current position for attention.

3.1.1.1 Place the cursor at the first data entry field to which the user must provide input, and advance the cursor to the next data field when the user has completed entry in the current field.

3.1.1.2 If the placeholding cursor blinks, the default rate should be 3 Hz. User selectable blink rate should be between 3 and 5 Hz.

3.1.1.3 Use only one placeholding cursor in each window in which the user is entering alphanumeric characters.

3.1.1.4 Make a placeholding cursor the height or width of the alphanumeric character adjacent to it.

3.1.2 Pointing Cursor

The pointing cursor has the advantage of permitting the user to point at display information and select an item. This direct-manipulation approach presents the users with commands that do not have to be learned, reduces the chance of typographical errors on a keyboard, and keeps their attention on the display.

3.1.2.1 Do not make the pointing cursor blink.

3.1.2.2 Make the pointing cursor completely graphic. Do not use a label.

3.1.2.3 Do not move the pointing cursor without input from the user.

    3.1.2.3.1 Ensure that the step size of cursor movement is both horizontally and vertically consistent.

3.1.2.4 Use a cursor to enable the user to move the focal point of input or attention within a display.

3.1.2.5 Make the pointing cursor available at all times. It should not obscure other, critical information.

3.1.2.6 Use crosshairs when fine positioning accuracy is required.

3.1.2.7 Use multiple cursors only if they are required by the task.

    3.1.2.7.1 Make multiple cursors visually distinctive.

    3.1.2.7.2 Provide a visual indication of the cursor that is being controlled.

3.2 Text

The user interface presents text, for example in menus, labels, help windows, and message areas. The user may need to enter brief text, as in naming a file or making control entries. The user may need to enter continuous text, as in writing a comment or maintaining an online event log. The user needs simple editing capabilities (e.g., for correcting typographical errors and making word substitutions) that do not require going into a separate edit *mode*.

3.2.1 Text Fields

Present text fields in a consistent format, from one display to another.

3.2.1.1   Enable the use of text fields for the execution of commands, such as spell check, grammar check, search, find, and replace.

3.2.1.2   Ensure that control entries (e.g., keyed menu selections or commands) are distinguishable from displayed text to prevent the user from entering controls as text.

    3.2.1.2.1   Permit users to specify units of text as (e.g., words, paragraphs) modifiers for control entries.

    3.2.1.2.2   Highlight specified units of text to indicate boundaries of the text affected by control entries.

3.2.2 Continuous Text

Give users reasonable control over justification, line spacing, page structure (e.g., headers, margins, tab stops, and footers), and print options.

3.2.2.1   Left-justify all lines of continuous text.

    3.2.2.1.1   Do not permit right-justification with nonproportional spacing.

3.2.2.2   Maintain constant spacing between words. Do not use proportional spacing.

3.2.2.3   Use 150 percent of character height as the default line spacing.

3.2.2.4   Display continuous text in upper and lower case letters (i.e., mixed case.)

3.2.2.5   Provide automatic line breaks for entry/editing of unformatted text.

    3.2.2.5.1   Permit the user to override automatic line breaks by inserting page or section breaks when formatting and editing text.

3.2.2.6   For predefined page structures, provide the standard format automatically.

3.2.2.7   Allow users to label and store frequently used text formats and segments for future use.

3.2.2.8   Provide automatic pagination, but permit the user to override pagination in order to specify page numbers anywhere within a document.

    3.2.2.8.1   Enable users to control for the number of lines in a paragraph that will be permitted to stand by themselves as "orphans" or "widows" at the top or bottom of a page.

3.2.2.9   Provide a capability for the display of annotations to displayed text.

    3.2.2.9.1   Make annotations easy to distinguish from the text itself.

3.2.2.10 Permit the user to specify portions of the text for printing (e.g., a single page or range of pages).

    3.2.2.10.1 Allow the user to display text as it will be printed, including underlining, boldface, subscript, superscript, special characters, special symbols, and different styles and sizes of type.

    3.2.2.10.2 Inform the user of the status of requests for printouts. For example, notify the user when a printout has been completed.

3.3 Fonts and Typography

The legibility of displayed text is a major UI issue. Reading from the screen can be considerably slower compared to reading from paper. The following guidelines assume adequate display contrast, depending on lighting conditions.

3.3.1 Font Size and Styles

Improve legibility by the use of well-formed letter shapes and type sizes that are appropriate for viewing distances.

3.3.1.1 For a nominal viewing distance of 18 inches, the *minimum* recommended size for a font is 0.08 inch (just slightly less than 1/16th of an inch).

3.3.1.2 Where alphanumeric characters are displayed, select font styles to allow discrimination of similar characters, such as letter l and number 1, letter Z and number 2.

3.3.1.3 Do not use varying sizes or styles of fonts for any reason other than coding (e.g., text as labels, text as data, text as command input).

3.3.1.4 Use selected fonts in a consistent fashion throughout the interface, and provide upper and lower case with full descenders.

3.3.1.5 Avoid type faces that have extended serifs, internal patterns, or that are striped, italicized, stenciled, shadowed, or three-dimensional, or fonts that appear like handwritten script or like Old English script, and fonts that are distorted to look tall and thin or wide and fat.

3.4 Tables

In general, users should not be required to search through lengthy tabular data to find required values. That is a job for the software. The following guidelines apply when there is no alternative to tabular presentation or when a brief table will support task performance.

3.4.1 Information Presented

Present information that compares detailed sets of data in a recognizable order. A consistent design is required to facilitate scanning and assimilation.

3.4.2 Headings

Use row and column headings that reflect information the user had before consulting the table.

3.4.2.1 For large tables exceeding one screen, provide column and row labels in all displayed sections of the table.

3.4.3 Arrangement

Arrange rows and columns according to some logic (e.g., chronological, alphabetic).

3.4.4 Scanning Cues

Provide adequate separation between columns (i.e., at least three spaces) and between groups of rows (e.g., a blank line inserted after every fifth row).

3.5 Lists

Display a series of related items in a list to support quick, accurate scanning.

3.5.1 Number of Columns

A single column is usually recommended; that is, each item in the list starts on a new line.

3.5.1.1 For a more compact display of a long list, use multiple columns. When using multiple columns, order items vertically within each column.

3.5.2 Order of Items

Maintain the same order of items for each instance of a particular list. Base the order of items on natural logic, such as frequency of use, related functionality, or the normal sequence of user actions. If there is no apparent logical basis for ordering items, list them alphabetically.

3.5.2.1   If a single item in a list continues on to another line, mark the item to indicate the continuation of the item, for example use an ellipsis (...).

3.5.2.2   If the list is very long, use a hierarchic structure to partition it into a set of more compact lists.

3.5.3 Orderly Format

Attention to alignment and labeling can improve UI consistency.

3.5.3.1   Align decimal points when listing numbers with decimal values.

3.5.3.2   When decimal values are not used, numbers are flushed right.

3.5.3.3   Alphabetical listings are flushed left.

3.5.3.4   Labels describe the contents of the lists and are flushed left or centered.

3.6 Pushbuttons

Maintain consistency in the design of pushbuttons. Although pushbuttons can vary in size and shape, the design of a particular type of pushbutton should remain consistent throughout an application. Standard names and uses for common pushbutton functions are listed in Table A.3.

Table A.3   Names and Uses for Pushbutton Functions

Names	Uses
OK	Confirms any information changed in a window and the window is closed
Apply	Any changes in a window will occur and be displayed in the window
Reset	Cancels any changes that have not been submitted
Cancel	Closes a window after no changes were submitted
Help	Displays contextual help for an item or help for an entire window

3.6.1 Pushbutton Captions

Provide captions on pushbuttons, specifically stating the actions they are intended to perform.

3.6.2 Information Prior to Action

If additional information must be supplied by the user before the system can carry out a pushbutton action, provide an ellipsis (...) after the pushbutton caption to indicate that a query will be presented.

3.6.3 Arrangement of Pushbuttons

To the extent possible, arrange pushbuttons by frequency of use. For example, position frequently used action buttons to the left of or above other displayed buttons. When the same buttons are used for different windows, consistently place them in the same location, and keep related buttons together.

3.7 Icons

Icons are pictorial representations of objects or actions that reflect the controlling metaphor of the application (e.g., desktop, office environment, artist's studio). Although it seems obvious that icons should look like what they represent, this is not always easy to achieve in practice. An icon that means one thing to a developer may mean something entirely different to a user. It is important to pre-test icons with users to verify that the icon set conveys the intended meanings.

3.7.1 Representation

Use icons that have clear meanings to their shape and pictorially reflect the objects or actions represented. To the extent possible, use icons that are already familiar to users.

3.7.1.1   Make each icon represent a single object or action.
3.7.1.2   Make each icon a simple, closed figure. Use as few graphical components as necessary. Avoid ornamentation.
3.7.1.3   Do not use purely abstract designs for icons.
3.7.1.4   Use the same icons for the same objects and actions across applications.

3.7.1.5 If it is necessary to create a new icon, consult standard symbol sets available from the American National Standards Institute (ANSI) and other sources to find established icons that may meet the need.

3.7.1.6 If no existing icons are satisfactory, create shapes that are meaningful to users, easily recognizable, and visually distinct from each other.

3.7.1.7 Use humor in icon design only if all users will get the joke and none will be confused or offended.

3.7.2 Size

Make the icon big enough to be seen, recognized, and selected easily.

3.3.2.1 Make all of the icons within a related set the same size.

3.3.2.2 Determine size requirements imposed by UI style guides, GUI software, and standards for legibility.

3.7.3 Number

For most applications, display fewer than 20 icons simultaneously on the same screen.

3.7.4 Labeling

Give each icon a text label corresponding to the object or action. Do not let the label obscure the icon.

3.7.4.1 Place the caption or label directly beneath the icon.

3.7.5 Grouping

Group related icons using similar shapes and colors to depict a common relationship.

3.7.5.1 Provide a default arrangement, but permit users to rearrange icons within the context of their tasks.

3.7.6 Highlighting

Highlight icons selected by the user.

3.7.7 Documentation

Provide a glossary in online help containing a list of standard icons and their associated objects and actions.

3.7.8 Testing

Prior to implementation, measure the effectiveness of icons by testing them, with a representative group of users, for quick recognition and ease of learning. Redesign and retest until usability objectives are met.

3.8 Labels

The quality of labeling employed throughout a user interface can impact user performance. Labels should be as meaningful and detailed as possible.

3.8.1 Wording

Give each data field, data group, message, pushbutton, icon, and window a descriptive label or caption, generally not a number.

3.8.1.1 Spell words in full, using the simplest possible words as labels. Do not use contractions, abbreviations, or punctuation in labels (unless absolutely necessary for meaning or to accommodate space restrictions, or unless the label chosen is an accepted standard in the users' environment).

3.8.1.2 Display labels and titles in mixed case.

3.8.2 Location

Locate an item's label as close as possible to the item it describes (e.g., adjacent to the item, immediately above or below the item).

3.8.2.1 Integrate labels with graphics, using the same type style for labels and text.

3.8.3 Orientation

Display labels in a left-to-right (horizontal) orientation. Do not display labels vertically or in any other off-horizontal orientation.

3.8.4 Differentiation

Differentiate labels from other screen elements in a unique and consistent manner (e.g., bold, underlined).

3.8.5 Spacing

Separate labels from one another by at least two standard character spaces.

3.8.6 Consistency

Make labels consistent in wording, location, orientation, differentiation, and spacing throughout an application or set of applications.

3.9 Checkboxes and Radio Buttons

Use *checkboxes* or *radio buttons* to present multiple options. Multiple options are often presented in panels of checkboxes or radio buttons, but their use is not interchangeable. Checkboxes are used to allow the user to select several options. Radio buttons permit only one selection from a group of options.

3.9.1 Labeling

Descriptions of alternative choices for checkboxes and radio buttons should be fully and clearly spelled out and positioned to the right of each box or button.

3.9.1.1   Display descriptors (labels) in mixed case.
3.9.1.2   Capitalize the first letter of each major word in multi-word labels.

3.9.2 Choice Indication

Indicate that a choice has been made, in the box or button, by means of a checkmark, fill-in, or highlighting.

3.9.3 Checkboxes

Use checkboxes for nonexclusive options. When options are not mutually exclusive, checkboxes allow for more than one selection to be made.

Checkboxes are usually displayed as square or rectangular boxes with option labels inscribed alongside each box.

3.9.3.1 Provide labels for each set of checkboxes.

3.9.3.2 Arrange checkboxes in logical order so that the most frequently used boxes are at the top or at the left, depending on how the boxes are oriented.

3.9.3.3 A columnar orientation is generally preferred for checkboxes, with the boxes aligned to the left.

    3.9.3.3.1 If there is limited space, a horizontal orientation may be used, with adequate separation (three spaces) between each box.

3.9.3.4 Within a group of checkboxes, make the boxes equal in height and width.

3.9.3.5 Label style and orientation should remain consistent to the extent possible.

3.9.3.6 Use the method of indicating selected options consistently across all panels of checkboxes in an application or set of applications.

3.9.4 Radio Buttons

Use circular or diamond-shaped radio buttons for mutually exclusive options. Avoid using rectangular radio buttons because they may be confused with checkboxes. When options are mutually exclusive, radio buttons permit the selection of only one item at a time.

3.9.4.1 Provide labels for each set of radio buttons.

    3.9.4.1.1 If a screen or window contains only one panel of radio buttons, the screen or window title can serve as the panel label (if there is no question of user confusion).

3.9.4.2 Limit to eight the number of options presented in a panel of radio buttons.

    3.9.4.2.1 When nine or more options must be presented, consider using a scrollable list or a drop-down list.

3.9.4.3 Arrange options in a logical or expected order, beginning at the top of the panel.

3.9.4.4 Left-align the radio buttons and their labels in the preferred columnar format.

    3.9.4.4.1 If the buttons must be arranged horizontally, provide at least three spaces between an option label and the next button.

3.9.4.5 When a particular option is not available, display it as subdued or grayed-out in relation to the brightness of the available options.

3.9.4.6 Make the selection target area include the radio button and its label.

        3.9.4.6.1 When the cursor has been moved to an option, making it available for selection, highlight only the label (not the button) using a technique such as reverse video, reverse color, or a dashed box around the label.

3.9.4.7 Use the method chosen to indicate selection consistently across all panels of radio buttons in the application or set of applications.

3.10 Dialog Boxes

Dialog boxes ask users to specify preferences and to acknowledge messages from the system.

3.10.1 Dialog-Box Basics

There are two basic categories of dialog boxes: (1) modal and (2) modeless. Modal dialog boxes require a response before the user can take any further action. Modeless dialog boxes allow the user to perform parallel dialogs. Switching between the modeless dialog box and its associated window is permitted. Palettes and toolbars are modeless dialog boxes.

3.10.1.1 Give each dialog box a title.

3.10.1.2 Match pushbuttons to the function of the dialog box.

3.10.1.3 Size dialog boxes to be smaller than application windows.

3.10.1.4 Locate each dialog box uniquely, depending on the scope of its relationship to system or application elements.

3.10.2 Message Boxes

When a warning of an unexpected event (e.g., printer out of paper) or information regarding an irreversible state is presented to the user, a message box provides space for user acknowledgment.

4.0 Guidelines for Screen Layout and Design

This section concerns the orderly design to support the exchange of information between the user and the computer. Of interest are screen format and content, such as where information is placed, how information is structured, and what information is included. Achieving consistency in screen design throughout an application's user interface is a key challenge for the development team.

4.1 General Layout

The objective is to achieve a screen layout that meets users' information requirements while appearing well organized and uncluttered.

4.1.1 Presentation of Information

Present information in a directly usable form; the user should not have to cross-reference other resources or perform mental transformations of data.

4.1.1.1 To the extent possible, put all the data related to one task on a single screen. Users should be able to see the entire page on which they are working.

    4.1.1.1.1 If all the required data will not fit on a single screen, divide it into logical units so that the data needed first is presented first, followed by a screen or screens containing the data needed later in the task.

        4.1.1.1.1.1 Indicate display continuation when display output is presented on more than one screen.

        4.1.1.1.1.2 Label each screen of a multi-screen display to show its relationship to the others.

    4.1.1.1.2 Display functionally related data items on the same screen. Do not require the user to jump back and forth within a set of screens or windows to find required pieces of data.

4.1.1.2 Reserve special areas of the screen for:
- Commands
- Status messages
- Input fields

Locate these areas consistently on all screens.

4.1.1.3 To the extent possible, do not require users to perform mental comparisons or other analyses of data. Present the information integrated into the form needed for task performance (e.g., trends over time).

    4.1.1.3.1 When there is no alternative to requiring users to detect similarities, differences, trends, and relationships across sets of data, format the screen so that the data is grouped to facilitate analysis and comparison.

4.1.2 Emphasis between Elements

Use contrasting display features to emphasize differences between elements:

- Different screen components, such as dialog boxes, windows, and menus
- Items being acted upon
- Urgent items

4.1.3 Visual Guidance through Grouping

Guide users through the screen with bordering lines formed by display elements, and provide symmetry and balance through the use of white space.

4.1.3.1 Group data in ways that support the users' logical train of thought in performing their tasks.

    4.1.3.1.1 Group particularly important data items, and display them at the top of the screen.

    4.1.3.1.2 Group data items that are used more frequently than others, and display them near the top of the screen (below the important items referred to in 4.1.3.1.1).

    4.1.3.1.3 When data is used in some spatial or temporal order, group by sequence of use.

    4.1.3.1.4 When sets of data are associated with particular questions or are related to particular functions, group each set to illustrate those functional relationships.

    4.1.3.1.5 Use general-to-specific grouping when there are hierarchical relationships among data elements, with general elements preceding specific elements.

    4.1.3.1.6 If there is no other known logic for grouping data, based on the cognitive task analysis, use a standard grouping technique (e.g., chronological, alphabetical).

4.1.3.2 Use grouping to make the screen appear as an organized collection of smaller identifiable elements.

    4.1.3.2.1 Demarcate groups of information by spacing, drawing lines, color coding, or some other means. Be careful not to clutter the display with too many lines or colors.

        4.1.3.2.1.1 For critical tasks, use at least one character space above and below, and two character spaces before and after the critical information.

4.1.4 Visual Appearance

Be consistent with visual appearance and procedural usage.

4.1.4.1 Place recurring data fields in consistent relative positions within displays.

4.1.4.2 When appropriate for users, use the same format for input and output. (Determine appropriateness through the task analysis and discussions with users.)

4.1.4.3 When appropriate, match data-entry formats and source-document formats. (Determine appropriateness through the task analysis and discussions with users.)

4.1.4.4 In general, keep *screen density* below 50 percent and preferably less than 25 percent.

4.1.4.4.1 In displays used for critical tasks, minimize screen density (the ratio of filled to unfilled pixels).

4.1.5 Output Displays

Based on results of the task analysis, provide the user with whatever data is needed for any transaction, making such data available for display. Use task analysis to determine detailed information requirements for the user. Users should not have to recall data from one *output display* to the next.

4.1.5.1 Continue to provide prior data when necessary so that users do not have to remember previous values when they are interpreting new data.

4.1.5.2 Use familiar, task-oriented terms on displayed data and labels. Ensure that carefully chosen words and the same grammatical structure are used consistently within and across displays.

4.1.5.3 Use complete words instead of abbreviations, whenever possible.

4.1.5.3.1 When using abbreviations, choose those that are most commonly used and familiar to the user.

4.1.5.3.2 Do not use the same abbreviation for different words; make sure abbreviations are distinctive.

4.1.5.3.3 Minimize punctuation of abbreviations and acronyms; for example, display USA instead of U.S.A.

4.1.5.3.4 Use a standard method to form abbreviations.

4.1.5.3.5 Special abbreviations are used only when they are required for clarity. If an abbreviation must deviate from the standard method for forming abbreviations, make the deviation minimal. Keep abbreviations as short as possible.

4.1.5.3.6 When abbreviations or acronyms are required, provide a dictionary of terms in online help and in the user's guide.

4.1.5.4 Define the frequency of displaying a data field as required or optional. A required field is always displayed whenever a screen is used. An optional field is displayed when information is requested but not necessarily required. Alternatively, display both required and optional fields, but code them differently (e.g., place a parenthesis around the label of an optional field).

4.1.6 Entry Screens

If forms of any type are used for data entry, they should be compatible with those used for data output. Use the same item labeling and ordering for both. Data should be entered in units that are familiar to the user.

4.1.6.1 Ensure that screen titles reflect the names of the data elements. Clarification of titles on system worksheets may be required.

4.1.6.2 Minimize the amount of data that the user must enter.

4.1.6.2.1 The user should not have to enter the same data more than once. Correct items are saved and there is no need to enter that data again while changing incorrect items.

4.1.6.2.2 Preserve the context of each data-entry transaction.

4.1.6.3 During data entry, display feedback for each keyed entry within 0.02 seconds.

4.1.6.3.1 Design data-entry transactions and associated displays so that users are able to remain with one method of entry. If data entry is assigned to specific areas, provide clear visual definition of the entry fields.

4.1.6.3.2 Provide a sufficient number of lines and line length to support entry and editing tasks.

4.1.6.3.3 Permit users to change previous entries by delete and insert ("cut and paste") methods. If direct character substitution ("typeover") is included, make the data changes consistently available wherever character substitution is required.

4.1.6.3.4 For cancellation of data entry, have the computer confirm completion of a transaction with a message stating that the cancellation was successful or that there was an error.

4.1.6.3.5 When the user requests changes or deletion of the data, offer the option of maintaining the old value before making the change.

4.1.6.4   Provide the user with the means for selection and entry (e.g., point to and click on; move to and select) of a position on a display, or of a displayed item.

4.1.6.5   To aid the user in entering data in a hierarchic structure with various sections and levels of detail, provide computer aids, such as:
- Question-and-answer dialogues or form filling to maintain data relationships
- Arrows on flowcharts that automatically connect lines
- Indicators of current positions when panning a map

    4.1.6.5.1   For orientation, consider displaying a defined data structure with branches and levels labeled for reference.

    4.1.6.5.2   For complex data structures, provide computer prompts, so that the user can make appropriate data entries at different levels.

4.2   Alphanumerics

The display of continuous text, numbers, and combined alphanumeric codes raises numerous design and layout issues. Designers and developers should have a detailed understanding of user needs for alphanumeric displays before proceeding with any particular approach.

4.2.1   Continuous Text

Reading from a computer screen can be noticeably slower than reading from paper. The challenge in designing and displaying continuous text is to support the user's reading speed and comprehension.

4.2.1.1   If the user needs to read continuous text from the screen, present at least four lines of text at a time, displayed in mixed upper and lower case.

4.2.1.2   Present text in wide lines containing between 40 and 60 characters per line. Avoid narrow columns of short lines.

    4.2.1.2.1   Make the display space wide enough to present full lines of text. Do not require horizontal scrolling to "uncover" hidden text.

4.2.1.3   Number paragraphs, and separate them by at least one blank line.

4.2.2   Letter Combinations and Special Characters

4.2.2.1   Do not use restricted alphabetic sets for alphabetical data entry.

4.2.2.2   When *special characters* are chosen for keying (e.g., @, /, =, #), select characters that do not require frequent keyboard shifting.

4.2.3 Numbers

Present data in digital form only if the user needs specific numerical values.

4.2.3.1   Use six or fewer characters in numeric codes.
4.2.3.2   Use Arabic (not Roman) numerals when numbering items in a list.
4.2.3.3   Right-justify integers for ease of viewing and scanning.
4.2.3.4   Give the user the option to enter or omit the decimal point at the end of an integer. The system should recognize an entry of "45" and an entry of "45." as equivalent.
    4.2.3.4.1   If a decimal point is required for data processing, program the computer to append one as needed.
    4.2.3.4.2   When displayed in columns, decimal numbers should be decimal aligned.
4.2.3.5   Permit the user the option of entering or omitting *leading zeros* for general numeric data. In a field that is four characters long, "45" should be recognized by the system without requiring the user to enter "0045."
4.2.3.6   Separate long numbers into groups of three or four digits. Use either standard separators or spaces. For example, social security numbers and telephone numbers use hyphens; bank account numbers are often divided by spaces.

4.2.4 Scales

Use a linear scale for numerical data, not the more difficult to interpret logarithmic scale or nonlinear scales.

4.2.4.1   Begin scaling numeric data at zero.
4.2.4.2   Use a familiar, meaningful approach to determining scale intervals. For example, use standard intervals of 1, 2, 5, or 10 to label scale divisions.

4.2.5 Alphanumeric Codes

To aid user comprehension of textual and numeric codes, such as acronyms and abbreviations, use meaningful codes in preference to arbitrary codes.

4.2.5.1   Do not choose frequently confused characters and character pairs. For example, the letters O and I should not be used in codes because they can be confused with the numbers zero (0) and one (1). Similarly, the number 8 can be confused with the letters B and S.

4.2.5.2   When the user must recall alphanumeric codes, limit the code to five characters.

4.2.5.3   Group letters and numbers together, rather than interspersing letters and numbers.

        4.2.5.3.1   Group characters in blocks of three to five characters, separated by at least one blank space or other separating character.

4.2.5.4   Use either all upper case or all lower case for alphanumeric codes.

4.2.5.5   Use punctuation in alphanumeric codes only when the code might be confused with a word.

4.2.5.6   When designing alphanumeric commands, consider the effects of possible typographical errors. Ask whether mistyping a command will produce another valid but undesired command.

        4.2.5.6.1   Prevent the entry of inappropriate characters into a field (e.g., an alphabetic character into a field reserved for numeric characters).

4.3 Graphics

Displaying data in graphical formats can often, but not always, aid the user's visual detection and comprehension of relationships within the data. If the displayed data reflects spatial or temporal relationships, consider displaying it graphically instead of using numerical tables or textual descriptions. Because the benefits of graphics are task dependent, any planned graphical display should be tested for usability.

4.3.1 Visual Balance

To make displays readily scannable, balance their elements in as organized a pattern as possible, and maintain that organization across the application. Base the organizing principle on users' expectations and on their understanding of the logic underlying the displayed information.

4.3.1.1   Balance the left side of the display against the right side, and the top against the bottom, as shown in Figure A.1. Consider using a layout grid as an aid to achieving both visual and conceptual balance of displayed elements.

        4.3.1.1.1   Use symmetry (an even distribution of elements to the left and right of center) to convey stability.

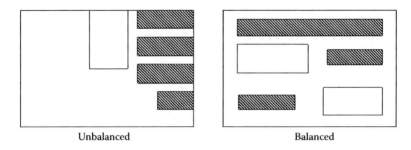

Unbalanced	Balanced

Figure A.1   Visual balance.

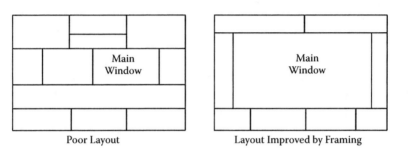

Poor Layout	Layout Improved by Framing

Figure A.2   Use of framing.

    4.3.1.1.2 If using an asymmetric layout to emphasize contrast or to convey movement, balance the distribution of displayed elements through the use of factors such as color, size, and shape.

4.3.1.2 Display short messages in wide, shallow spaces.

4.3.1.3 Display graphics in square or slightly rectangular areas. Use recommended proportions of length to width (e.g., 1:1, 1:1.414, 1:1.618). Avoid irregular shapes.

4.3.1.4 Frame the central display area with smaller functional elements (Figure A.2).

4.3.1.5 Leave at least one character space between the contents of a window and the window borders.

4.4 Hypertext and Hypermedia

Hypertext documents are based on a design metaphor that likens the screen to a deck of cards or a series of planes through which the user is able to scroll or pan. The primary features of a hypertext system are nodes (e.g., text, graphics, sound, video) and links between nodes. In hypermedia systems, the user controls traversal among nodes.

4.4.1 Access to Information

Provide alternative means for the user to access information in a hypermedia document (e.g., following links, searching, or using contextual cues).

4.4.2 Links

Links between nodes enable the user to move in a nonlinear fashion through the available information. A common problem to avoid is the presence of so many links that the user becomes overwhelmed.

4.4.2.1　Base the creation of links between related information on the user's need for information in some particular context.

4.4.2.2　Indicate the presence of links by use of a link marker (such as an icon) or by highlighting.

4.4.2.3　Present linked graphical materials with appended text defining the graphical material and its text links.

4.4.2.4　To the extent possible, provide links across media (i.e., in addition to text linking, use graphics linking, sound linking, and video linking).

4.4.3 User Orientation

To avoid user disorientation in navigating hypermedia documents, employ (1) maps or browsers that indicate the user's position within the network; or (2) tags, markers, or milestones that represent locations within the network.

4.4.4 Collaborative Authoring

In collaborative authoring of hypermedia documents, use an authoring system that provides ways to read, link, and edit the document while allowing authors to protect their work from unauthorized access or changes.

5.0 Guidelines for Interaction Styles and Data Protection

Depending on the user's task environment, one or more styles of interaction may be appropriate. The varieties of interaction styles include alphanumeric dialogs (e.g., fill-in forms) as well as graphical dialogs (e.g., menu selection and direct manipulation). Many user interfaces combine textual and graphical styles. The key design challenges are to match the interaction style to the user's task domain and to protect the integrity of the data.

5.1 Fill-In Forms

Fill-in forms are used to enter predefined items into labeled fields. These screens resemble paper forms that are completed by filling in the blanks. The screens provide necessary cues so that novice users can correctly determine what must be keyed, enter the appropriate information, and then review it. Major issues include design of entry fields and transactions.

5.1.1 Compatible Forms

Design forms so that data items are ordered in a way that is familiar to the user.

5.1.1.1   If transcriptions from source documents are used in data entry, ensure that form-filling displays are compatible with such documents in terms of item ordering, data grouping, labeling, etc.

5.1.2 Entry-Field Basics

Design data-entry fields consistently within and across applications. That is, use consistent approaches to labeling, prompting, highlighting, justification, and spacing.

5.1.2.1   Label each data field to inform users of entries to be made.
      5.1.2.1.1   Keep labels close to associated data fields; separate them by at least one space.
      5.1.2.1.2   Ensure consistency in field labels by using the same label for the same kind of data entry.
      5.1.2.1.3   Protect field labels from keyed entry by having the cursor skip over them when the user is spacing or tabbing.
      5.1.2.1.4   Use descriptive wording, standard terms, codes, and abbreviations when labeling data fields. For more clarity, employ additional cues in a data field label.

Example: | Birth Date mm/dd/yy: _ _ / _ _ / _ _ |

5.1.2.1.5   Include a unit of measurement as part of the field label when that unit (e.g., $, °, mph) is part of a particular data field. The units of measurement employed should be familiar to the user. When alternative units of measurement are used, provide space to distinguish the units that are entered.

Example: | **Weight:** _ _ _   **(lb/kg)** _ _

5.1.2.2   In form-filling, require one explicit entry action at the end of the transaction sequence for the entry of logically related items, to avoid the separate entry of each item.

5.1.2.2.1   Allow the user to enter multiple data items without keying special separator or delimiter characters.

5.1.2.2.2   Permit the user to review, cancel, or back up multiple data items entered as a single transaction.

5.1.2.3   If using a delimiter, be consistent in the employment of a standard character. Choose a character that does not require shifting keys or one that does not occur as part of any data entry.

5.1.2.3.1   Do not require users to remove delimiters or otherwise enter keystrokes for all positions within a variable-length field.

5.1.2.4   Select a standard means of prompting users for keyed entry, such as highlighting the entry field with beveled edges or shadows.

5.1.2.4.1   Ensure that the method used for highlighting is visually different from screen error messages.

5.1.2.4.2   Highlight entry fields consistently across screens.

5.1.2.5   Clearly distinguish between required and optional entry fields. For example, dashes might indicate required fields, and dots, optional fields.

Example:
| Requirement No.: _ _ _ _ _ _
| User: _ _ _ _ _ _
| Date: ....
| Time: ....

5.1.2.5.1   Provide a means for indicating when a fixed or maximum length is specified for data entry (Figure A.3).

5.1.2.5.2   Use field delineation cues, such as coding the labels of required and optional entry fields.

5.1.2.5.3   If the data entry does not completely fill the markers because data entry length is variable, ignore the remaining field markers in computer processing.

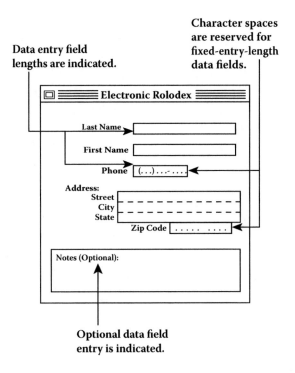

Figure A.3   Data entry design.

5.1.2.5.4   Do not accomplish data entry by overwriting a set of characters within a field.

5.1.2.6   To speed data entry, offer default values that can be defined for data entry in a specific task.

5.1.2.6.1   In the event of a series of defined default values, permit the user to accept defaults for all entries or to default until reaching the next required, non-default entry.

5.1.2.6.2   When it is not possible to predict what default values will be useful, permit the user to define, change, or remove default values for any data-entry field, without changing default definitions for subsequent transactions.

5.1.2.6.3   At the beginning of a data-entry transaction, display default values in the appropriate fields.

5.1.2.7   Provide automatic updating to free the user from entering the same data twice.

5.1.2.8   Limit data items to five to seven characters when the user must code data or enter numbers.

5.1.2.8.1 If the data items must be longer, partition them into shorter clusters for entry and display. For example, ten-digit telephone numbers are partitioned into three groups: XXX-XXX-XXXX.

5.1.2.9 Use a consistent approach to the justification of data-entry fields.

5.1.2.9.1 Left-justify the caption and the entry fields, with one space between the longest caption and the entry field. Alternatively, right-justify the captions and left-justify the entry fields.

```
┌─────────────────────────┐  ┌─────────────────────────────┐
│ Organization:  _ _ _ _ _│  │ Logon Account Code: _ _ _ _ _│
│ Account Code: _ _ _ _   │  │     Report Number:  _ _ _    │
│ Password:      _ _ _ _  │  │            Date:  _ _/_ _/_  │
└─────────────────────────┘  └─────────────────────────────┘
```

Alternative justification of caption and entry fields.

5.1.2.10 For horizontal viewing, provide a minimum of five spaces between the longest entry field in one column and the left-most caption in the adjacent column. For vertical viewing, provide one blank line between groups of related information.

```
┌────────────────────────────────────────────┐
│ 1. Project #: _ _ _ _ _   4. Project #: _ _ _ _ _ │
│ 2. Project #: _ _ _ _ _   5. Project #: _ _ _ _ _ │
│ 3. Project #: _ _ _ _ _   6. Project #: _ _ _ _ _ │
└────────────────────────────────────────────┘
```

Horizontal spacing of entry fields.

```
┌──────────────────────────────────────────────┐
│ Employee Number:          _ _ _ _ _            │
│ Social Security Number: _ _ _  _ _  _ _ _ _    │
│ Grade:                    _ _                  │
│ Department:               _ _ _ _ _ _ _ _ _    │
│ Division:                 _ _ _                │
│                                                │
│ Title:                    _ _ _ _ _ _ _ _ _    │
│ Years in Service:         _ _                  │
│ Salary:                   _ _ _ _ _ _          │
└──────────────────────────────────────────────┘
```

Vertical spacing of entry fields.

5.1.3 Command Keystrokes

Across interaction styles, when speed of command input is important, use command keystrokes (i.e., a limited number of keystrokes combined with pressing a command key to access a command language term).

5.1.4 Function Keys

Use function keys for tasks with unique control entries or as an adjunct to other interaction styles for functions that occur frequently, that must be made quickly, and that must be made with minimal syntax errors.

5.2 Question-and-Answer

A question-and-answer interface is a combination of menu and fill-in form interfaces in a dialog style. The dialog proceeds in a step-by-step continual interaction. Typically, prompting is included with the question. Sometimes questions and answers are scrolled on the screen, enabling the user to view much of the dialog. In other cases, new questions individually refresh the screen, omitting from view previous questions and answers.

Question-and-answer dialogs are used for the following situations:

- Tasks require routine data entry.
- Data items are known and ordering can be constrained.
- Users are novices and new to the system.
- Computer response time is relatively fast.

5.2.1 Wording of Questions

Ensure questions are in clear, simple language. The grammatical form should be consistent throughout.

5.2.1.1 Avoid negatives such as, "If the claim is not related to an accident, check here." Phrase the question in a positive manner, such as "Check here if the claim is related to an accident."

5.2.2 Mnemonic Codes and Abbreviations for Answers

Use simple mnemonic codes for answers to questions. The user should not have to perform several translations to correctly answer a question. For example, when the user is asked for marital status, the user indicates married or single through a simple *mnemonic code.*

5.2.2.1 When a question requires only two possible answers as in the question, "Are you an employee (e) or a visitor (v)," provide mnemonic codes such as "e" for "employee" and "v" for "visitor."

5.2.2.2 Minimize typing requirements by requesting abbreviated rather than spelled-out answers, such as "m" for married and "y" for yes. Avoid capital letters when not necessary (for example, do not require "M" for married and "Y" for yes).

5.2.3 Recapitulation of Prior Answers

Display interrelated, computer-posed questions so that answers to previous questions are visible to the user. This often helps the user in answering questions that follow.

5.2.4 Visible Titles

Display the dialog title continuously, despite questions scrolling off the screen as the dialog progresses.

5.2.5 Visual Coding of Dialog Parts

Use visual cues and white space so that the user can distinguish between questions, prompts, instructions, and user input. Capital versus lower-case letters, indentations, and spatial location are some other methods that can be used to identify dialog parts.

5.2.6 Navigation Instructions

Include instructions for using navigation capabilities; otherwise the user may never discover and make use of them.

5.2.7 Scanning Capabilities

Provide the user with the capability to return to and edit previous answers, scan through future questions, quit the session before completion of dialog, and re-enter the dialog at the point where the user left off.

5.3 Menus

The key objectives of menu design are to minimize the user's search-and-selection time and to optimize the user's ability to navigate through the menu structure.

5.3.1 General

Consider using menus when:

- User tasks involve selecting from a constrained set of alternative actions.
- User tasks require only occasional data entry.
- Users have little experience or training.

■ Computer response is reasonably fast.

■ Commands from a large command set are used infrequently.

5.3.1.1 Locate menus and menu options consistently when they appear in different displays.

5.3.1.2 Provide a means for the experienced user to bypass the menu structure by using direct keyboard commands. Display alternative keyboard commands (*accelerators*) to the right of the menu option label. Do not use arbitrary numbers for accelerator codes.

5.3.1.3 If logical grouping of options is not possible, display up to eight options that are appropriate to any particular transaction.

    5.3.1.3.1 If selection must be made from a list of more than eight options or if sequential selection is required, consider using a hierarchic menu structure.

    5.3.1.3.2 If logical categories can be established for a set of more than eight options, as many as 64 categorized options may be presented in one menu.

5.3.1.4 Dim (or gray out) unavailable or invalid options.

5.3.2 Phrasing Menu Options

Use direct, unambiguous wording that reflects the actions to be executed. Use verbs or verb phrases (not nouns or noun phrases) to denote actions (e.g., edit, view, insert).

5.3.2.1 Where possible, use wording that is familiar to users, but do not use familiar terms to mean something different from their common usage in the user community.

5.3.3 Formatting Menu Options

Menu options can be formatted linearly in a vertical or horizontal list or spatially in a circle, rectangle, or other geometric shape (e.g., pie menus). The following guidelines apply to the layout, organization, and grouping of vertically formatted menu options.

5.3.3.1 Format the menu list as a single column, wide enough to accommodate the widest option plus its keyboard accelerator.

5.3.3.2 Arrange menu and submenu options in separate, cascading columns, with the options listed under each other, and left-justified.

5.3.3.3 Use logical sequence, criticality, or frequency of use to establish the ordering of options in a brief menu.

5.3.3.3.1 Make the most likely selection in a menu list the default option.

5.3.3.3.2 Within hierarchic menus, permit immediate access to critical or frequently selected options.

5.3.3.4 If basing menu organization on frequency of use, place the following options at the bottom of the menu:
■ Less frequently used options.
■ Destructive commands, such as Delete or Exit.

5.3.3.5 Within a longer menu, group logically related options and draw a solid line between groups. Make the solid line the same color as the option labels.

5.3.3.6 If there is no inherent logical order in a set of menu options, alphabetize the options, but do not place options for opposing actions adjacent to each other. For example, the Delete option should not be next to the Save option.

5.3.4 Pull-Down Menus

Pull-down menus appear in response to the user's selection of a menu option from the menu bar. They are also called "drop-down" menus. Pull-down menus should be used when space is limited, when users need to see the menu options only when selecting them, and when required information on the screen will not be obscured by the menu. Pull-down menus include various types of options (e.g., command actions, settings or toggles, submenus, or cascades).

5.3.4.1 Use pull-down menus to open top-level menus listed in the menu bar.

5.3.4.2 Place the pull-down directly below the option selected from the menu bar. The higher-level option serves as the title for the pull-down.

5.3.4.3 Present the pull-down in the same foreground and background colors used in the menu bar. (These colors should contrast sufficiently with the background of the application area/screen body.)

5.3.4.4 Outline the pull-down with a border or drop shadow.

5.3.4.5 To the extent possible, present all options to minimize scrolling.

5.3.4.6 Present the options in initial capital letters followed by lower-case letters ("mixed case") or in self-explanatory graphics (e.g., fill-in patterns, colors), as appropriate to the user's task.

5.3.4.7 Display a pull-down menu until the user makes a selection.

5.3.4.8 Do not place instructions in pull-down menus.

5.3.4.9 If a pull-down option leads to a second-level, cascading pull-down, follow the option label with a right-pointing arrow. Position the cascading pull-down to the right of the highlighted option in the previous pull-down.

The recommended number of levels of cascading pull-downs varies between one (Apple) and three (DEC windows). To support the user's sense of orientation within the menu structure, it is best to minimize the number of levels.

5.3.5 Pop-Up Menus

Each window or displayed object can have an associated pop-up menu that appears, on demand, in response to a user action (e.g., point and click on a designated screen area or menu icon). Visually, a pop-up menu resembles a pull-down menu, but it is not associated with the top-level menus listed in the menu bar. A pop-up menu typically contains five to ten options presented in a vertical listing. In some environments, pop-up menus can cascade and can include keyboard accelerators.

5.3.5.1 Provide some indication or cue to the existence of a pop-up menu (e.g., highlight the portion of the display that can be selected to access the hidden menu; provide a textual message indicating that a hidden menu is available; or change the shape of the cursor when it is located in a "clickable" or selectable area).

5.3.5.2 Place a pop-up menu directly below the pointer used to select it and near the object or higher-level menu that is being manipulated.

5.3.5.3 Display a title for each pop-up menu.

5.3.5.4 When an option in a pop-up menu leads to a cascading menu, place a right-pointing triangle after the option label.

5.3.5.5 Make the pop-up distinct from the screen background by giving it a contrasting, yet complementary, background or by giving it a solid-line border.

5.3.5.6 Highlight an option selected from a pop-up menu. In particular, continue to highlight an option that leads to a cascading menu. The highlighted option serves as the title for the cascading menu.

5.3.5.7 Because of the variation in usage and implementation of pop-up menus across different environments, check your UI software style guide before incorporating pop-up menus in your application's user interface.

option-button menus (closed)

option-button menu (opened)

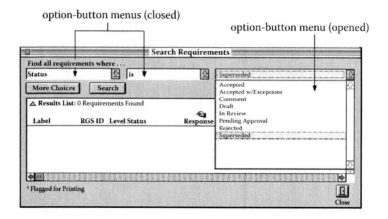

Figure A.4 Option-menu buttons.

5.3.6 *Option-Button Menus*

When screen space is limited, use an option-button menu to present a brief set of specialized menu options (Figure A.4).

5.3.6.1 Implement an option-button menu so that it opens like a pull-down menu, allowing the user to see all of the possible options.

5.3.6.2 Distinguish an option-button menu from a pushbutton.

5.3.7 *Graphic Menus*

Graphic menus are sometimes called palettes. A *palette* is a set of unlabeled symbols, typically presented within small rectangles. Symbols may be icons, patterns, characters, or drawings that represent an operation. When activated, a symbol provides access to a software tool (i.e., a set of specialized software functions). Palettes are used widely in drawing and painting packages but have proliferated even in word-processing applications. A major problem for the user is not knowing what the symbols mean.

5.3.7.1 Ensure that symbols are self-explanatory, as they are not labeled.

5.3.7.2 Because selection of a symbol (tool) sends the user into a *mode*, display a reminder of the mode that is in effect (e.g., by changing the shape of the pointing cursor).

5.3.7.3   Allow the user to move and resize the palette.

5.3.7.4   Reflect settings for the active window in the palette.

5.3.8 Tear-Off Menus

A *tear-off menu* can be "torn" from the menu bar and moved to another location on the screen where it can remain on display. Tear-off menus are also called "tacked" or "pushpin" menus.

5.3.8.1   Keep a tear-off menu posted so that the user can make multiple selections before dismissing it.

5.3.8.2   Use a graphic tear-off menu, instead of a fixed palette, to save display space and provide greater flexibility.

5.3.9 Aiding Menu Navigation

One of the biggest problems for users of menuing systems is getting lost in the menu structure. A key objective of menu design is to support the user's ability to navigate both forward and backward through the menu structure. The following aids to menu *navigation* can be used singly or in combination, depending on the nature of the user's goals, tasks, and information requirements.

5.3.9.1   Provide graphical or textual aids to assist users in maintaining their orientation within the underlying menu structure. (Graphic aids include designated font styles, line types, or colors for different menu levels. Textual aids include numbering schemes and descriptive titles).

        5.3.9.1.1   Provide visual cues indicating the user's current position within the menu structure and the path the user has traveled through a hierarchy of menus.

        5.3.9.1.2   Consider displaying a small schematic of the menu structure, highlighting the path taken as the user proceeds. The schematic serves the function of a road map.

        5.3.9.1.3   Consider providing a textual list of the options already selected, as an alternative to the highlighted menu map.

5.3.9.2   Display the primary navigational aid continuously or make it available from a pull-down menu.

5.3.9.3   Keep the top-level menu options available in the menu bar.

5.3.9.4   In a hierarchical menu, allow the user to return to the next higher menu level or to the top-level menu with a single control action.

5.3.9.5   Provide visual indicators, such as ellipses (...), to make menu options that branch to other submenus distinguishable from menu options that will immediately perform an operation.

5.3.9.6   Provide support for various user search strategies.
    5.3.9.6.1   Provide the capability to move both forward and backward through the menu structure.

5.3.9.7   Allow the experienced user to use optional shortcuts, such as *direct access, type ahead, jump ahead,* or *user-developed macros,* to speed up traversal of the menu structure.

5.3.9.8   Consider various strategies for repositioning search automatically when the user has reached a terminal node in a hierarchical menu without finding the target menu option.
    5.3.9.8.1   Reposition search to the next higher level that affords the widest breadth of selection.
    5.3.9.8.2   Provide a capability for users to mark points in the menu structure where they might want to return and a capability to return to such a point by issuing a command.
    5.3.9.8.3   Reposition to intermediate "*landmarks*" instead of forcing the user to return to the root node to restart a local search.

5.3.9.9   Sequence menus according to the logical flow of control required by the user's task.

5.3.9.10   Consider allowing users to create their own pathways through the menu structure (e.g., by adding horizontal and diagonal links within the original structure).

5.4   Direct Manipulation

For the user, graphical representations are often much easier to retain and manipulate than are textual or numeric representations. By means of *direct manipulation,* the user senses that the displayed environment is acted upon with actions that are rapid, and with results that are continuously visible.

5.4.1 Manipulation Techniques

Techniques of direct manipulation include open/close, minimize/maximize, drag-and-drop, resize, and scroll. Many direct-manipulation tasks are initiated by the user's action of pointing and clicking on screen-control graphics or icons.

5.4.1.1   Continuously display graphical reminders of actions that can be performed.

Figure A.5   Examples of slider bars.

Figure A.6   Examples of spin buttons.

5.4.1.2   Provide feedback both about the action to be performed and about the action as it is performed.

    5.4.1.2.1   If a selection action is to be performed, highlight the selected object.

    5.4.1.2.2   If the action is to be a movement, alter the pointing cursor's shape and highlight the object to be moved. Continue to highlight the object as it is moved.

    5.4.1.2.3   In a drag-and-drop action, move the entire object as the user drags it; do not allow the object to lag behind the pointing cursor.

5.4.1.3   Permit the user to cancel a selection before executing the associated action.

5.4.1.4   Provide smooth, even tracking between the screen pointer and the input device (e.g., mouse, trackball).

5.4.1.5   Immediately display the results of users' direct manipulations.

5.4.1.6   Consider using a slider bar (Figure A.5) and button to allow the user to set values represented along a scale.

5.4.1.7   Consider using a spin button (Figure A.6) to allow the user to select from a long list of options that increase or decrease uniformly, in constant intervals.

5.4.2 Browsing

The coordination of multiple windows that can appear, change contents, and close as a result of user activity is a design that is useful for browsing. Techniques for browsing depend on the task for which the design is developed. Types of multiple window coordinations and procedures for browsing are as follows:

- *Synchronized scrolling.* The scroll bar of one window is linked to the scroll bar of an adjoining window. When one scroll bar is moved, it causes the other to scroll its window contents. This allows the browser to compare the contents of both windows simultaneously.
- *Hierarchical browsing.* Selecting an item in the first window with a pointing device can lead to the display of an adjoining window that contains more detail. The development of coordinated windows that display different levels of information is regarded as a finer-grained approach.
- *Direct selection pointing.* Direct selection pointing at an icon, a word in the text, or a variable name in a program results in the pop-up of an adjoining window with information about the icon, word, or variable name.
- *Two-dimensional browsing.* A map, graphic, photographs, or other image is presented in a high-level view. The details of that view are then simultaneously presented in magnified form in another, larger window.
- *Dependent-windows opening.* The opening of dependent windows that are conveniently located on a display is one option of browsing. When browsing a program, opening a main procedure results in a dependent set of procedures opening up as well.
- *Dependent-windows closing.* With a single action, the closing of a window results in the closing of all its dependent windows. The advantage of dependent-window closing is the one-step process of removing those windows from the screen that are no longer applicable, such as dialogs, messages, and help windows.
- *Save or open window state.* Saving the state of a display as it appears on the screen with all the windows intact is a feature useful for browsing. The implementation of a *Save By...* menu item to the *File* menu permits the user to access that state for future reference.

5.5 Data Protection

Whenever a proposed user action will interrupt a transaction sequence, it is necessary to provide the automatic protection of data. If potential data loss cannot be prevented, warn the user and require confirmation prior to implementation.

Data integrity can also be advanced by limiting access, by building protection around dangerous operations, and by maintaining security procedures. Providing an "undo" function and effective online help are major ways to protect data and transaction sequences from the unintended consequences of possible user actions.

5.5.1 *Sequence Control*

The various interaction styles support the completion of transactions and the sequencing of transactions. A transaction is one complete exchange of information between the user and the computer. Transactions include keystrokes and their immediate display, as well as command entries (e.g., Save, Print) and their execution. A sequence is a series of user actions combined with computer logic that results in the initiation, interruption, or termination of transactions.

Key design objectives are to maintain consistency among control actions, limit the need for control actions, reduce loading on the user's memory, and provide flexibility for adaptation to a range of user needs. Sequence control should be in the hands of the user, with system control subordinated to user control.

5.5.1.1 Use the structure of the user's task to design a sequence of related transactions. A sequence of transactions should form a logical unit from the user's point of view and should provide the control options needed at any point.

    5.5.1.1.1 Provide transaction options that match expected user goals and tasks.

5.5.1.2 Provide multiple, flexible means of sequence control so that users can accomplish necessary transactions involving data entry, display, and processing, or can obtain guidance as needed.

    5.5.1.2.1 Give users more than one method of controlling scrolling and paging.

5.5.1.3 Permit users to control transaction sequencing by explicit action (Figure A.7). Defer computer processing until that explicit user action is taken.

    5.5.1.3.1 Provide a means to override control lockout due to processing.

5.5.1.4 Provide immediate system acknowledgment of every control entry.

5.5.1.5 Permit users to key a sequence of commands or option codes as a single massed or "stacked" command entry.

5.5.1.6 Provide interrupt or abort functions to terminate transactions.

    5.5.1.6.1 Consider the need for the following types of interrupts, in addition to backup and undo:

        ■ Cancel: abort a command or operation.

        ■ Review: return to the first display in a sequence and permit the user to step through the sequence.

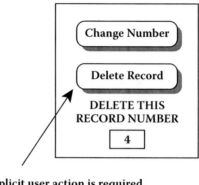

Example:
Explicit user action is required,
especially for data destructive
operations

Figure A.7   Requiring explicit user action.

- Restart: cancel all entries made in the transaction sequence and return to the beginning of the sequence.
- End: conclude a repetitive transaction sequence.
- Pause: interrupt the transaction sequence.
- Continue: resume a paused transaction sequence without any change to data entries or control logic.
- Suspend: preserve current transaction status when the user leaves the system, and permit resumption of work at that point on re-entry.

5.5.1.6.2   If different types of transaction interrupts are provided, designate each interrupt function as a separate control action with a distinct name.

5.5.1.6.3   Display paused or suspended status.

5.5.1.7   Provide prompts for resumption of a transaction sequence.

5.5.1.7.1   Permit users to search for specific line numbers and literal strings of alphanumeric characters.

5.5.1.8   Minimize the number of screens required to complete a transaction.

5.5.2 Access Security

Include a simple, prompted log-on process to protect data from unauthorized access.

5.5.2.1   Provide for user selection of passwords, and use software to enforce periodic changing of passwords.

5.5.2.1.1   Do not display entered passwords on the screen.

5.5.2.2 Establish user authorization for data display, entry, or change at initial log-on. Do not require additional authorization when the user attempts to display data, enter data, or make changes to data.

5.5.2.3 Limit the number and rate of unsuccessful attempts to log-on.

5.5.2.4 To protect highly sensitive information, require another authentication of the user's identity after ten minutes of inactivity.

5.5.2.5 When a record of data access is required, have the system maintain the records automatically (i.e., do not expect the user to keep records manually or through the system).

5.5.3 *Dangerous Operations*

Maintain the integrity of the data. Build protection around dangerous operations, such as accidental file deletion.

5.5.3.1 Prior to command execution, require users to confirm that they want to perform a critical, potentially hazardous, or potentially destructive command (including commands that would destroy stored data).

    5.5.3.1.1 If a complete file is to be deleted, provide sufficient information for the user to confirm that the file is to be deleted (e.g., file name, description, size, creation and modification dates).

    5.5.3.1.2 Label a confirm action clearly and distinctively.

    5.5.3.1.3 Make explicit the effects that will follow a confirmation.

    5.5.3.1.4 Require the user to wait for computer prompting before entering a confirmation (i.e., do not buffer the confirm affirmation).

5.5.3.3 Require the user to select a dangerous operation instead of making it a default. (*Note:* This may be a deviation from design consistency, but it is necessary in the interest of data integrity.)

5.5.3.4 Deactivate potentially destructive function keys or other devices when they are not needed.

5.5.3.5 Protect display-formatting features, such as field labels and delimiters, from accidental change by users.

5.5.3.6 Provide clear and consistent procedures for potentially dangerous transactions (e.g., global operations or those involving data change or deletion).

5.5.4 *Information Security*

When displayed data is classified or controlled, display a prominent indication of their status.

5.5.4.1   When displayed data must be protected, maintain computer control over the display (e.g., do not allow users to change a "read-only" field), and display the status of the screen (e.g., read-only).

5.5.4.2   When classified or controlled data are to be displayed at an uncontrolled workstation, provide a rapid means of temporarily suppressing the screen display if privacy is threatened.

6.0 Guidelines for Display Control and Window Design

Resolving issues of data selection and presentation is a key concern of the development team. These display-control issues become even more complex in a windowed environment. Key human-factors issues center on the design of window appearance and behavior (i.e., "look and feel"). A design objective is to minimize time spent in window management or "housekeeping."

Check the style guide that applies to your environment's UI development software to determine how much latitude you have in changing the look and feel of windows in your application.

6.1 Display Control

Designers are expected to determine as many user requirements for specific tasks as possible. Because *all* user requirements cannot be anticipated by the designer, give users the flexibility to tailor their displays online by controlling data selection, data coverage within a display frame, data updating, and data suppression.

6.1.1 User Control

Support user control by permitting users to control the amount, format, movement, and complexity of displayed data. Within data-protection constraints, users should be allowed to change displayed data or enter new data.

6.1.1.1   Indicate display-control options clearly and appropriately for selection by the user. (Determine appropriateness from the task analysis and from discussions with the user group.)

6.1.1.2   To the extent possible (without crowding), include data relevant to the user's current transaction in one display frame or page.

6.1.1.3   Provide an easy and consistent means of moving through the data, such as windowing, panning, paging, or scrolling.

6.1.1.3.1   Use scrolling to support the expert user's search through continuous text. Do not use paging or windowing for this purpose.

6.1.1.3.2   Use paging for the user's search of logically grouped information, such as data forms. Do not use panning or scrolling for this purpose.

6.1.1.3.3   Use up/down arrows to indicate vertical scrolling direction and previous/next or left/right arrows to indicate paging direction.

6.1.1.4   Provide a zoom in/out capability to support the user's detailed examination of graphical displays (e.g., maps, pictures, diagrams).

6.1.2 Selection of Data for Display

Enable the user to select data for display. In determining the means for specification of data output, either by the user or automatically, consider the following recommendations:

6.1.2.1   For general data processing systems, enable users to specify the data for displayed output.

6.1.2.2   For specific information handling applications, always allow users to select data to meet task requirements.

6.1.2.3   If the designer cannot exactly determine the particular categories required by users at different stages of their job, permit users to select the categories they need for any information-handling task.

6.1.2.4   Responses to simple requests for data display should not take more than 0.5 to 1.0 second.

6.1.2.4.1   If a response must be delayed, notify the user when display output is complete.

6.1.3 Update

When displayed data changes dynamically with external events, permit the user to request an update of the change(s) and to control the update rate.

6.1.3.1   Consider highlighting data changes that result from automatic updating of a display.

6.1.3.1.1   Maintain the highlighting briefly but long enough to call the user's attention to any changes.

6.1.3.2   Ensure that changing data values are readable.

6.1.3.3   If the user must determine trends over time or make predictions based on changing data, provide integrated trend displays and predictive displays.

6.1.4 Suppression

Permit the user to suppress displayed data not required for the task at hand.

6.1.4.1   After data have been suppressed from a display, remind the user of the suppressed data.

6.1.4.2   Enable the user to restore suppressed data quickly to its originally displayed form.

6.2   General Window Appearance

The appearance of *windows* in a given application is generally controlled by instructions built into the user-interface development software. In some cases, it may be possible to exercise options on window appearance or to customize some aspects of window appearance.

6.2.1 Window Components

Typically, a window is a square or rectangular area of the screen that contains a *window frame*, a *menu bar*, an *application area*, and *window controls*. Optionally, a window can include a *command area* and *a message area*. The components of the window frame are sometimes called "decorations." Decorations can include a title bar, maximize and minimize buttons, a resize border, and a window menu button. A specific set of window controls may be required and built into the UI development software. Other window controls are optional.

6.2.1.1.   Display a brief, unique, and descriptive title at the top center of *each* window unless directed otherwise by a UI toolkit style guide.

   6.2.1.1.1   Continue to display the window title while the user scrolls data in the application area.

6.2.1.2   Tailor the size of the application area to the user's needs.

6.2.1.3   Provide window controls to support the following actions:
   - Opening and closing a window
   - Moving a window
   - Re-sizing a window
   - Shrinking a window to an icon

- Scrolling through window contents
- Zooming in and out

6.2.1.3.1 Provide standard buttons by which the user can control the size of the window (from minimum through variable to maximum).

6.2.1.3.2 Comply with the default appearance and placement of scroll bars for your environment. (Some windowing systems allow users to control placement of scroll bars.)

6.2.1.3.3 Display scroll bars in full contrast only for the active window (that is, the window that displays the user's current input).

6.2.1.3.4 Make optional window controls consistent in appearance with the required controls.

6.2.2 Primary and Secondary Windows

An application's *primary* or *main window* displays the essential data that the user needs to interact with the application. Additional, *secondary windows* convey context-specific information. Secondary windows may be called "transient" or "child" windows. A dialog box can be used to create a secondary window.

6.2.2.1 Limit the number of secondary windows to avoid creating navigation problems for the user.

6.2.2.2 Locate related window components in the same place from parent to child.

6.2.2.3 Use a secondary window to temporarily add data (such as help screens, menus, or other features) to a display, or as a means to control or display divergent information, or to segregate and control separate operations.

6.2.3 Tiled and Overlapping Windows

When windows are strictly tiled, they abut on each other's borders but do not overlap. The look is two-dimensional. When windows overlap, the window nearest to the apparent foreground is the active window. It may obscure data "beneath" it or be made transparent so that underlying data is visible. The look of overlapping windows is close to three-dimensional, like that of papers stacked on a desk.

6.2.3.1 Use *tiled windows* to support user performance when any of the following apply:

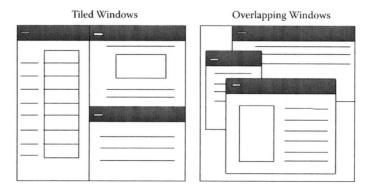

Tiled Windows   Overlapping Windows

Figure A.8   Tiled and overlapping windows.

- User activities focus on a single task.
- Tasks require minimal manipulation of windows.
- Users are novices or use the application infrequently.

6.2.3.2 Use *overlapping* windows when:
- User activities cut across independent tasks.
- Tasks require frequent window manipulation.
- Users are expert or use the application frequently.

6.2.3.3 Use a variant of tiled or overlapping windows to limit clutter and promote efficiency while supporting access to several sources of information (Figure A.8). Variants include *non-space-filling tiling, piles of tiles, automatic panning, window zooming*, and *cascades*.

6.2.3.4 If using overlapping windows, ensure that window overlays are nondestructive; overlaid data is not permanently erased.

6.2.3.5 For tiled windows, indicate the active window by means of a technique such as highlighting the window border, altering the background color slightly, or changing the labeling.

6.2.3.6 For overlapping windows, indicate the active window by moving it to the forefront upon activation by the user.

6.2.3.7 For overlapping windows, use a neutral background pattern instead of complex patterns that create unintended visual effects.

6.2.4 Decision-Supportive Window Design

The user's decision-making tasks will often require the integration of various kinds of information from multiple sources. Data can be given on different scales or in different units. From the perspective of the user's information-processing capacities, an objective of window design is to increase the user's ability to integrate such multiple sets of information. If the different sets of data must be kept separate and not integrated automatically, various windowing strategies can promote user productivity.

6.2.4.1 Consider using the suggested windowing strategies under the conditions specified as follows:
- When the user must consider different data sets in making a decision, place the required data sets in separate windows that can be displayed simultaneously.
- When it will benefit users to see the same data at different levels of analysis, display each level in a separate window.
- When the user can benefit from different perspectives on the same object or event, show each perspective in a different window. Perspectives might be more or less concrete or abstract (e.g., looking at a spacecraft design from various angles, considering different attributes of the spacecraft, or taking an historical or predictive view of spacecraft operations).
- When changes made in one window affect data in other windows, link the affected windows so that the rest of the window set is updated by the changes.

6.2.4.2 Decide which of the decision-supportive strategies to use on the basis of a good understanding of the user's functions and tasks.

6.2.4.3 Use combinations of the decision-supportive strategies that will best support user decision making in particular situations.

6.2.4.4 If the user must interact with a sequence of displays in close temporal proximity, use separate windows that can be displayed simultaneously.

6.2.5 Related versus Independent Windows

To promote the user's conceptual grouping, design related windows or sets of windows so that they share family characteristics. To promote differentiation of unrelated windows, windows or window sets that are independent of each other should reflect their differences partially through their appearance. (Independent windows may also behave differently.)

6.2.5.1 Use identical attributes for related windows (e.g., size, shape, color of foreground, background, and border).
6.2.5.1.1 Give independent windows contrasting attributes (e.g., different sizes or shapes, different colors in foreground, background, or borders).

6.2.5.2 Place related windows close to each other.

      6.2.5.2.1 Use spacing to segregate independent windows from each other.

6.3 General Window Behavior ("Feel")

The behavior of tiled or overlapping windows can be entirely controlled by the windowing system, or some behaviors can be controlled by the user. For example, the user can control the basic windowing actions (e.g., open, resize, move), as well as placement of scroll bars. *Panning* strategies can be automatic or under user control. Although user-controlled placement of windows and window elements requires additional decision-making and housekeeping, some amount of optional user control can improve subjective satisfaction with the user interface.

General design objectives are to limit the extent of window manipulation and to preserve predictability in windowing behavior by (1) minimizing manual activity for window-manipulation tasks, and (2) aiming for consistency across windowing operations.

6.3.1 Window Manipulation

Systems vary in the steps required to perform window-manipulation actions, but the actions themselves have become relatively standardized. The windowing system in use usually controls the behavior of controls located in the window frame.

6.3.1.1 Provide common window-manipulation actions, as listed in Table A.4. These actions are typically performed with a mouse, but keyboard alternatives may be provided.

      6.3.1.1.1 Following the user's open action, open the new window as close as possible to the *current focus* without obscuring the current focus. For example, when the user selects a control-panel icon, display the open control panel just below its icon. If the user requests help with a fill-in-form field, display the help window to the side of the field without obscuring the field.

      6.3.1.1.2 Open and close windows as smoothly and rapidly as possible.

      6.3.1.1.3 Upon resizing, reformat text, graphics, or icon layouts so that they remain visible, up to some standard limit set by project consensus.

Table A.4 Window Manipulation

Opening and Closing Windows	
Create	Displays an entirely new window
Delete	Removes a window from the screen
Open	Replaces an iconic window with the full-size window it represents
Close	Replaces a window with an iconic window
Bring-To-Front	Moves a window to the most forward plane of a screen with overlapping windows
Push-To-Back	Moves a window to the most rearward plane of a screen with overlapping windows
Changing Windows	
Move	Repositions a window in its two-dimensional plane
Resize	Shows more or less of the data in a window by contracting the window or expanding it to its maximum size
Zoom	Expands to maximum size with one action
Rescale	Shows more or less of the data in the window by changing the scale of the image in the window
Scroll	Selects a different portion of data for viewing without resizing
Name/Rename	Defines or changes the name of a window
Make Active (Change Focus)	Designates a window as the one available for interaction

6.3.1.1.4   Protect against any obscuring of critical information during window resizing.

6.3.1.1.5   Provide visual feedback during movement of a window.

6.3.1.1.6   Follow a standard panning sequence.

6.3.1.1.7   If the user must frequently perform long mouse movements, provide keyboard alternatives for windowing actions.

6.3.1.1.8   Consider controlling window manipulation by user task actions, without requiring the user to perform direct window-manipulation actions.

6.3.1.2   Allow keyboard and mouse input to affect only the active window.

6.3.2 Aiding Window Arrangement and Navigation

To reduce housekeeping and support the user's sense of orientation, provide some built-in aids to window manipulation and navigation between windows.

6.3.2.1 Design for maximum ease and efficiency of navigating between windows.

6.3.2.2 Consider providing a way for the user to move around among open windows with minimal manual activity.

6.3.2.3 Consider providing a capability for the user to call by name a window or a particular configuration of windows (a *window macro*).

6.3.2.4 When windows are allowed to overlap, provide powerful commands to support the user's tailored arrangement of windows on the screen (e.g., create, name, and recall specific sets of windows).

6.3.2.5 Within a set of windows (parent and children), offer an indication of how far the user has progressed through the set and how many windows remain in the set.

6.3.2.6 For a set of overlapping, open windows, allow the user to request an iconic or graphical map depicting all the open windows.

6.3.2.7 When a map of open windows is available, allow the user to designate the active window by selecting a map element. Bring the selected window forward without requiring the user to resize or move other windows.

6.3.2.8 Consider opening or closing child windows when a parent window is opened or closed.

7.0 Guidelines for Visual Coding Techniques

Color is a major technique for supporting the user's quick detection and discrimination of displayed data elements or groupings of data. Other visual-coding techniques include variations in brightness, flashing, line style, symbols, sizes, and shapes. Each of these techniques can be misused or overused. A rule of thumb is to use visual coding for functional, not decorative purposes. The key challenge for designers is to use these techniques in ways that enhance users' task performance (Table A.5).

7.1 Color

Color is used for several functional purposes in screen design:

Table A.5   Attention-Getting Techniques

Technique	When to Use	When Not to Use
Color	A powerful attention-getter is needed	Several colors are already used on the display
Blinking/ Flashing	User must respond immediately	Message does not require immediate attention or text is lengthy
Bold	Captions or titles should stand out	There are more than three levels of bold
Reverse video	Purpose is to indicate a selected item or error	Text is lengthy
Size	A code is needed for relative quantity or importance	There are five or more levels of size codes
Font	Text items should stand out	There are more than two to four different character types
Underlining	Purpose is to draw attention to key words for instruction or to distinguish fill-in fields from text	Too frequent use reduces legibility
Shape	Purpose is to communicate urgency	Use of shapes is not based on established standards
Special characters and icons	Purpose is to draw attention to items on a screen	Space is limited (graphic symbols take up additional screen space)
Proximity	White space can be used to associate items with each other (grouping)	There is no need to associate items
Borders	Purpose is to identify meaningful groups, create sense of closure, and focus attention	Identified groups, closure, and focus of attention are not required

- ▪ To establish relationships between displayed objects
- ▪ To help the user distinguish between displayed objects
- ▪ To communicate the organization of information
- ▪ To call the user's attention to system states

If color is overused, these purposes are defeated. Likewise, if color is used for decorative purposes, these functional purposes are compromised.

Table A.6 Color Combinations to Avoid

Saturated red and blue	Saturated red and green
Saturated blue and green	Saturated yellow and green
Yellow on purple	Green on white
Yellow on green	Blue on black
Magenta on green	Red on black
Magenta on black	Yellow on white

7.1.1 Number of Colors

Limit the number of colors to be used. Preferably, use four or less.

7.1.1.1   Use task performance requirements as the basis for determining the number of colors to present simultaneously. In general, minimize the number of colors presented together on the same screen.

      7.1.1.1.1   Use color to support visual-search tasks and symbol-identification tasks.

7.1.1.2   Use no more than six distinct colors or three shades of gray if the user must recall the meanings of colors or shades.

7.1.1.3   Use no more than six distinct colors if the user must perform rapid visual searching based on color discrimination.

7.1.1.4   If functional requirements dictate the use of more than the recommended number of colors or shades of gray, display a legend of color or shade meanings.

7.1.2 Pairing Colors

Avoid the color combinations listed in Table A.6.

7.1.3 Foreground and Background Colors

Consult Table A.7 for recommended foreground and background colors.

     Use a medium achromatic background (e.g., dark or medium gray) to maximize the visibility of foreground colors.

7.1.3.1   Consider the effects of varying levels of saturation (color intensity) and the effects of varying levels of lightness (amount of white mixed with the color) on the discriminability of colors and on color interactions.

      7.1.3.1.1   Avoid combinations that are similar in lightness (e.g., navy blue on black, yellow on white).

Table A.7 Foreground and Background Colors

Foreground					Background					
	Black	Blue	Green	Cyan	Red	Magenta	Brown	White	Gray	Beige
Black	—	—		R		R		R	R	R
Blue	—	—			—	—	—	r	r	r
Green	—	r	—	R	—				—	—
Cyan	R			—					R	R
White	R								—	—
Bold Green	R								R	R
Bold Cyan	R	R		—	R	R			R	R
Bold Magenta	R		R			—			R	R
Yellow	R	R	—	R		R		—	—	—
Bold White	R	R	R	R				—	—	—

R = recommended; r = some saturations acceptable; — = avoid this combination

Table A.8   Colors to Use for Thin Lines

No. of Colors	White Background	Black Background
1	Red or green	Yellow, cyan, or green
2	Red and green Magenta and cyan Red and blue	Green and magenta Yellow and magenta Cyan and magenta
3	Red, blue, and green	Cyan, magenta, and yellow

7.1.3.2   Maintain adequate contrast between foreground and background colors to enhance color perception and perceived image resolution.

    7.1.3.2.1   Increase contrast if the screen will be viewed under dim lighting conditions.

    7.1.3.2.2   Consider using complementary colors (yellow on dark blue, or magenta on green) to maximize color contrast, if appropriate for the user's task environment.

7.1.3.3   Consult authoritative sources for guidance on measuring color uniformity, color contrast, and color differences.

7.1.3.4   Test selected colors with users to verify that the colors can be easily discriminated from each other. Color contrast should be at least 7:1 for foreground versus background.

7.1.4 Colors for Thin Lines

Consult Table A.8 for colors to make thin lines easily perceivable.

7.1.5 Redundant Use of Color

Be sure that the information coded by color is coded in some other manner for the sake of color-deficient users.

7.1.5.1   Before adding color to a display, design for its use in monochrome. Then, use color as a redundant code to enhance an otherwise logical, well-organized design.

7.1.6 Consistent Use of Color

Use color consistently with common meanings for the user's culture (e.g., in Western cultures, use green for good or normal, yellow for caution, and red for danger or warning).

7.1.6.1   If the user community has previously established meanings for various colors, retain those meanings. Do not use a color to signify a different condition than it signified in the previous system.

7.2 Brightness

On either monochrome or color displays, variations in brightness can be used to attract the user's attention and to differentiate between categories or levels within a category. On a color display, variations on the continuum from dull to bright (brightness) are indistinguishable from variations in lightness (the range from white through gray to black).

7.2.1 Suggested Uses

Use brightness coding for task-related purposes.

7.2.1.1   Consider using high brightness to call attention to errors in data-entry fields and to highlight answer fields on question-and-answer screens.
7.2.1.2   Consider using brightness coding to differentiate between adjacent items of information or to code state conditions (e.g., on/off, standby-run).
7.2.1.3   Consider using "reverse video" (i.e., brightness inversion) to highlight critical items requiring user attention.
       7.2.1.3.1   Return to a normal brightness when the user has responded.

7.2.2 Levels of Brightness

Use only two levels of brightness coding (bright and dim) separated by at least a 2:1 ratio.

7.3 Flashing or Blinking

Flashing or blinking is a powerful attention-getter but should be used only rarely. Overuse of flash or blink coding has a high potential to distract the user. Data or text that the user must read should never blink or flash because a blinking object is, by definition, not displayed continuously and can be read only when it is displayed.

7.3.1 Suggested Uses

Use flash or blink coding only to indicate an urgent need for user attention and response or to indicate the active location for data entry (i.e., place a blinking cursor at the point where user input will be accepted).

7.3.1.1 Allow only a very small area of the screen to flash at any moment.

7.3.1.2 Instead of blinking the data or text, place a small square or rectangle next to the critical information, and blink just that shape.

7.3.2 Levels of Flashing

Use no more than two levels of flash or blink coding:

- Slow = less than 2 Hz
- Fast = 3 to 5 Hz

7.3.3 Length of Intervals

In general, use equal "on" and "off" duty cycles.

7.3.3.1 Consider "winking" rather than blinking by using an "on" cycle that is substantially longer than the "off" cycle.

7.4 Line Coding

Lines or "rules" aid in focusing the user's attention on related information and serve to separate unrelated groupings of information. Line borders delineate the boundaries of menu bars, display-control options, and entire windows. Line coding should be used sparingly.

7.4.1 Line Attributes

Use line thickness, width, and height or length to convey functional meaning.

7.4.1.1 Use line coding by type (e.g., solid, dashed, dotted), by width, or by other attributes to indicate association between elements.

7.4.1.1.1 Limit to four the number of variations in any one line attribute (e.g., four thicknesses, four lengths).

7.4.1.1.2 Minimize the possible interactions caused by varying line attributes. For example, use horizontal lines of equal width and vertical lines of equal height where possible.

7.4.1.2 Use line-length coding for applications involving spatial categorizations in a single dimension (e.g., velocity).

7.4.1.3 Use line-direction coding for applications involving spatial categorizations in two dimensions (e.g., altitude, bearing).

7.5 Special Symbols

Use special, standard symbols (e.g., asterisk, arrow) to draw the user's attention to specific items in alphanumeric displays.

7.5.1 Mappings

Make special symbols analogous to the event or system elements they represent, based on established standards or conventional meanings.

7.5.2 Consistent Meaning

Assign consistent meanings to special symbols within and across applications.

7.6 Symbol Sizes

Use size coding only on uncrowded displays.

7.6.1 Number of Sizes

Use no more than three symbol sizes for coding. A larger sized object should be 1.5 times the height of the next smaller object (e.g., character, symbol, shape).

7.7 Shapes

Use shape categories (e.g., circle, triangle, square) to code related objects and to support the user's ability to discriminate between various categories of displayed data.

7.7.1 Redundant Coding

Map shapes to colors (e.g., red circles, green triangles) to achieve redundant coding (i.e., meaning is conveyed both by shape and color).

7.7.2 Distinctiveness

Use a distinctive shape to call attention to a single type of displayed object.

7.8 Type Styles

Variations in type styles include the use of bold, underlining, and different fonts.

7.8.1 Bold

Use the heavy intensity of bolding for strong emphasis.

7.8.1.1 If more than one level of bold is available, avoid using more than three different levels whose meanings the user must remember.

7.8.2 Underlining

Use underlining for mild emphasis, not for urgent or critical information.

7.8.2.1 Use underlining to emphasize key words, titles, or headings.
7.8.2.2 Use underlining to distinguish fill-in fields from surrounding text or labels.

7.8.3 Fonts

Use multiple fonts to convey moderate emphasis and to help the user discriminate among categories of displayed information.

7.8.3.1 Limit to two or three the number of different fonts displayed on any one screen. Do not exceed four fonts.
7.8.3.2 Use variations within one font (e.g., size, style) to convey levels within a category of information. For example, large, bold letters for high-level titles; smaller, bold letters for second-level titles; and still smaller, underlined letters for third-level titles.

7.9 Three-Dimensional Effects

The GUI toolkits typically provide widgets with three-dimensional features, such as drop shadows and beveled edges. Three-dimensional features cause objects to appear closer to the user. Closer objects (i.e., those in the foreground) take on greater importance than background elements. The user's attention goes naturally to screen elements that seem closer because they have become important in the context of the task. Such features should be used sparingly on any one display screen to avoid canceling out their effects.

7.9.1 Drop Shadows

Consider using drop shadows to make important elements appear closer to the user.

7.9.1.1 Place shadows at the lower right of icons and buttons, as if light were coming from the upper left.

7.9.1.2 Place shadows along the bottom and right side of a pull-down menu, dialog box, or window to attract the user's attention.

7.9.2 Beveled Edges

Consider using beveled edges to bring important screen elements into the foreground. Beveled edges can be used on icons, buttons, menus, dialog boxes, and windows.

7.9.2.1 Shade the bottom and right beveled edges to enhance the three-dimensional effect.

8.0 Guidelines for User Guidance and Feedback

Providing effective guidance and feedback to the user contributes to meeting several general objectives of user-interface design:

■ Consistency of operational procedures
■ Efficient use of system capabilities
■ Limited memory load on the user
■ Reduced learning time
■ Flexibility in supporting different classes of users
■ Error prevention

User guidance includes prompts, warnings, error messages, status information, and online help. A key design goal is to reflect the user's (not the designer's) understanding of the system. Meeting this goal requires review and usability testing by potential end users who have not been involved with system development.

8.1 Prompts and General Guidance Messages

Prompts are advisory messages that help in navigating through the user interface. General guidance messages inform the user about available actions and suggest actions to be taken by the user.

8.1.1 Distinctive, Consistent Prompts and Messages

Ensure that prompts and general guidance messages are distinct from displayed data and used consistently throughout the application.

8.1.1.1   Use consistent, concise phrasing, and minimal, consistent punctuation in prompts and general guidance messages.

8.1.1.2   Use positive, clear wording and the active voice in prompts and general guidance messages.

8.1.1.3   Make prompts and user guidance explicit to eliminate the need for the user to memorize lengthy sequences or refer to references.

8.1.1.3.1   Do not include codes or references to external sources in prompts.

8.1.1.4   Do not present prompts and general guidance in a person-like or personal manner. Do not use the first ("I") or second person ("You").

8.1.1.5   Where possible, provide prompts for required formats and acceptable values for data entry.

8.1.2 Explanations

Use brief prompts and messages to explain required input, commands, error messages, system capabilities, display formats, procedures, and steps in a sequence.

8.1.3 Prompting for Coded Data Entry

Prompt the user for required formats and provide values for valid data entries. For example, prompt the user to enter a color selection:

```
┌─────────────────────────┐
│  Color: _____           │
│               r = red   │
│               b = blue  │
│               g = green │
└─────────────────────────┘
```

8.1.4 Optional Guidance

Permit users to request prompts and general guidance, as needed, depending on their level of experience.

8.1.4.1   Design prompts and general guidance with the novice user in mind.
8.1.4.2   Allow expert users to "turn off" prompting and guidance.

8.1.5 Location of Prompts

Locate prompts where the user is expected to input data, whenever possible; otherwise place prompts in a standard message area.

8.2 Cautions and Warnings

Display of cautions and warnings should be consistent throughout the system.

8.2.1 Cautions

Use cautions for operations and actions that might have the following kinds of results:

- Permanent data loss
- No data loss, but undoable consequences
- Conflict with the operations of others
- Need for excessive processing time

8.2.2 Warnings

Use warnings for operations and actions that might have the following kinds of results:

- Permanent data loss
- Data loss and undoable, with some exceptions (e.g., saving an edited file using the same file name as the unedited file does not require a warning)
- Threat or compromise of information, such as proprietary information
- Non-interruptible processing
- Invocation of ancillary system actions (e.g., automatic deletion or overwriting of an original file when executing a renaming command)

8.2.3 Visual and Auditory Display

Present distinctive cautions and warnings through both visual and auditory display.

8.3 Error Messages

Use error messages to inform the user of incorrect command or data entry.

8.3.1 Location

Present the error message at the point of the error or in a consistently located message area.

8.3.2 Style

Make error messages specific, informative, and brief.

8.3.2.1 Use neutral wording in error messages. Keep the phrasing positive and professional.

8.3.2.2 Phrase error messages in terms of the current task.

8.3.3 Information Content

Include the following information in the error message:

- Why input was rejected
- What corrective actions may be taken in subsequent operations
- Format requirements, if formatting conventions were violated

8.3.4 Detailed Explanation of Error

Permit the user to request a more detailed explanation of the error and additional information about the ongoing operation.

8.3.5 Error Correction

Allow the user to correct an error immediately after it has been detected.

8.3.5.1   If an error cannot be corrected, design the system so that other transactions can still be initiated. Permit the user to store and later retrieve the transaction with an error.

8.4 System and Status Information

System or status messages should not be humorous or sarcastic, nor should they be presented in the first ("I") or second person ("You").

8.4.1 Message Scope and Content

Display messages to indicate the following conditions:

- Keyboard lock
- Log-on denial failure
- File writing operations
- Making remote connections
- Printing progress/spooling
- Complex time-consuming operations
- Processing delay
- Save operations
- Mail/data transmission
- High time shared system loads
- Complex processing completion

8.4.1.1   Include the following information:

- A description of the system state
- Directives for user action
- Consequences, if any, of failure to follow directives

8.4.2 Message Location

Present system and status messages in a consistent location.

8.4.3 Operational Mode

Inform the user of the current operational mode when the mode might affect the user's actions.

8.5 Task-Related Job Aids

Job aids support user productivity and performance by providing task-related guidance.

8.5.1 Content

Job aids should include an on-line dictionary of abbreviations, acronyms, and codes, as well as allowable options and value ranges. Online help is a major job aid.

8.5.2 Dialog Aiding

Provide context-specific information on semantics and syntax of any available user dialog. Include a structured listing of the following command information:

- Each command available
- The associated menu options and keystroke alternatives (accelerators)
- Uses and consequences of the command

8.5.3 Online Help

Provide context-sensitive, self-explanatory help that permits rapid access to information about specific interactions, tasks, messages, or commands. Include help on questions users are likely to have about all parts of the application.

8.5.3.1 While the user is viewing help in a separate, reserved window, display as much as possible of the user's current task display.

8.5.3.2 If the user is executing a particular command and requests help, provide information on that command (e.g., the effects of that command, alternatives to that command).

8.5.3.3 When an error occurs, and the user requests help, provide a useful description of the error and suggest at least one recovery technique.

8.5.3.4 If an online reference manual is available, open the manual at the topic corresponding to the current context when the user requests help.

8.5.3.5 Use a help icon on the screen and designate a function key as the help key. Use the help icon and the help key consistently throughout the application.

Acknowledgments

Adapted from Goddard Space Flight Center, Data Systems Technology Division. *User-Interface Guidelines,* January 30, 1996.

Appendix B

Web-Based System Design Guide

Task 1: Determine Organizational Readiness and Impact

Undertaking the design and development, adoption, or purchase of an X-Internet system has strategic implications for organizations. Making the decision to implement a system will have an effect on information technology strategies and infrastructure, budgeting and planning, personnel and staffing, and policy. The decision can also have an effect on how the organization sees its role as a provider of data and how it chooses to service its constituents and develop relationships with them. The strategic impact of such a project will vary, depending on the size and structure of the organization and its existing resources.

The decision to embark on the implementation of a system, and whether the system should be developed, adopted, or purchased, depends on interrelated factors. Identifying the best approach depends on analyzing the characteristics and objectives of the organization to identify the positive and negative effects of development, adoption, or purchase. The following guidelines are designed to provide a decision-making framework. No specific recommendations are made. However, by reviewing the information contained in these guidelines, an organization will be much better positioned to make an informed choice regarding which option is most appropriate for them.

Addressing the elements listed in the following checklists will allow agencies to build a profile of their capacity to implement a Web-based data dissemination tool. Organizations can then build capacity where it does not exist or is insufficient. Such areas might include:

- Staffing
- System support
- System security
- Training
- Organizational support for technology
- System compatibility
- Standards and confidentiality
- Funding
- Data concerns
- Users

Steps for identifying areas for strengthening include conducting a stakeholder analysis, documenting costs, assessing staffing, and examining implications for organizational policies and processes.

Step 1: Identify and Engage Stakeholders

To assess the effect of developing, adopting, or purchasing a Web-based system, identifying its direct or indirect effects on the organization is necessary during development and after it is implemented. Key stakeholders (e.g., internal staff or end users) should be identified and included in the initial decision-making process. Experience demonstrates that organizational support is a critical element in development, adoption, or purchase of a system. The project team is likely to include members from different parts of the organization, and creating an environment of interdepartmental cooperation is essential for success.

Organizations also might want to involve external stakeholders (e.g., suppliers, clients, etc.). This will depend on existing relationships and the extent to which the organization prefers to keep decision making an internal process at this early stage. The degree to which external stakeholders are affected or involved will vary, but understanding their roles, requirements, motivations, and commitment is important.

Senior management concerns include:

- What is driving the demand for a Web-based system?
- Who needs the system and its data? Who are the potential users?
- Is its priority high enough to warrant investment in the project?
- What are the present organizational goals?
- Will the implementation of a system further the organizational goals?

- Do organizational goals need to be reassessed or reprioritized?
- Will the implementation of a data dissemination system fulfill the needs of internal and external users of the data and reduce the number of queries, freeing staff to focus on other activities?
- How will a Web-based approach help fulfill the needs of internal and external consumers?
- Does an alternative or better technical approach than a Web-based tool exist?
- What are the policy concerns associated with conducting this project and how substantial/problematic are they?
- How will this project move the organization forward in achieving its goals?
- How can users' needs be institutionalized in designing and implementing the system?

IT concerns include:

- Does a need exist?
- What are the concerns that would need to be addressed related to existing hardware, operating system software, and Web server applications?
- How will the project interface with existing system functions (e.g., Web applications or databases)?
- Are any changes anticipated for existing systems, applications, and functions that would have implications for a X-Internet system?
- Who should have the decision-making authority and responsibility for content, datasets, technical development, and maintenance?
- How well do current data dissemination efforts meet users' needs? What additional needs do users have?
- Does the IT department have the staff capacity and expertise to undertake the acquisition or development of a new dissemination system?
- What are the implications for IT department collaborations with other departments in the organization? Who else would need to be involved?
- Given the current financial environment, is funding to support the development or acquisition of a system feasible?
- What is the potential for cost savings or cost offset?
- What level of funding is available to support indirect costs related to making the system operational (e.g., software upgrades, personnel costs such as training fees, or staff time spent in training)?
- What funding is available to support ongoing maintenance costs?

- If additional full-time equivalents (FTEs) are required, can they be funded?
- Will additional funding be needed? What are the potential sources?

Given the answers to these questions, an organization can quantify the benefits to be gained from undertaking an effort to implement a system. More detailed assessments of user needs are described in Task 2.

Step 2: Assess Costs

Identifying the costs involved in current data dissemination efforts is an important step in assessing the cost-benefits. To assess these costs, consider the resource expenditures in dollars and staff time to:

- Produce printed reports
- Respond to telephone inquiries
- Develop static tables or reports for posting on a Web site
- Maintain current hardware, operating system software, Web server applications, and system functions

The costs associated with the current level of effort should be compared with the estimated costs associated with whichever approach the organization wants to deploy, after that decision has been made. Information regarding cost implications of developing, adopting, or purchasing a Web-based data dissemination system are discussed in Task 3.

Step 3: Assess Staffing

Certain concerns should be explored regarding IT staff needs for system development, adoption, or purchase. Assessing whether the IT department has the staff capacity and expertise to undertake development or acquisition of a system is important.

Does staff capacity include:

- Technical support staff to resolve server or system problems as they arise?
- Sufficient staff to perform all needed development and maintenance work for the system?

Does staff expertise include adequate experience in:

- Maintaining the specific server (e.g., Apache Web server), database (e.g., Microsoft® SQL Server™), and additional software (e.g., statistical analysis software) that comprise the system?

- Establishing security protocol and backup plans for ensuring protection against data loss or system interruption?
- Programming in the languages selected for the database and application?
- Identifying data confidentiality and data integrity concerns related to the system?
- Planning for adequate server resources to support the number of anticipated users?
- Planning for adequate server support for the amount of data in the system?

Step 4: Consider Existing Organizational Policies and Procedures

Organizations should also consider their organizational policies and procedures and assess how these affect the management and progress of the project. General considerations include the following:

- What organizational channels must be navigated to move the project forward?
- How best can this be achieved?
- What are the approval processes?

Conversely, organizations also need to consider whether the technical approach they choose will conflict with organizational policy. This is a critical area, especially when adopting or purchasing an X-Internet system. The specifications of the system must be examined thoroughly to ensure that it meets organizational policy regarding data presentation standards, confidentiality, and security. A thorough requirements definition (see Task 2) is necessary to avoid incompatibility with organizational policy and extra costs incurred in retrofitting the system for compliance. Issues to explore in identifying current organizational needs and constraints include:

- What statutes and rules govern data collection and dissemination activities?
- Do written policies and guidelines exist that need to be reviewed?
- What is the approval process for determining what data are made available and in what formats?
- Who are the internal decision makers? What departments need to be involved?
- Do external partners need to be involved in decisions?

Task 2: Define the Project

Whether the organization is developing, adopting, or purchasing a system, the second major task is to define the project. Key components in this section are defining the system requirements and developing a project strategy.

To define system requirements,

- Gather background information and related materials.
- Understand users and their tasks to guide or assess interface design.
- Establish business rules to guide database design and system programming.
- Create a requirements definition.

Gather Background Information

Whether a system is developed, adopted, or purchased, as much background information and documentation as possible should be gathered. An organization that adopts a system from another public organization or purchases a system from a developer must be familiar with the tool's goals, design, development, and performance to ensure it is obtaining a tested and sound system that meets its data dissemination needs.

An organization that develops its own system should gather background information related to tasks and data needs from its staff, any documented inquiries or requests from the general public, and documentation from other similar systems.

Understand Users' Needs

Understanding users and their tasks will enable the organization to develop or select an appropriate system. Examples of user tasks might be "Generate reports on disease trends by county" or "Find geographic data related to disease outbreaks in my area." When developing a system, understanding and prioritizing user tasks is key to good interface design. When adopting or purchasing a system, clearly articulating user tasks will ensure that the organization selects a system that is designed to meet their users' needs.

Establish Business Rules

Business rules define processes, data, and constraints. Data validation — programming designed to identify errors in data — typically enforces the business rules. For example, a business rule might be "All users must enter a unique e-mail address to register." To enforce that rule, the system might be programmed to check that something was entered in the "e-mail" field; that what was entered conforms to rules regarding e-mail addresses (e.g., username@domain.com); and that the e-mail address entered is not already stored in the database.

Create a Requirements Definition

Developing a project strategy involves construction of a project plan and system design documentation for the database and Web application. Not all of the detailed steps might be relevant to every project. When a system is adopted or purchased, for example, system documentation might be acquired rather than written. However, certain project management steps (e.g., requirements definition) are necessary to every process to determine whether a system is suitable for adoption or purchase. Going through all steps thoroughly and ensuring that the relevant activities are undertaken is necessary.

Requirements definition is the first critical step in establishing a framework that guides the development, adoption, or purchase of a system that meets the needs of the project. System requirements will reflect the needs of stakeholders and users, and they should be analyzed closely so that appropriate technical solutions can be developed.

The project is likely to begin with a core set of requirements that will form the basis for project planning and design and development activity. However, the initial set of requirements is likely to be modified and the changes need to be managed.

At each stage of development, the requirements definition document should be consulted to ensure that the project plan reflects the requirements. After the system is deployed, its success will be gauged by the system's ability to meet stated requirements.

This substantial undertaking is key whether developing, adopting, or purchasing a system because the definition will provide information for the criteria used to determine which system to adopt or purchase, or how to develop it. The following sections describe the key components of the system that should be considered in the requirements definition.

Step 1: Define the Purpose of the Site

The purpose of the site must be clear from the outset so that the project team can maintain its focus through the different stages of planning and development.

- Develop an overall statement of intent.
- Clarify the purpose of the site to make developing project goals and, eventually, measuring the effectiveness of the tool easier.

Step 2: Identify System Users

A system's users are the persons who will actually use the X-Internet system to accomplish tasks and must be identified before beginning a design or evaluation process. The types of users determine a great deal about the system (e.g., the platform, data required, or best way to present the data). Representative users might include technical support staff, administrators, managers, and customers — all persons who will use the system or its products (e.g., the general public, employees, etc.).

User inquiry, also called user and task analysis, is a collection of methods designed to gather information related to how users accomplish tasks. Project teams often make assumptions about users that might not be accurate. To assess user needs, involving users directly is necessary. User and task information can be gathered before design begins or throughout the development process. It can also provide key information for assessing systems for adoption or purchase. Gather information from users directly to allow the project team to create realistic scenarios that reflect real needs.

User and task analysis might yield information regarding:

- User goals (what they are attempting to accomplish with the task)
- What they do to accomplish their goals
- Characteristics they bring to the task (who they are and where they came from)
- Environment in which they accomplish goals and tasks
- Their skills and experience
- Their needs

Steps in user inquiry can include the following:

- Assemble a team that regularly interacts with system users (if the system already exists), or is involved in the design effort (if it is a new system or Web site).
- Use brainstorming techniques to identify known and potential users.
- List characteristics of individual users and groups of users.
- Use this information to create task and user characteristic matrices to model the anticipated user community. Field-study and other user and task analysis techniques should either support or refute these models.
- Test the design team's assumptions through interaction with users.

Questions to answer include:

- Who is your target audience? [Choose the typical users and profile each in detail. Include information such as occupation, technical expertise, education level, age range, sex, online frequency, online activities, what kind of equipment they have, and what kind of Internet connection they have. Do as many profiles as you need. Use Web logs from an existing site to get information regarding your users.]

■ What are the typical tasks the users might perform with the tool? [For example, register, log on, search for information on maternal and child, make a query, look for help, and contact the organization. Server log data from an existing system can be used to support or refute some of your task analysis. For example, you can tell which pages were visited, for how long, and how frequently.]

Step 3: Set Goals

Determine the system's goals to help identify which functions are priorities and need to be imported or developed first. Whether developing, adopting, or purchasing a system, add features incrementally to keep the initial work manageable and to allow for testing and consolidation of the system at each stage. Define both short-term (six months to a year) and long-term (longer than a year) goals.

The type and number of an organization's development goals will determine how they are tracked, measured, and prioritized. For example, a long-term organizational goal might be to move a client/server-based system to the Web. This larger goal would have its own set of composite goals, each with its own measurements and priorities. Immediate priorities within that goal might include gathering user data regarding the old system or identifying design specifications for the new Web interface.

Project Goals Should Be Measurable

An example of a measurable goal is to specify the number of persons who will use the system within a defined period of time. For example, "200 queries per month will be made to the data system." This goal could be quantitatively measured by the number of persons registered to use the tool, or a measurement obtained from the system database. Measurements could include:

■ Percentage increase in total unique visitors
■ Decrease in the amount of requests for paper copies of publications
■ Decrease in the amount of phone time spent finding data for requestors

Quantitative measurements can also be obtained from Web server logs. Server logs are text files that list requests made to a Web server. New products continue to enter and leave the marketplace for this type of software, but current products include WebTrends® and WebQA™. Analyzing the logs before adding a new system will provide a benchmark for measuring the success of the system. Check the configuration of the Web site's servers to determine whether they will need to be reconfigured to gather more or different types of data. The logs can be difficult to read but can be analyzed by commercial software that produces statistics.

Measurements for goal achievement will change on the basis of the goal. Success of a system redesign might be measured by an increased number of registered users or by an increased number of "page views." The organization should establish methods for measurement and achievable standards for success in meeting its goals.

Step 4: Assess the Technical Environment

An assessment should be made of existing technical expertise and equipment to answer specific questions. If adopting or purchasing a tool, consider the following:

- Will it work on the current servers and network?
- Will current staff be able to support and maintain it?
- If current staff cannot support it, how will the system be supported?
- How much maintenance, if any, is required?

If designing a tool, consider the following:

- Can current staff build it?
- Will current staff be able to support and maintain it?
- Will a consultant be hired to build it? If so, can current staff support it after it is delivered?
- How much maintenance, if any, is required?

Step 5: Establish Data Confidentiality Policies

- Data confidentiality policies should be consistent with federal privacy regulations and state legislation pertaining to data privacy and the release of data, which differs from state to state.

Step 6: Establish System Security Policies

Web site security should be a primary concern when hosting and managing a system that uses the Web to disseminate data. This might include restricting access to:

- Data
- User information and profiles
- Server logs
- Search logs
- E-mail documentation at the organizational level

Every Web application should have a defined security policy — even if this policy allows unrestricted access by the general public. Develop a security policy that enables the owners of the system and the data to make conscious decisions regarding the availability of the data and how an attack by hackers can be handled.

Answer the following questions when establishing security policies:

- Should users register to receive data?
- After users are registered, should data be password-protected so that only a unique identification number and password allow access to the records?
- Should users enter their user ID and password for each session?
- How should database security be handled?
- Which firewall software should be used?
- Should different levels of user access be predetermined and the data delivered to them customized based on their level of access?
- Should time-out features be included? Often used as a security device, time-out features assume that an error has occurred in specified situations and shut down a program. For example, a user's failing to use a program for more than 30 minutes might trigger the time-out feature.
- How should an attack by hackers be handled?
- How should the system be backed up?

Establishment of security policies and practices should also include a means of auditing and monitoring to ensure that system security is maintained. This could include creating checklists that are followed by technical support and project staff on a regular basis, analyzing backup tapes, or periodically updating virus and hacker protections.

Step 7: Establish Business Rules

As data confidentiality and security (Steps 5 and 6, respectively) are basic requirements to developing, adopting, or purchasing a system, they set the stage for establishing business rules. If a rule affects data confidentiality or security, those concerns and the business rule should be brought into alignment.

A business rule is a statement that sets data integrity constraints that apply to a field in a database or a relationship between tables in that database. Business rules are based on how an organization views and uses data, which reflect the way the organization functions. The goal of a data integrity constraint is to enforce a business rule within a database or application.

Building a Web application involves making choices regarding data — what types of data will be disseminated, how they will be disseminated, and how they will be reflected in the interface that the user sees. To establish the choices that need to be made during database design, the organization should compose a formal set of business rules. The rules will influence data selection, how relationships between tables in a database are constructed, and what reports the database produces. The rules might also affect security and confidentiality concerns.

Step 8: Develop System Design Document

After completing the relevant information-gathering activities described in Steps 1 through 7, develop a system design document that synthesizes all of the requirements and information into a clear statement composed of the functional and organizational requirements of the system. A system design document should be developed detailing a technical approach that ensures the development, adoption, or purchase of a system that:

- Meets the high-level goals of the organization and the goals of the project
- Provides identified users the ability to perform the required tasks.

The system design document should also:

- Identify software design parameters (Web application and business rules and database design)
- Identify software and hardware needs

Step 9: Develop a Project Strategy

The project strategy transforms the requirements definition into a plan of action. The project strategy interprets the information contained in the definition and describes how it will shape the dissemination system and the steps needed to complete the project.

The organization should complete a project plan whether it is developing, adopting, or purchasing a system. All of these approaches will affect current technical environments, workflow, and staffing. This should be addressed in the project plan so that the integration of the system into the organization's operations will be smooth.

The project plan should document what the system is expected to do (defined requirements) and how this will be achieved. The plan should include:

- Activities
- Schedule and sequencing
- Critical path
- Milestones
- Resources and budget
- Project staffing and management information

All staff working on the project should agree on the project plan. Progress can then be monitored, any changes to the scope of the project can be factored in, and the effect of the project can be measured. The plan provides a vehicle to communicate with those involved in the pre-planning stages. It can also be used to coordinate changes and as an overall measure of the progress of the project. Keep a copy of the project baseline on paper or electronically so you can compare progress.

The project baseline consists of the first project plan's milestone descriptions and dates. With most projects, deadlines shift, requirements change, and unforeseen events occur. Keeping a copy of the original timeline as a baseline to compare with the actual development progress might be helpful. Managing and coordinating these activities is time-consuming and management time should be factored into the overall cost of the project.

Revisit the Requirements

After a project plan has been developed, review the requirements definition statement. Staff should conduct this review to ensure that the system is still the same as was originally defined and that it can be realistically implemented by using the project plan.

Task 3: Select the Approach

Completing the following steps will help determine whether an organization should develop its own system or adopt or purchase an existing system.

Step 1: Determine the Functional Capability of Each Approach

After the system requirements are defined and a project strategy is developed, the functional capability of the proposed approach to meet the requirements should be assessed. If acquiring an existing system, either through adoption or purchase, it should be assessed to determine the following:

- Can it meet the primary and secondary purposes defined for the site?
- Is it suitable for our target audience?
- Does it support the user tasks identified?
- Is it compatible with existing platforms?
- Does it meet requirements for confidentiality?
- Is comprehensive documentation available?

Step 2: Identify Staff Resources Necessary To Implement the Approach

The cost of resources and their availability has been a major concern to organizations that have already developed or adopted Web-based data dissemination tools. They expressed concerns regarding the difficulty of staffing their initiatives and in recruiting staff with the appropriate technical skills. Organizations should consider their capacity in this area and establish how an implementation project can be supported.

Questions to consider to identify staff resources needed include:

- What are the short- and long-term staffing requirements for the project, and can they be supported?
- What will be the effect on IT support functions and how will project staff interact with the IT department?
- Do staff have the skills to meet programming requirements for the new tool?
- Are staff available in-house to work on the project and can they be diverted from their present tasks?
- Do staff have the appropriate technical skills and depth of technical knowledge?
- Can the organization compete with the private sector on salary and compensation to hire appropriate technical staff? If not, how will the right staff be recruited?
- Do other sources of suitable labor (e.g., university students, interns) exist?
- Do consultants need to be hired?

- Are sufficient training resources available, or will they need to be acquired?
- Can the organization still function effectively and achieve organizational goals, or will this project have an impact on other activities?

If the organization is developing a system, project staff must evaluate the effect of creating training and help mechanisms as well as their associated costs. If adopting or purchasing a system, the project staff must determine whether the donating/licensing entity will provide training support and technical assistance. If not, the adopting organization should be prepared to develop these services. Concerns to explore include the following:

- Does the donating/licensing organization provide initial training and technical assistance?
- Does it provide ongoing technical assistance?
- Is online help available?
- Are fees charged for training/technical assistance?

Step 3: Estimate the Cost of Implementing the Approach

To identify costs accurately, the following items must be considered:

- *Proprietary systems.* Assess all of the costs associated with the adoption or purchase of a system (e.g., purchase costs, annual fees, or licenses). Conduct thorough research regarding systems or technologies under consideration and obtain system documentation. Identify any compatibility concerns and the costs associated with integration and customization.
- *Hardware.* A new system can increase the workload on existing servers, demand additional network resources, or require personal computers for all staff. Identify the load on existing hardware, including servers, desktops, laptops, and network hardware, and any additional hardware requirements.
- *Software.* Assess the system's capability with existing applications, databases, proprietary software, network software, operating systems, statistical software, and geographic information system (GIS) software.
- *Security.* Identify any additional costs to ensure system and data security.
- *Licenses.* Consider fees for upgrades and long-term licensing.
- *Maintenance.* Consider software, database, network, etc.

- *Customization.* This might be needed, if the organization is adopting a system.
- *Staffing support.* Identify costs associated with implementing the selected approach.

After these costs have been estimated and defined, they should be compared with the costs associated with the current level of effort for data dissemination activities. This comparison will help ensure that the new approach is cost-effective, or identify that the approach is possibly not realistic for the organization.

Step 4: Determine Whether the Selected Approach Will Meet Organizational Needs and Constraints

The steps taken in Task 1, Determine Organizational Readiness and Impact, will have laid the groundwork for determining organizational needs and constraints. At this juncture, revisit the steps in the decision-making process to determine if the plan meets the original goals.

Task 4: Design Data Presentation Formats

Organizations must consider standards for data presentation. The organization must first ensure that the system adheres to the data presentation standards, including confidentiality, that are in place. Second, they must decide how best to display information on the computer screen.

Step 1: Maintain Adherence to Data Presentation Standards

As will be discussed in Task 5, the data presentation standards in place must be considered. Before launching a system, determine the established rules protecting confidentiality of data and ensure the appropriate personnel know them. If a system is being developed or purchased, ensure that programmers know these standards and program the system accordingly. If a system is being adopted, determine whether the system will need to be modified so that the standards can be followed.

Include documentation of data element standards for users of the system. This is a rationale by which system developers and managers label each category of data that resides in the database; among other features, standards should provide guidance on how to name each data element and where those elements should reside in the database structure. This documentation should be contained in a separate section that is clearly marked. In addition, including messages in the query output is helpful in explaining standards when they are enforced and marking these data with special characters. For example, in the case of cell suppression, which is a technique that can be used to maintain the confidentiality of data regarding individual persons or establishments, providing a message that explains why the data was not returned will help the user understand that the query was not faulty.

A few common examples of instances where standards for statistical calculation and data presentation should be developed and adhered to include:

- Cell suppression criteria
- Age adjustment methodology
- Confidence intervals
- Data smoothing methodology
- Geographic units of analysis (relative to a mapping component)
- Methodology for handling unknown or missing data

Step 2: Organize Data Presentation

The presentation of the query options and output on the computer screen are critical features of a user-friendly system. In presenting data, usability principles should be followed. Task 5 describes usability testing procedures for use before, during, and after system development. In addition to those procedures, other methods can be used for ensuring system usability. By adhering to basic rules or heuristics, organizations can ensure that their system has user-friendly query interfaces and output screens.

Task 5: Implement the System

Different steps must be taken when implementing the chosen system. Although certain overlap exists between implementation steps for designing a system and adopting or purchasing a system, important distinctions must be made. Therefore, the following section is broken down into two main components:

1. Designing and developing a new system
2. Adopting or purchasing an existing system

After requirements definition has occurred and information gathered has been translated into a project strategy, initial system design and prototyping can begin. During this phase, prototype information architecture is developed and tested, graphical user interface (GUI) prototypes are developed and tested, and finally, the database and Web application are developed to defined coding standards.

In this section, Steps 1 through 3 relate to design, and Steps 4 through 16 relate to development.

Concept Prototyping and Design

Concept prototyping should be conducted before any programming begins to produce a more user-centered design. In the prototyping stage, usability pitfalls and problems are anticipated, identified, and fixed inexpensively.

After the prototypes have been tested and approved, they can be made production ready, meaning that the files are ready for the programmers. The programming stage is less problematic if the prototypes have clean, commented, accessible HTML code.

Prototyping typically entails:

- Conducting user testing with the preliminary prototypes on paper or in HTML, when changes can be easily made
- Assessing the usability of the system, and testing different approaches
- Creating a look that reflects the organization and gives the user the best information to complete tasks
- Reviewing the prototypes for potential accessibility problems

Design Stages

The basic design process might involve the following:

- Produce an initial set of Web pages called a wireframe. A wireframe is a plain-looking graphic that shows a Web page layout (e.g., the content, navigation, etc.). It does not show colors or actual images. The wireframe will demonstrate how the site might be organized (e.g., navigation, browsing screens, and search results) and suggest content for the pages. The wireframe should not show actual content, the site's look-and-feel (e.g., colors or fonts), or a functional back end (e.g., database). The wireframe will help the project team visualize the possibilities for the Web-based query system interface.
- Produce "graphic composites" (flat electronic images). These are rapidly drawn but high-quality sketches intended for presentation; also known as graphic comps. The composites will illustrate ideas for how the site could look, including colors, fonts, logos, etc.

The design of the graphic user interface and the information architecture will be dictated by the information gained during requirements definition and by input from stakeholders and end users regarding the aesthetic preferences of the organization. This part of the process is an iterative one, and the design of the user interface should be tested with users to ensure optimal usability. Testing and redesign might need to be done multiple times until the most usable design is identified. Thus, the wireframe should be kept as simple as possible, so that it can be developed and changed quickly. The design can then be built out.

Following are the critical steps and elements in designing a user-centered interface and an effective and easily maintainable Web application.

Step 1: Design Web Pages for Usability

Usability is the measure of the quality of a user's interaction with an interface.

Usability tests frequently answer questions such as these:

- Can the users achieve their goals with this site?
- Can they accomplish tasks successfully?
- How long does it take them to complete a task?
- How long did it take them to get there? What steps did they take?
- Do they understand what the site's capabilities are?
- What do they want to do that they cannot?
- What do they find confusing or frustrating?

Usability testing is often seen as an expensive undertaking that calls for labs with two-way mirrors and video equipment, carefully screened subject groups, and expert analysis. The perceived expense and difficulty of the testing process often discourages people from conducting any usability tests.

Step 2: Design Web Pages for Accessibility

Designing for accessibility means designing pages and systems that can be accessed by persons with different disabilities. Nearly one fifth of all Americans have a severe or functional disability. Although persons with disabilities can derive great benefit from having easy access to goods and services online, many Web pages are not accessible.

Although a number of automated tools for assessing accessibility have been developed, accessibility evaluations cannot be completely automated. Comprehensive accessibility reviews might incorporate a combination of automated tests, guideline reviews, user tests, browser tests, and reviews with assistive technology. Assistive technology is software or hardware designed to assist persons with disabilities in carrying out daily activities. A knowledgeable evaluator should analyze the results.

Consider accessibility early. Accessibility concerns are much easier to correct if diagnosed early. They are even easier to correct when accessibility is considered during site or system design. During early design meetings, project teams should:

- Involve staff responsible for accessibility evaluations.
- Identify the guidelines or standards to be applied, and establish a target conformance level.
- Agree on a review schedule.
- Distribute training materials on accessible HTML, so developers can implement accessibility correctly and learn to conduct spot reviews of their work.

A good list of evaluation software products is available at http://www.w3.org/WAI/ER/existingtools.html. This Web site also lists guidelines for conducting accessibility evaluations at http://www.w3.org/WAI/eval/.

After a site has been launched, every content update must comply with accessibility guidelines and achieve the conformance level selected during the design process. To accomplish this, project teams should:

- Articulate the conformance level to be maintained during future updates.
- Determine who monitors and updates the site, and train them to test updates for accessibility.
- Establish a schedule for follow-up evaluations of the complete site or system.
- Purchase or download software to facilitate evaluation and make the software available to whoever maintains the system.
- Provide a mechanism for user feedback (e.g., e-mail, e-mail form, mail-to link, or an address).

Step 3: Create Graphic Composites

To get an idea of how similar tools look, make a list of sites that are appealing. Identify elements that are useful or attractive. Consolidate ideas and give this information to the graphic designer, together with any existing logos, graphics, or other elements that must be part of the system. The designer should provide two or three design alternatives.

The sample design is usually a layered, digital file that shows the elements of the page: logos, navigation, titles, example illustrations, and some mock body text. It should provide an idea of the color scheme, the grid (where elements will exist on the screen), the fonts, and the tone or feel of the page. In its finished form, the design will indicate all the information necessary to create the page in HTML.

After the main look-and-feel has been agreed upon, the designer should create mockups of the lower-level pages and how the elements change from section to section. For example, a home page might look different from a second-level page, which in turn looks different from a third-level page. There should be a design for each of these showing the differences.

Development

Development should be approached methodically and carefully. Each step is proposed because it ensures the success of the next step. The use of templates, validation, testing, code reviews, file standards, coding standards, and the style guide are part of the process because each has been found to benefit the development process and the final product. A template is a shell structure, coded in HTML, ColdFusion®, or another language, into which individual page content is inserted. Templates represent a working model of a system in development; they often include a fully functioning GUI and a partially functioning back end.

At the end of programming, the system will still be an ongoing project. Maintenance, additions, and changes will occur; the care with which it was initially programmed will help or hinder this process. The following steps are recommended for development.

Step 4: Create User-Friendly Interface

The system interface should be clean and easy to follow. Consider the following when creating the system's interface:

- Ensure that links and buttons are clearly defined so users know what to expect when clicking on them.
- Make error messages easy to understand so that users know what caused the error, how to fix the error, and how they can prevent such errors in the future.
- If users are required to register to use the database, explain why they must do so.
- Specify whether or not payment is required for using the system.

- Keep text simple, preferably at a 6th- to 8th-grade reading level. If content is aimed at an audience with a specialized vocabulary, be sure to use terms familiar to that audience.
- Provide definitions and help for users.
- Make help links context specific (e.g., the Help link on a query page should provide information regarding querying, whereas the Help link on an output page should provide information concerning tasks that can be performed in the output screen).
- Allow users to accomplish tasks with the least number of steps possible.
- Use the correct form element for the questions. For example, if the user can select more than one option in a brief list, use checkboxes. If the list is long, consider using a drop-down list or breaking up the list in some way. Try to limit the number of form elements that are present in a single form. For more information on designing forms for usability, see http://formsthatwork.com.
- Avoid causing multiple browser windows to open because users are sometimes unaware that they are opened and can be unsure how to close them.
- Show contact information clearly on every page.
- Use fonts that are 11-point or larger. Where possible, use relative font sizes to allow users to control the size of the text in their browser.
- Keep the color scheme uniform throughout the site.
- Select foreground and background colors to achieve high contrast (e.g., do not use light yellow on a white background). This will increase the readability of the site.
- Test the Web site using multiple browsers and browser versions because the appearance of the Web site might change, depending on what browser is used to view it.
- Set a browser compatibility standard and require compliance.

Step 5: Conduct Image Slicing

After the designs are finalized, they should be "sliced" into images that are placed in table cells so that the images look seamless. At the same time, the slicing allows the changing elements to be swapped as the user moves to different sections. After you decide where to cut the images, a software program optimizes the image (compresses the image into as small a file size as possible), slices the image, and creates the HTML slice code to put the slices back together in a table.

Step 6: Create Templates

The sliced code can then be inserted into a complete HTML file (with no page-specific content), creating a template. The template matches the page design visually as closely as it can. All functionality should be added to the template at this point, including dynamic element codes, META tags, rollovers, forms, etc. User feedback via observation and testing can be incorporated quickly across the site by updating a template. This encourages continual improvement. Templates offer certain advantages; they

- Provide tools to page developers to streamline the development process
- Generally include required HTML elements (e.g., META tags, Cascading Style Sheets (CSS), and predefined layout strategies that allow developers to focus on content rather than recurring presentation elements)
- Encourage consistency between pages
- Provide consistent tools and strategies in the template to encourage the creation of pages that contain common elements presented in the same way
- Encourage consistent application of the site's architecture
- Provide a means to centralize site navigation, which discourages developers from extending the site's architecture without considering its effect on the whole site
- Greatly reduce the cost of iterative design, which improves usability

Step 7: Use Cascading Style Sheets (CSS)

Cascading style sheets (CSS) can be used for adding style (e.g., fonts, colors, or spacing) to Web documents. Image slices, part of the HTML templates, combine with style sheets to form the foundation or shell of the system. The content for each page, which might include text, additional images, or data, is incorporated into this shell. By attaching style sheets to Web documents, developers can change the format without adding new HTML tags. Users can override stylistic decisions that prevent them from accessing a site's content by either turning styles off or substituting their own style sheets.

Cascading style sheets offer certain advantages; they

- Separate content from presentation
- Provide benefits to users (e.g., consistency, usability, and accessibility) while improving the development process
- Support future technologies and diverse users

- Allow the presentation of information in a format appropriate for any device or user with the use of alternate style sheets
- Improve accessibility by encouraging the correct use of HTML elements
- Reduce the need for "tag misuse" to gain control of presentation elements (e.g., using Table as a presentation element rather than a structuring element)
- Improve usability by rendering pages faster and more consistently
- Reduce the complexity of page code, eliminating tags (e.g., FONT and BOLD), nested layout tables, and spacer images (this reduction in presentation code produces pages that are compliant with upcoming HTML standards, and backwards-compatible in browsers that do not support certain features)
- Override presentation elements that users have trouble perceiving

Step 8: Conduct Validation and Test Guidelines

After the templates look correct, they should be validated and tested according to the accepted guidelines of the project. Refer to the organization's policy for validation and testing guidelines, particularly for accessibility.

HTML and CSS validation is fairly simple now because the W3C has posted validators online. HTML documents can be submitted at http://validator.w3.org/, and CSS files at http://jigsaw.w3.org/css-validator/, for immediate feedback.

Step 9: Implement Code Review

The main reason for validating and reviewing the Web-based data dissemination tool's code is to ensure users see what you want them to see on their browser. The two main browsers, Netscape® Communicator and Microsoft® Internet Explorer, do not always agree on how certain codes appear on their browsers; therefore, Web developers have to write code that works on both. The W3C (World Wide Web Consortium) has guidelines (www.w3c.org) regarding how to write HTML and CSS code that works on both browsers.

Step 10: Designate File and Directory Naming Standards

After the code within the system has been validated and reviewed, attention must be given to organizing the discrete files that comprise the system, including how files are named and grouped for easy maintenance and updating.

The X-Internet system should use logical and consistent directory structure and file-naming conventions to make maintenance easier and to reduce errors. Conventions should conform to existing organization standards.

If the structure is intuitive, maintaining the site will be easier. Keep files neatly organized in multiple sub-directories based on the system's information architecture. Include a sub-directory for images and a sub-directory for dynamic elements (elements in a Web page that are updated every time someone requests the page. Examples are the results of a search, or a button that reads Login or Logout, depending on whether or not the user has already logged in).

For example, a site divided into sections called About the Organization, News, Statistics, and Links might have a directory structure such as:

Root directory (contains home page and other top-level pages):

- about/
- news/
- stats/
- links/
- images/

Within each sub-directory that represents a section, the section's home or default page should be named "index" or another name conventionally accepted as a default. Sections that feature multiple pages in a series could have files "index," "index2," "index3," etc. Sections that feature interactive tools can benefit from file naming that reflects the function of the page, (e.g., e-mail or validate).

Ensure that the site's physical structure (i.e., where the HTML files are, where the images are, and how the folders are nested) is based on the information architecture. If the structure is intuitive, maintaining the site will be easier.

Step 11: Determine File Naming Conventions

Naming conventions can contribute greatly to the readability and maintainability of code. These guidelines will help you choose meaningful names for your code elements.

- Set a project standard for naming files, variables, and objects (e.g., projectname_requirements.doc).
- Use variable names that clearly indicate the content of each variable (e.g., "first_name").
- Use familiar vocabulary (e.g., use "last_name" rather than "surname").

- Match form field names and variable names to the corresponding database field name.
- Use naming conventions that conform to the syntax of the programming language.
- Use lowercase file names in 8.3 format (i.e., eight characters for the name and three for the appropriate extension).

Although certain platforms now allow for long, case-insensitive file names, programmers should strive to maintain the lowercase, 8.3 format for file names. Two primary reasons exist for this approach. First, the 8.3 format can be used on all of the platforms currently in use and ensures that the file name will be readable. Second, in certain cases, Windows® has demonstrated difficulties with restoring long file names from backup. Therefore, by using long file names, the programmer is introducing instability into procedures to back up the application.

Circumstances might exist in which the programmer cannot use this 8.3 format because of constraints of the specific programming language or the server environment. For example, the Macromedia® ColdFusion® application architecture requires the existence of a file named Application.cfm. The uppercase "A" is required if the application is deployed on a UNIX® server. Exceptions to this standard should be based on compelling language- or platform-specific requirements.

Step 12: Implement Coding Standards

Using comments in your code provides valuable information, both to yourself and to other programmers who may be unfamiliar with your code. For the best coding, follow these guidelines:

- Include standard information (e.g., name, date, file name, purpose, and update).
- Break up sections of the code by using comments.
- Comment on exceptions to the standards.

Someone unfamiliar with the code needs to know who worked on it last and when, to determine whether that person is still available to provide guidance.

Too often, the comments at the top of a file remain unchanged, despite major revisions to the code. Noting all substantial modifications at the top is best. Then, the next programmer does not have to search through the code. If applicable, include the version number and notes concerning the history of the file.

Divisions should be clear to the reader so that the different sections of the code can be identified easily. Use asterisks or a full line of a repeated symbol to differentiate sections. Certain persons also find that always beginning their comments flush left is helpful, and provides a visual contrast to the indented code around them.

Step 13: Engage in HTML Production

Production starts after the templates have been validated and tested. That means formatting the content, placing it into the templates, and saving it as new files. In production, the HTML coders should use the original templates and a style guide to ensure the pages are consistent across the site.

Step 14: Create Style Guide

The style guide (see Appendix A) defines how each recurring element should be formatted and used. The guide should explain which fonts to use; how titles, headings, subheadings, footnotes, and captions should look; how to prepare pictures; and where elements go. It should show everything that a graphics standards manual would show for a magazine, for example. In addition, it should detail how to code elements, what ALT tags (i.e., used in HTML coding to describe in words any graphic images on a Web page) to use for images, what comments to use in certain sections, and how to use the cascading style sheets. Using a guide will make production quicker and more consistent. After production, the guide will be used for creating new pages.

For production and maintenance, the guide should include:

- How to modify and use the templates
- How to add or modify graphics; where the original graphics files are located
- How the Web server is set up and where the files are located
- Naming conventions for:
  - CSS files and codes
  - Files and folders
  - Images
- HTML code conventions
- Other coding conventions as needed (e.g., Perl, Common Gateway Interface (CGI) scripts, ColdFusion® includes)

Step 15: Create User-Friendly Query Functions

The system's query functions should allow for data searches to be conducted with ease. Consider the following when creating the system's query functions:

- Create different query interfaces for users with different levels of experience — for example, one for beginning users who want a simple query, and one for advanced users who want to conduct complex queries.
- By default, have users start with a simple query interface. Enable more expert users to skip over the beginner interface.
- Write the accompanying text and instructions for simple queries at a 6th- to 8th-grade reading level. For all queries, write text and instructions in the simplest language possible.
- Use tables rather than body text to allow users to construct queries quickly. Users will more easily select items from a bulleted list than a paragraph to build a query.
- Describe the content of the datasets, so that users can determine if the data are relevant to their query.
- Clearly state disclaimers and limitations of the data, either on the query page or on a link from the query page.
- Allow users flexibility in selecting age range and year variables.
- Allow users to query death by name of primary diagnosis as well as by ICD-9 or ICD-10 code.
- When possible, allow users flexibility in defining areas of geographic analysis (e.g., building neighborhoods by aggregating zip codes).
- Identify which variables cannot be used in combination because they will produce illogical or circular queries, will result in person-identifiable results, or are not supported by the system.
- Allow users to download acceptable data sets to perform more sophisticated analyses if it does not violate confidentiality standards.
- Provide a clear way to submit data by way of a submit button, in an easy-to-find location. For long pages, a "submit" button at the top and bottom of the screen is acceptable, but both should perform exactly the same function and be identifiable as such.
- Provide a query progress bar during processing of the query, so that users can see that the system is actively generating results from the query. This is especially important for large datasets, when the query may take some time to process. This information will only be provided while the system is building the results screen, so easier-to-build results will mean the information is more quickly presented and departed from the screen.
- Maximize system performance to increase speed of queries. Usability expert Jakob Nielsen recommends that pages take no longer than ten seconds to load, based on the most prevalent connection speeds of system users (e.g., cable modem, T-1 line, or dial-up modem).

Step 16: Design Usable Outputs

The system's output functions should provide users with data that is clearly distinguishable and well-organized. The output functions should also be flexible to meet users' data reporting needs. Consider the following when designing the system's output functions:

- Identify the query variables on the output pages.
- Use colors or other mechanisms such as size or position to differentiate between the output and the query variables.
- Allow users to select multiple output formats simultaneously (e.g., allowing users to create a table and a graph from the same query).
- Allow users to easily manipulate output after the query is complete (e.g., changing colors or labels on graphs or otherwise modifying the appearance of graphs, charts, tables, and maps).
- Allow users to further query their outputs (e.g., creating nested tables).
- Ensure that outputs can be downloaded and printed with ease and integrity.
- Allow outputs to be downloaded in multiple formats and clearly define those formats.
- Provide surrounding language, interpretation of the output, and instructions for additional steps and options (e.g., printing and downloading) on the output page.

Task 6: Test the System

Testing the system is a necessary step in the system development, adoption, or purchase process. Testing and quality assurance focus on functionality of the site, quality and accuracy of query output, and accessibility.

The testing plan should have been considered in the project plan, but it should be reviewed before starting the formal test.

Step 1: Test the System

Testing helps programmers fix problems before the system has real users and data. Any system, no matter how well coded and standardized, will have problems that only testing can catch. Testing conducted by a designated system tester will find problems that programmers and others familiar with the system might overlook. Testing should be done across the common user environments defined in the requirements definition, in the following order:

- System testing:
  - In defined user environments (browsers, platforms)
  - With live data
  - With scenarios
- Content check
- Fixing testing failures
- Test fixes

Step 2: Publicize the Launch Date

When the system and site are ready to go live, let the users know. Tell them when it will be live and where it is, and solicit their feedback. Send out e-mail, publish notices, and post notices on Web sites that users will be likely to see. If applicable, inform the public relations department. Also enlist the help of stakeholders and end users to publicize the launch date.

Ensure that information concerning the new system is added to your existing site's META information (key words, phrases, and description paragraphs). Then re-register with the search engines that refer users to the site. Referring search engine statistics can be found through the Web logs.

Step 3: Promote Training on the System

The need for training should be addressed whether developing, adopting, or purchasing a system; implications for each approach are described in the following.

Developing a System. A large part of developing a system is developing training and documentation. A Web content specialist or technical writer should walk through the system with the interface designer and programmers to write the documentation. Writing the Help section can begin as soon as the overall functionality is planned and certain pieces have been programmed. As each section is finished, the writer should add to the online help system or printed manual, and the entire documentation should be reviewed after testing and deployment, to ensure that it is consistent with the final system.

Adopting a System. One of the benefits of adopting a system is that a similar organization already has experience with it; the best training might be from current users. Arranging for staff from the donating organization to come on-site to provide training and technical assistance might be possible. Another alternative would be to have staff from the adopting organization observe system users. The system builders might also have documentation that would be helpful for training purposes. At a minimum, they should be able to recount their own lessons learned in using the system.

Purchasing a System. Frequently, software designers and vendors offer training on their software. The majority of programs also have online help and other documentation. The vendors might include on-site training for a fee or include it with the purchase. This should be a factor in deciding which system to buy.

Beyond initial training, developing a plan for training that reaches local departments and other users statewide is essential. The training should be provided on an ongoing basis, particularly considering staff turnover. Certain states have addressed the need for training through train-the-trainer programs so that local or regional trainers are available. Also enlist the help of stakeholders and end users to promote training on the system. In addition to training on the use of the Web-based data dissemination system, training for local public users should address appropriate use and interpretation of statistics.

Task 7: Evaluate the System

Evaluation of the system applies to developers, adopters, and purchasers and should encompass a series of elements/phases, including:

- Usability/user testing
- Accessibility and assistive technology testing
- Validation and browser testing

Additionally, stakeholders and end users should be involved in the evaluation process, including preparing recommendations as a result of the evaluation.

Developing a System

The process of evaluation will depend on budget, time limits, organizational support, whether or not a contractor is involved and the contractor budget, personnel, and a variety of other possible concerns. Evaluation should be conducted during development, to establish that the design meets user needs and does not break down in required environments. (That is, after the operating system and Web server environments have been decided, the system must function normally within them.) Standards for success need to be established before testing, preferably before the development process is initiated.

Whoever manages development should establish a realistic timeline and budget for specific types of evaluation. Both accessibility testing and usability testing should be conducted early and often during the development process (the process of gathering user data is part of the usability engineering life cycle). Browser testing and validation should occur after development, but before the final accessibility compliance audit (which should be conducted just prior to launch). Staff should be aware that evaluation occurs throughout the project and not only at the end of the process.

Contracting versus In-House Evaluation

If a contractor has been used to build the Web system, the contractor might conduct its own set of evaluations. However, unless the state or local organization asks for user testing or accessibility reviews, they are probably not going to happen. Usability and accessibility testing still are not standard steps in the majority of development processes. An extra fee might be charged for evaluation services, and it is one more area of expertise to assess before hiring a contractor.

If the project manager wants to handle evaluation externally, he or she should know which evaluation methods are desired (e.g., accessibility, user analysis and testing, log analysis, and browser testing/validation) and select contractors who have that expertise. Samples of the contractor's work should be obtained to assess whether the contractor has the necessary experience and expertise to evaluate a Web system.

The organization can also have a contractor design and build the system, but choose to conduct certain types of tests internally. In that situation, the project manager will need to know when during the development process evaluation should occur, and coordinate that with the contractor. The benefit of internal usability testing is greater control within the organization. The majority of agencies also have a ready source of test subjects in their project staff. Internal user testing requires organizational support and funding, which can sometimes be a barrier.

Web contractors usually conduct regular browser tests. The organization should establish a standard set of browsers for which testing is required, and decide what features should be tested (e.g., JavaScript™ disabled, style sheets disabled, text magnification, etc.). A standard for success or failure can thus be established.

Web contractors are not usually experts on accessibility and usability. However, many can conduct simple tests that provide useful feedback about the usability of the system. If evaluation is handled externally, determining whether the contractor has experience with that type of evaluation, how often and at what points in the process they intend to test, and what methodologies they intend to use are all important. This is also helpful for keeping track of the development budget. Setting up a usability lab with a minimal budget (e.g., $2000) for user testing will be difficult. If a contractor sets up log analysis software to gather information concerning Web site visits, that will only gather certain types of information. Knowing what kind of data is needed to justify the expense of the system to organizational decision makers is important.

Purchasing a System

If a system is purchased, usability and accessibility testing should have occurred before purchase. The company that produced the application should have conducted user testing. Browser testing will probably be required once the site or system is populated with the purchasing organization's data to test the data (this assumes that the system is viewable in a commercial Web browser).

Accessibility testing should be the responsibility of the developer, because this type of solution is supposed to be delivered ready for installation, similar to a commercial software product. Managers should ask about implementation of state or local accessibility requirements before purchasing a product, because the buyer should ensure access for users with disabilities.

If the product does not meet stated guidelines, the buyer should consider purchasing another product or hiring a contractor instead. If the purchased system is still their preferred solution, then they should work out the cost of additional development with the product developer, who should recognize that the accessibility modifications will be desirable to other consumers and adjust fees accordingly.

Evaluation Techniques

The following are basic techniques that can be used to monitor the performance of the deployed system. They can be used for developed, adopted, or purchased systems.

Step 1: Perform Log Analysis and Monitor System Use

Server log files record activity on a Web server. They provide information on where visitors to the site are coming from, which pages they visit, how long they stay, and which browsers they use. What data is collected depends on how the logs are set up by IT staff.

The project manager and technical staff should work together to select log analysis software (a review of log analysis software can be found at http://webdesign.about.com/cs/traffic/). If a contractor is involved, discuss which tools they use for server log analysis (if any), and how the reports will be accessed. Responsibility for log analysis might depend on where the system or Web site is hosted (e.g., will it be hosted on the contractor's server or the organization's server?). Contractors might provide access to reports from their Web servers on an agreed-upon schedule.

Server logs should collect data regarding:

- Who visits the Web site
- How users move through site pages — how the user goes from one page to the next (using what page element — link, button, etc.)
- How much time users spend on a given page (e.g., if they spend a lot of time in one place, either the content meets their needs, or they are very confused. If many visitors spend lots of time on one page, that content may need to be moved up to a higher level within the site architecture, so visitors can find it quickly and easily.)
- The location from which visitors leave the site or system (e.g., if users are hitting the home page and leaving again immediately, a problem exists.)
- Task completion — logs can tell you what files were requested and whether the request was successfully filled. (This is not the same thing as user testing; logs can tell you whether someone got what they asked for, not whether they wanted something that was not there in the first place or whether what they asked for turned out to be the wrong thing.)

Recognizing that server log analysis is not entirely accurate is important. Certain requests are never logged, and other requests should not be counted. For example, if the same person visits the site multiple times, is each visit counted? Determine whether the organization wants to know how many unique visitors accessed the pages, or how many times the pages were accessed.

Concerns to be aware of when using log analysis are described in the following:

Caching. Web browsers store pages in their cache so that the user does not have to load the pages anew every time one is requested. If a page is in the cache, the browser calls it up from the cache instead of requesting it from the server. Thus, no new visit is recorded.

Proxy Servers. Internet service providers (ISPs) often use proxy servers (servers that intercede between a Web browser and a Web server). Proxy servers also cache pages. If the proxy server has a page in its cache, it will load it instead of requesting it from the Web server.

IP Address Confusion. Certain software equates a unique IP address/browser with a unique user. This may not be accurate because (1) ISPs might assign a new IP address each time a user connects, resulting in an overestimate of users; or (2) certain users might share IP addresses, resulting in an underestimate of users (e.g., when a number of users are behind a firewall, they may all show up as the same IP address on Web server logs of sites outside the firewall).

Robots. Robots are computer programs that visit Web sites to catalog them for search engines. It is possible to filter out visits from robots, but the filter will have to be updated to catch new robots.

Step 2: Obtain User Feedback

Methods of obtaining user feedback include:

- E-mail
- Customer service calls
- Interviews
- Surveys
- Usability tests
- Group discussions/focus groups
- A prominent contact phone number presented on every page of the site

All these methods can be effective, and different methods can be used together to achieve maximum effect.

Task 8: Maintain the System

Even a well-designed and programmed site will need maintenance. Users will find errors that were not foreseen. Software can be added to a server that creates conflicts with the system. The managers will want to see whether the site is achieving the goals defined in the requirements definition stage. They will also need to check and adjust how search engines are finding and indexing the site.

Eventually, any site will have things added to it. New modules must be tested for errors, and should be tested with users. Can users find the information? Do the new modules make things easier or introduce new problems? All this should be considered in the maintenance plan.

A Web site that does not have a well-conceived maintenance plan will soon become confusing. The maintenance plan is part of the requirements definition but it should be reviewed when the site is implemented because, during development, concerns might have arisen that were not considered in the original plan. After approximately one year, the maintenance plan should be reviewed again to see that it is still on target, and changes should be made, if needed.

After deployment, ongoing maintenance will be required and a maintenance plan should be implemented, which includes:

- Schedule for running log-analyzer software and running online surveys to acquire user feedback
- Schedule for optimizing strategic keywords (META tags and HTML)
- Incorporation of answers to questions from users into the site content
- Periodic user testing to ensure site upgrades do not diminish user experience
- Checking of site search capability at least weekly — site searches often become disabled without being noticed unless they are checked
- Examination of technical support logs and application server logs for Web server errors, and performance times
- Database backup plan
- Periodic database optimization, including consistency checks, index maintenance, and analysis of queries for efficiency

For systems that are adopted or purchased, these concerns may not be relevant, depending on the system parameters and the types of maintenance features that have been built into the system by the donating or licensing organization.

Appendix: Design Guidelines

The following design guidelines are most useful when designing the architecture and the look of the site, and should be taken into consideration as early as possible.

The following table describes which sections should be considered at each stage of development:

Section	Web Development Stage
Navigation	User and Task Analysis Wireframes Concept Prototyping Graphic Composites
Menus and Toolbars	User and Task Analysis Wireframes Concept Prototyping Graphic Composites
Fonts	Graphic Composites HTML Templates HTML Production
Form Elements and Controls	Concept Prototyping HTML Templates
Mechanisms for Feedback	Graphic Composites HTML Templates Programming
Color	Graphic Composites HTML Templates
Web Style	Concept Prototyping Graphic Composites HTML Templates HTML Production Programming
Graphics	Graphic Composites HTML Templates Programming

Navigation

- *Make navigation easily learned and consistent.* The user will give up if he or she must spend too much time learning to navigate the site. Make the navigation easily learnable and clear, and then apply it consistently throughout the site.
- *Navigation must demonstrate its context.* On the Web, navigation must clearly indicate where users are, where they have been, and how to get back where they started. An example of this would be a grayed-out button in a navigation bar, which is often used to illustrate a user's present location.

- *Do not make the user go through too many steps to get to content.* If users must click through two or three pages before arriving at the information they need, they might give up. Too many levels and sub-levels can be confusing. Users should not have to click through more than three screens to reach their goal.
- If a series of data entry forms is used, *clearly indicate the user's present location* in the series, and how many screens the user must complete before data entry is complete.
- *Provide feedback.* Page navigation and controls must demonstrate that the user's situation has changed. The user needs feedback to understand what he or she has done, and what effect it has had.
- Always provide a link back to the home page.
- *Provide different means of navigating the site.* In addition to top and side navigation menus, provide a site map or index. If possible, provide a "breadcrumb trail" (a series of links at the top of a Web page that demonstrates how users arrived at their current location).
- *Provide an e-mail contact link on every page of the site.* The link might lead to a feedback form, or might simply be a mail-to link. Users must have contact information on every page of the site.

Menus and Toolbars

- *Use succinct and clear menu titles.* Choose titles that clearly indicate page content.
- *Limit the number of items in a global navigation menu.* Try to keep menu items to nine or less. A number of subheadings might fit under each item in the menu.
- *Use drop-down lists sparingly.* Drop-down lists are used on the Web for different purposes, including allowing users to fill in forms and providing lengthy drop-down lists for navigational purposes. Users often find interactive drop-downs that change as they make selections confusing.
- Disable menu items when they are unavailable.
- *Do not use navigation menus to jump users to another site or open an e-mail link.* Global navigation links should open pages within the site.
- *Order menu items appropriately in terms of importance to the user.* Organize related menu items into groups.
- *All navigation menu items must be accessible by keyboard.* The user must be able to use the Tab key to access menu items. This does not mean that JavaScript™ menus may not be used, only that the menu items must also be available elsewhere in HTML.

- *Establish a tab order from top to bottom and left to right of the page.* This is rarely a problem on the Web, but pay attention to the structure of layout tables so the tab order of menu links makes sense, and groupings of links are not lost.
- *Use standard navigation menus on all pages.* The top-level navigation menu should be available from any page on the site. This will brand your content and provide users with a consistent means of moving about within the site.

Fonts

- *Avoid overspecific use of fonts in Web site or system design.* It is often best to accept a default font that will work on all users' machines. If a specific font is used, list alternatives to increase the probability that one of the fonts will be available on the user's machine. Limit the number of typefaces used in an interface. Too many fonts can contribute to visual clutter.
- *Avoid using uppercase text unless it is in reference to a database variable or HTML code.* On the Web, uppercase text implies emphasis.
- *Do not override the user's font selections.* Use style sheets to format text wherever possible. Cascading style sheets (CSS) ensure that the developer can separate content from presentation. If style sheets are used, the text must still be legible even if they are turned off.
- *Avoid using bold and italic.* Use bold and italic text occasionally for emphasis. Use it rarely and consistently.

Form Elements And Controls

- *Establish consistent system or site navigation*, with a link to the main menu on all pages.
- Include the organization or department name on all pages.
- *Include brief directions* (if possible, less than 100 words) on query use on the first screen of the system. Educate the user through hypertext links and context-sensitive help.
- Allow users to refine results without initiating a new query.
- *Preserve the user's work* (especially with pick lists and text entry boxes) so users do not have to start over or review past entries.
- Use the appropriate form element for a task:
  - Use checkboxes for toggling between two choices. If the checkbox is checked, the option is selected. If it is not checked, the option is not selected.

- Use drop-down combo boxes when users should make one selection from a series of options. A single selection drop-down box is appropriate when the user may only select one item from a preset list, and the user cannot add new items to the list.
- Use multiple selection checkboxes when more than one selection is available, and the user may not add new items to the list.
- Do not use input and submission methods that cannot be used with older model browsers and assistive technology, or provide an accessible alternative.

■ *Provide accelerators for expert users and simplified elements and controls for novices* (e.g., provide complex query construction for researchers and static tables for the general public).

■ *Use standard controls. Maintain system conventions when creating or using controls.* When a series of buttons is presented in a screen or form (e.g., Add, Cancel, and Apply), it should be presented in the same order on every screen on which they appear. Consistency in presentation will increase the usability of system forms. Use consistent capitalization and justification on all submit image buttons. In Web-based forms, explicitly associate form controls with their labels using HTML markup. This can be achieved using the LABEL element.

■ *Required fields must be indicated visually through an image or character.* For example, required fields could be marked with a red asterisk. The "required field" indicator must also be available to users who cannot see the page.

Mechanisms for Feedback

Minimize error messages by preventing errors whenever possible. To minimize user errors:

- Disable invalid menu items and form controls, and make the inaccessibility of the item or control obvious to the user.
- Inform the user if incorrect data entry has occurred, so he or she can correct the error.
- Where possible, present lists of options to prevent data entry errors.

If an error occurs, provide a clear and simple error message that explains how the problem can be fixed. Good error messages tell the user what the problem is and how to fix it. They also provide information on who to contact if the error cannot be corrected. Keep it brief and to the point.

- *Do not use humorous or sarcastic language in error messages.* Do not imply that the error is the user's fault. Do not use system error language or error numbers.
- *Feedback on status.* Provide visual feedback for available and unavailable selections. If a form field is unavailable for data entry, the system should indicate that.
- *Let users know when they are about to be timed out of a system.* Give them the option of requesting additional time.

Color

- *Do not override users' color selections.* This is especially important for users with impaired vision, who may need to view pages in high contrast.
- *Ensure that background colors and text provide sufficient contrast for legibility.* There must be a 90 percent contrast difference to read text clearly. A light background with dark text is easiest to read.
- *Use color to emphasize key items and draw attention to them. Use it sparingly.* Do not use color alone to create the emphasis or draw attention. Do not use color on unimportant background items, as it may distract users.
- *Use color to group similar items and differentiate between dissimilar items.* Contrasting colors can emphasize difference, and using the same color on a series of pages can demonstrate that they are related. Also use some means other than color (e.g., text) to indicate the relationships.
- *Limit use of colors in color-coding. Do not attach meaning to more than three colors,* because users will not be able to remember the meanings. The more colors used, the more distracting and less effective they are.
- *Test colors* on different monitors and different browsers, with different settings, to check legibility and effectiveness.
- *Use browser-safe colors.* The browser-safe palette contains 216 colors out of a possible 256. The palette is useful for flat-color graphics and logos, and areas in an image with a lot of a single color.

Web Style

- *Titles and headings.* Use titles, page headings, and subheadings consistently in Web pages and systems. Structure articles with two or three levels of subheadings, because sub-headings help assistive technology interpret the page content. Consistency in headings and titles will also help users navigate and provide a meaningful title for bookmark pages.

- *Use page titles.* Page titles are included in the TITLE element of an HTML document. The page title is generally the first thing users see when the page loads, and the title will show up as the text of any bookmark the user sets.
- *Page titles should not be longer than 40 to 60 characters.* Page titles should not all begin with the same word. Different pages should use different titles; the same title should not be used for every page of a site or a section of a site. Eliminate articles (a, an, and the) from page titles.
- *Include the name of the organization or Web site in each page title.* The title should be a concise and plainly worded description of page contents. A unique title should be used on each page. New information should precede old information (e.g., the title of the page would appear before the name of the site, if both were included).
- *Heading text has to make sense when the rest of the text is unavailable.* Clearly explain the content of the page or article. Using different levels of subheadings will increase usability for individuals with disabilities.
- *Users do not like to read online.* If the article is longer than half a page, users might print it out rather than reading it on the computer screen. Documents written for reading on the Web must be concise and formatted to facilitate scanning. The "inverted pyramid" writing style used in journalism, where important information is placed at the beginning of the first sentence so it can be easily found, works well. Developers can also highlight key words, use meaningful sub-headings, use bulleted lists, limit themselves to one idea per paragraph, and load their writing by beginning with the conclusion.
- For Web publishing, usability experts *recommend writing only 50 percent of the content you would for a print publication.*
- *Limit jargon.* Figure out who will read your pages, and target the level of reading difficulty accordingly. Write clearly and succinctly. Avoid hyperbole and marketing language. Avoid metaphor.
- *Avoid using too much markup in paragraphs.* Too many styles of typeface can make the page appear busy.
- Use hypertext to split up long information into multiple pages.
- *Do not construct sentences around link phrases such as "click here."* Avoid linking the text "click here;" instead, choose meaningful text that indicates the target of the link.

- *Inserting multiple links in a paragraph can distract users* from the page text. Only the most germane and useful links should be included in the body of the page text. All other supporting links can be included in groups of footnote links at the bottom of the document.
- If you are not using default link colors, *try to use link colors that match the text color.*
- *Use Spell Check.* Poor spelling or grammar will make users unwilling to trust your content. Be sure text and text equivalents are spellchecked and copyedited.
- *Provide a search feature on documentation pages.* After all, users only access documentation when they are unable to figure out something.
- *Provide examples* to help users implement instructions. Any instructions should be task-oriented and demonstrate the steps required to complete the task.
- *Use language familiar to the user* to describe actions or events (e.g., use language from the Windows® system screens to describe actions taken within the Windows® environment).
- *Repetition will provide users with clear expectations for page layout and behavior.* It will also "brand" the site with a consistent identity. Consistent layout and navigation will help users find what they need on the site, and avoid them having to decipher a new navigation design every few pages.
- *Reuse controls, buttons, and navigation elements* when designing new pages and prototypes. A consistent look-and-feel will increase user comfort with your content.
- *Place logos and navigation menus in a consistent location on the page,* and make them a consistent size throughout the site.
- *Use color consistently.* Make sure contrast is sufficient between text and background colors so that pages are legible.

English readers read from left to right, and from the top of the page to the bottom. This is the basis for most graphic design of print publications. On Web pages, the top of the page is the most important "real estate" on the screen. The top four or five inches of the page are all that is visible on the computer monitor. Important content should be visible in that space.

Graphics

- *Graphics should support the content, data, and purpose of the system or site.* Do not use graphics for the sake of adding images.
- *Do not use graphics that have negative cultural connotations.* Review and test graphics to be certain that you are not using

images that might have a different meaning to someone of a different culture. For example, in some cultures, a black box around a picture means that the person pictured is dead. The Web is a global medium. Be aware of the messages you are sending.

■ Place information on the screen, including graphics, based on a *hierarchy of information.* Ask yourself, "What does the user want to do first? Second? Third?" Place content accordingly.

■ *Use an appropriate image format for Web graphics,* either GIF or JPG. Choose the smallest image you can. Keep graphics small; under 24K in size is ideal.

■ *Use the fewest images with the smallest byte size that is appropriate to achieve an acceptable download speed.* Large images slow Web page downloads, especially for users with slow Internet connections. Breaking a large image into several smaller images will decrease download times; but if too many small images appear on a page, download times will still be problematic.

■ *All Web graphics should be optimized.* Optimizing reduces the bit depth of the image, resulting in a smaller byte size.

■ *Specify height and width attributes with the IMG element in HTML.* If you do this, placeholder text will appear in the browser window while the image loads. This allows the user to scan page content and complete tasks, whether the images have finished loading or not.

■ *Provide a text version of each image using the ALT attribute in HTML.* ALT text communicates the meaning or purpose of an image to users who cannot see the page or cannot see it well. ALT text should not be used to create ToolTip pop-ups in Microsoft® Internet Explorer. That the ALT text describes what the image does is more important than how it appears. If the button is used for navigation purposes (i.e., it is a link), then the ALT text should indicate the target of the link.

■ *Avoid using animated GIFs.* Animated GIFs can distract users from important page content.

■ *Do not import graphic elements from another Web site or print publication.* The images might not be in an appropriate format, and what works in print might not work on the Web.

Notes

This appendix is based on the Center for Disease Control's (www.cdc.gov) manual entitled "Web-Based Systems for Dissemination of Health-Related Data: A Guide for Public Health Agencies Developing, Adopting, or Purchasing Interactive Web-Based Data Dissemination Systems."

Appendix C

Audio and Video Production Values

Part of what goes into a rich Internet is audio and video. The intent of this appendix is to provide some guidance to non-experts on how to develop professional media files.

Guidelines for Digital Video

There is no commonly agreed-upon methodology to create digital video. Because the hardware and software involved is continually evolving, the digital video maker will have to stay on his or her toes to make sure that the videos produced are always on the "cutting edge."

The following discussion depicts a fairly common sequence of events that take places in the creation of a video on a PC (before encoding). Because the computer brings the creation process into the nonlinear age, none of these steps really has to follow in exact sequence. Assuming that the storyboarding process has been completed, the following steps can occur.

Gathering Source Material

Production facilities and personnel can be employed to create new footage for editing and manipulation, or stock footage can be gathered. The effect of the nonlinear editing process is obvious here because it allows editors to play "what if" with the story line in an unprecedented manner. Thus, additional footage may be shot at this stage, and more footage may be required later if the story line is allowed to evolve. The computer itself is capable of generating text, graphics, and even 2D and 3D animations.

Digitizing

Before any editing can take place, the source video must be converted into digital form by the computer and stored on disk. This process is known as *digitizing*.

Video input can come from many kinds of input devices, from consumer-quality VHS machines to traditional high-end tape equipment. However, the quality of the digital image directly depends on the quality of the medium from which it comes. While there are several digitizing methods, they all depend on the quality of the source device. Thus, the rental or purchase of a high-quality deck should be factored into the overall cost of equipment. Still frames to be included in the production can be created in the PC or brought in through a high-quality scanner.

Editing Nonlinearly

The nonlinear editing process has many advantages. Most software products handle the editing process by facilitating the creation in an offline model of the final video, rather than by actually compositing the video themselves online. This model contains information about how the video is to unfold over time. Various video clips are trimmed and then sequenced together with intervening transitions, wipes, and keys. Rather than manipulate the video files themselves, the model contains information about the files and the pointers to them.

Because the computer is a general-purpose tool, it can be used for more than just the editing process. Static graphic elements can be assembled by means of professional-quality graphics programs, text can be generated, and 2D and 3D animations can be created. Changes to all of these production elements can be made right up to the last minute.

The computer allows the editor to create and store a model of the video project without creating the actual video. Because this model can also be duplicated, and the duplicate can be altered without altering the original, it is possible to create several different models or previews of the same project.

After the creation process has ended, the resulting video model must be used to create or render an actual video. During the rendering process, the computer proceeds frame-by-frame through the model and performs all operations necessary to create a complete frame at the desired resolution and quality. This process can be quite time-consuming, depending on the complexity of the model and the duration of the video.

Because many compositing and special-effect computations are very processor-intensive, three ways to speed the rendering process are to (1) purchase a faster computer, (2) accelerate the current machine, or (3) take advantage of multiprocessor hardware and software to operate in parallel.

Broadcast-Quality Software

Software for personal computers and workstations now exists to create stills, edit video nonlinearly, create transitions, perform composites, render special effects, animate in two and three dimensions, etc.

No one package can do it all, however, so it is important to research the capabilities of different software products from different vendors. The minimum feature-set necessary to ensure broadcast-quality output is comprised of 24-bit color manipulation, sub-pixel positioning and anti-aliasing, Alpha channel support, and text generation that supports anti-aliasing of Postscript and TrueType fonts.

The most common representation of color in personal computers is familiar to video professionals as "component" video. Here, colors consist of three channels: red, green, and blue. Each channel is represented by 8 bits (1 byte), for a total of 24 bits per pixel. Programs that generate 24-bit color output are essential to broadcast-quality work because this color scheme can represent more than 16 million separate colors, more than the human eye can distinguish.

If your software has digital video effects (DVE)-like features, sub-pixel positioning is essential for achieving smooth-looking motion of video layers and important for compositing. To achieve broadcast-quality motion, it is necessary to compensate for the computer's limited screen resolution. This is created by the illusion that the number of screen pixels per inch is much greater than it actually is. Sub-pixel sampling is the frame-processing method that creates this illusion.

Anti-aliasing becomes important when the edges of any graphic object are diagonal to any degree, when rectangular shapes are rotated, or when smooth curves are desired, as with character generation. Similar to sub-pixel positioning, it is a method of compensating for the limited resolution of the screen. It accomplishes this by removing "jaggies," thereby smoothing diagonal lines and curves.

The Alpha channel contains transparency information for each pixel. Many video professionals are surprised to learn that some PC-based graphics software products, such as Photoshop, are more capable of creating and handling Alpha channel information than a more professional broadcast paint system. To the video professional, this transparency information is a key signal that defines which parts of the video frame are transparent, which are opaque, and which semitransparent.

The most common example of this can be seen on most newscasts. The character generator used to overlay the type on the screen contains an Alpha channel. The layering device uses the Alpha channel to determine which parts of the overlay (the letters) will be opaque and which parts will be filled with the background image (e.g., a reporter standing in front of City Hall). Uses for this include compositing 3D, computer-generated graphic animations into 2D backgrounds.

Recommendations for Video and Audio Capture

Video Considerations

The basic shooting goals for compressed video are to:

1. Limit the amount of picture content that changes from one frame to the next
2. Limit the amount of textured detail in the picture (clothing, backgrounds, etc.)

The following listing of tips naturally follow from these two basic goals. If possible, always use a stationary (tripod-mounted) camera, especially for "talking heads," office interiors, and even outside location shots. This is probably the single most important factor for high-quality compressed video.

- Plan for limited motion in and through the scene. For example, if you are shooting a talking head, put the person in a chair that cannot rock back and forth. If the subject is particularly animated, shoot from farther back to reduce the amount of motion in the frame.
- Have the subject wear bright colors. Red, pink, yellow, and light blue solids are good. Black and navy are bad because dark colors generate video "noise," which gets interpreted as changing frame contents and is thus unnecessarily encoded.
- Have your subject wear solids instead of patterns. Herringbone, checks, stripes, and prints all contain complicated edge details that must be encoded and compressed, thus taking precious bits away from the details you want to render, such as facial expressions and moving lips. These color and pattern recommendations also apply to background detail. It is preferable to shoot the subject in front

of a piece of uniformly colored, seamless paper than sitting in front of a bookcase filled with books or a window covered by venetian blinds.

■ Plan for "settle time" after transitions (e.g., titles, screen shots, cuts). Suppose you are creating a training video and shooting screen shots of a computer application. You show the mouse clicking on a menu item, and a sub-menu drops down. The sub-menu will be a bit blurry when it first makes its appearance. Wait a few seconds for the text to become clear.

■ Use large, clear fonts for titles, credits, supers, computer screen shots, etc. The picture is going to be small to begin with, and it will be difficult to read fine print in a compressed image. Larger text will make viewers much more comfortable. Avoid rapid-fire "music video"-style cuts, dissolves, wipes, pans, zooms, special effects, etc. Images that are not on the screen for more than a second or two will not have a chance to resolve themselves to clarity.

■ If you have the flexibility, short depth-of-field is preferable soft; out-of-focus backgrounds are easier to code than sharply defined complicated details and textures. Choose a shorter shutter speed and a wider aperture to reduce depth-of-field. Do not use automatic exposure controls — maintain constant brightness. For example, while shooting an interior location, as people move into and out of the scene, the background light level should not change. Changing background lighting levels will be interpreted as changes in frame contents and will be unnecessarily encoded. Brighter lighting gets coded better — avoid dark frame contents, large shadows, etc. Dimly lit areas can generate video "noise," which will be interpreted as changing frame contents and will be unnecessarily encoded.

■ Digitize video in uncompressed format. After connecting the video source to your computer's video capture board, capture digital video in uncompressed format. If your video is already compressed when passing it to the video processing software, the file that results will not be of as high quality as it would be if the software operates on uncompressed digital video.

Audio Considerations

Here are some tips for achieving high-quality compressed audio:

■ Use a good microphone to reduce or eliminate background noise as much as possible. For "talking heads," use a wired (not wireless) clip-on lavalier microphone. In crowded areas, use a shotgun or boom microphone — as directional as possible.

■ Do not use a camcorder's built-in microphone. These microphones generally pick up motor noise in the camcorder itself, in addition to omnidirectional sounds in a noisy environment.

■ Set microphone gain properly. If the gain is too high, clipping or distortion can result. If it is too low, the audio may be too faint to be encoded properly or heard upon playback.

■ Understand the limitations of the audio compression algorithm on which your software standardizes. The audio heard at the far end, when decompressed, will be of telephone "toll quality." The frequency range of the audio will be between 300 and 3400 Hz. Do not expect to hear high sibilant treble or booming bass sounds. G.726 audio lends itself quite well to a single human speaker, not as well to music, and somewhat poorly to a simultaneous combination of speech and music.

■ Avoid higher sampling rates, avoid 8-bit samples, and avoid stereo sampling.

Applications and Design Considerations in Using Audio

Several different types of audio output — speech, music, and sound effects — can be incorporated into audio on the Internet. To use each type effectively, developers must learn more about how each of the types can be used to improve their content.

Speech

Two types of speech are available for use: (1) digitized and (2) synthesized. Digitized speech provides high-quality, natural speech but requires significant disk-storage capacity. Synthesized speech is not as storage intensive but may not sound as natural as human speech.

Speech is an important element of human communication and can be used effectively to transmit information. One advantage of using natural speech is the power of the human voice to persuade. Another advantage is that speech can potentially eliminate the need to display large amounts of text.

Music

Music is also an important component of human communication. It is used to set a mood or tone, provide connections or transitions, add interest or excitement, and evoke emotion. Music, especially when combined with speech and sound effects, can greatly enhance the presentation of text and visuals.

Sound Effects

Sound effects are used to enhance or augment the presentation of information. Two types of sound effects are natural and synthetic. Natural sounds are unadorned, commonplace sounds that occur around us. Synthetic sounds are those that are produced electronically or artificially.

There are two general categories of sound effects: (1) ambient and (2) special. Ambient sounds are the background sounds that communicate the context of the screen or place. Special sounds are uniquely identifiable sounds, such as the ring of a telephone, that complement narration and or visuals.

Narration

To produce high-quality recorded speech, a script should be written and professionally recorded. To provide balance, both female and male narrators should be used. Nonprofessional narrators, such as corporate officers can be used to provide credibility. When content must be explained or information must be delivered accurately, a professional can be relied upon to follow the specifications of the script and deliver a professional-sounding audio track.

To be effective, a narrator should:

1. Vary intonation to motivate, explain, provoke, exhort, or empathize.
2. Use a conversational tone.
3. Be amiable, candid, sincere, and straightforward.
4. Avoid sounding arrogant, pretentious, flippant, disrespectful, or sarcastic.
5. Avoid a lecturing tone.

When recording narrative speech, be sure to eliminate background or ambient sound unless it is used to provide a realistic environment. On occasion, incorporating ambient sound can be effective because it can be used to help establish a mood or increase the feeling of reality.

Developing the Speech

Good writing techniques are essential to the development of successful Webcasting programs. Thus, to integrate speech as an effective tool, developers must learn to write an effective narration as part of a program script. General guidelines for this activity can be gathered from the techniques used for scriptwriting for other media:

1. Write the way people speak.
2. Use language the audience can understand.
3. Write as if the narrator were teaching or speaking with one person.
4. Write in a clear, straightforward manner.
5. Write in short sentences that can be spoken in a single breath.
6. Use second-person pronouns — you and your.
7. Use contractions and other simplified forms that are used in speech.
8. Emphasize clarity and simplicity.
9. Omit needless words.
10. Avoid slang.
11. Avoid oral presentation of figures and statistics.
12. Use humor when appropriate.
13. Present information in small chunks.
14. Emphasize the objectives or goals of the Webcast.
15. Interpret what the user is seeing rather than simply describe it.
16. Make the visuals and. narration go hand-in-hand; usually the visuals tell the story and the narration interprets, explains, or elaborates.
17. Adhere to time limits and length requirements.
18. Understand the capabilities and limitations of Internet hardware and software, especially as related to the use of speech.

Narration should be read aloud and then revised if it sounds awkward, stilted, or boring. To raise the level of user interest, quotes, conversations, conversations, and case studies could be included in audio scripts.

Selecting Music

Few articles or books have been written that provide detailed information or guidelines about the effective use of music in interactive programs. Some suggest that incorporating music begins with identifying the function of the music and making it an integral element of the script. Thus, the use of music should be considered as the program is being visualized and the script written. In general, music can be used to:

1. Establish mood
2. Set the pace
3. Signal a turn of events
4. Indicate progress and activity
5. Provide transitions and continuity

6. Evoke emotion
7. Accompany titles or introduction information
8. Emphasize important points
9. Support visual information
10. Add interest, realism, and surprise

Music can have a wide variety of effects on its listeners. It is not only "background," but also works in conjunction with the visual message to provide interest, excitement, tension, or realism. Because music plays an important storytelling role, it should fit the pace and mood of the presentation and appeal to the audience's lifestyle, taste, and workplace position. Guidelines to accomplish this include:

1. Make music an integral part from the start, rather than try to find music to "go with" imagery later.
2. Choose a music style that conveys the mood you wish to create.
3. Convey personality through instrumentation.
4. Use recurring themes as musical signatures to help the audience feel familiar with a characters, place, or segment.
5. Use tempo, dynamics, and pitch to establish energy levels.
6. Use different styles of music and instrumentation to suggest time periods, cultures, locations, and sense of place.
7. Use musical genres to communicate to specific audiences: for example, big band sounds for older audiences, or rap, metal, or pop for teenagers.
8. Know when to hold them, and when to fold them. Music should not compete with the narration or overwhelm the message of the program.

Selecting Sound Effects

Natural, ambient sounds are an integral part of our daily lives. We use them to help us interpret and assess our surroundings. For example, we listen to the "thunk" of a car door to find out if it has closed properly.

Sound, or non-speech audio, can provide different types of messages, including alarms or warnings and status or monitoring messages. Alarms and warnings are sounds and signals that interrupt and alert a listener. These sounds, such as fire alarms and police sirens, normally are loud and easily identifiable. Status and monitoring messages are sounds that give us information about ongoing tasks. The click of the keys on the keyboard is an example of these typically short sounds. Status and monitoring sounds fade rapidly from the listener's awareness and are significant only when they indicate a change — for example, when the sound does *not* occur.

There are several other categories of sound:

1. *Physical events:* we can identify whether a dropped glass bounced or shattered.
2. *Invisible structures:* tapping a wall helps us to locate where to hang a picture.
3. *Dynamic change:* as we pour liquid into a glass, we can hear when it is full.
4. *Abnormal structures:* we can tell when the car engine is malfunctioning by its sound.
5. *Events in space:* we can hear someone approaching by the sound of footsteps.

Not only can sound effects provide specific information about an environment or setting, but they can also be used to accomplish the following tasks:

1. Create atmosphere
2. Add realism
3. Emphasize important points
4. Indicate progress or activity
5. Increase interest
6. Establish mood
7. Cue or prompt users
8. Increase users' motivation

Three significant considerations should govern the use of sound effects:

1. They must be clear and easily identifiable.
2. They should not overwhelm the primary message.
3. They should be appropriate for the intended audience.

General Guidelines

1. To maximize the use of audio, carefully analyze the target audience, delivery environment, and content.
2. Clearly define why and how audio will be used.
3. Whenever possible, integrate audio into the whole program, and do it from the start of the project.
4. Develop detailed scripts or storyboards.
5. Allow users to control the audio.
6. Make sound effects meaningful.

7. Use the highest-quality audio possible, given the storage constraints of the Internet.
8. Collaborate with others who have experience using different types of audio.
9. Learn more about the use of sound, especially music.

Audio Hints

The staff members at Real Networks have become experts at squeezing out the best sound from the limited bandwidth of the Internet. Here is what they recommend:

1. *Use a good original source.* A high-quality audio source is probably the single most important variable in determining final audio quality. They start with satellite signals, audio compact discs, or digital audio tapes. When creating sounds from scratch, they use professional-quality microphones. You can make sound files from low-quality analog cassettes, tiny condenser microphones, or anything else — but the hiss and distortion in the resulting sound file will have a substantial adverse effect on clarity after the file is encoded.

   You should always encode from 16-bit (not 8-bit or mu-law) sound files. They also recommend digitizing at a 22,050-Hz sample rate.

2. *Set your input levels correctly.* Setting correct levels is absolutely crucial. When creating the original sound file, the input level should be set to use the full range of available amplitude, while avoiding clipping. Clipping is audible as a high-frequency crackling noise, and is what occurs if you try to send too much input to your soundcard (or any other piece of audio equipment).

   When digitizing with your sound card, first do several test runs and adjust your input level so the input approaches but does not exceed the maximum level. You can adjust this on the mixer page of your soundcard utilities. Look for the Input Levels or Recording Levels option. Most mixer pages have some sort of visual display where you can see how much sound is coming in. Make sure there are no peaks above maximum. These are generally indicated by a red light somewhere. Be conservative with your levels; you never know when someone will get excited and speak much louder, or when a great play at a sports event will make a crowd roar. Differences in volume levels can be evened out later.

   Sound files that do not use the full amplitude range will produce poor-quality encoded files. If the amplitude range of an existing file is too low, you can use your audio editor's increase amplitude or increase volume command to adjust the range before encoding the levels automatically.

Note, however, that better quality will be achieved if the levels are set correctly at the time of recording. The good news is that once you set your input levels correctly, they generally will not need to be reset. If you are reasonably consistent with your recording practices, you will save yourself a lot of trouble in the long run.

3. *Use high-quality equipment.* High-quality equipment will produce better results and save you a lot of headaches in the long run. Every piece of equipment in the audio chain, from the microphone to the soundcard to the software, will have an effect on your encoded files. If you intend to make sound a big part of your Web site, you should invest in professional-quality audio equipment. This need not be a crippling investment, but it does mean you will have to purchase from a professional recording equipment dealer, not your local computer/hi-fi/gadget store.

4. *Select appropriate material.* If you want to encode music for transmission over 14.4-Kbps phone lines, remember that the simpler the source, the better chance that the encoded version will be faithful to the original. There is not enough bandwidth in a 14.4 line to do justice to a harmonically complex signal (such as a full orchestra). Many folks have used music successfully in their 14.4 clips as background, where fidelity is not as important an issue.

5. *Correcting DC offset.* Sometimes when files are digitized, something known as *DC offset* creeps in. This is when the digitized waveform is not correctly centered around the 0 volts axis. Most of this is due to improper grounding of soundcards Some soundcards are worse than others; to see how bad your soundcard is, try recording silence. You should, in theory, see nothing in the waveform window, but you will probably see a flat line just slightly above or below the 0 volts axis. This is DC offset.

This can wreak havoc when you attempt to process the waveform, and can add a low rumbling sound to the encoded file. Luckily, most editors have a built-in facility to take care of this. Some call it "centering the wave" and are automatic; others allow you to adjust DC offset manually *(+1–)*. In this case, you will have to find out precisely what your DC offset is by running a "statistics" command or something similar. Then you will have to correct it. For example, if your average DC offset is 45, you will want to offset the wave by –45.

Obviously, if you are doing a live broadcast, you will have to live with whatever DC offset there is. Properly balanced wiring between all your audio components will help minimize this as well as any ground loops.

6. *Noise gating (or expansion).* Noise gating, or downward expansion, eliminates unwanted background noise that becomes audible during pauses in the audio (e.g., when an announcer pauses, or there is a gap between programs). Signals above a certain volume level are left alone, but below this level the signal is turned down or even off, depending on how heavy the gating or expansion is. Setting up a noise gate or expander is straightforward. Most budget compressors have a built-in noise gate.

   To use noise gating, set the threshold control so that the gating or expansion occurs when there is no desired audio, but not so high that the beginnings of words or music that you want to hear are chopped off. It takes a bit of time, but remember to err on the side of caution just in case the next person in the program has a softer voice.

   If your gate or expander has a range control, set this to around 5 to 10 dB. This means it will turn down the "noise" sections a little, but not turn them off altogether. That way you will hear if the gate is cutting something off that you want to hear, and you can then readjust the threshold setting accordingly.

7. *Compression.* One of the side effects of digital encoding is artifacts — sounds that were not there before encoding. These can be heard sometimes as rumbling or distortion in the signal. These artifacts appear at a relatively constant low level, whether the original soundfile was loud or quiet. Louder files tend to mask these quiet artifacts, so it is recommended to feed the encoder a loud signal. However, we are limited by the loudest section of the file being encoded. If we could turn down the loudest section, we could turn up the overall volume of the soundfile. A compressor helps us accomplish this.

   Compression reduces the difference between the loudest and quietest sections of the incoming signal. Sections that exceed a user-defined threshold are turned down. Now that these loud sections have been turned down, we can turn up the overall volume of the soundfile. How much the sections are turned up or down depends on how much compression you use.

   How much compression should you use? The exact settings will be determined by experience and by referring to the manual that comes with your equipment or software. However, for speech, it is recommended that you use moderate to extreme compression (4:1 to 10:1).

8. *Equalization.* Equalization (or EQ) changes the tone of the incoming signal just as you can on your home stereo or car radio. This is done by "boosting" (turning up) or "cutting" (turning down)

certain frequencies. Using EQ, we can boost frequencies that we like (where the important content is) and cut frequencies where there is noise or unwanted sound. By doing this, we can give the encoder a big hint about which sound information to keep. Encoding discards a lot of the high-end, or treble information. This can make files sound dull. To compensate for this, it helps to boost the middle frequencies or midrange. This will also make speech sound more intelligible.

Most good mixing boards will have a midrange EQ knob. Sometimes you can choose which frequency to boost; other times this is preset at the factory. If not, or if you are using a graphic equalizer or audio processing software, you will want to boost at around 2.5 KHz.

If your equipment does not have a mid-frequencies EQ knob, you can obtain a similar result by turning down the low and high EQ knobs and then turning up the overall volume (note, however, that this is not as effective as boosting the *mids,* which attacks the problem at its source).

The amount that you should turn up the midrange depends on your EQ equipment and source file. A little experimentation is necessary. Try adding some *mids* to a short section of a piece to be encoded and check it with the RealAudio Player. If it is a bit muddy or difficult to understand, try adding a little more. You can keep going until the knob will not turn anymore, or until the result starts to sound too harsh.

For digital audio encoded at a low Kbps, it is important to try to make the voice as full as possible in the middle frequencies. This is where the majority of speech information is contained. What we are trying to do is lift the voice away from any background noise.

Some signals can also be improved by rolling off (turning down) the bass frequencies. Side effects of encoding are sometimes audible as a lower voice "shadowing" the original. This is particularly noticeable with women speakers. When this effect is too prominent, try rolling off the bass and encoding the result. The artifacts will not disappear, but sometimes they will be quieter. Be careful not to make the voice sound too thin or brittle.

For audio played back at low Kbps, much more of the fidelity of the original recording is retained, so you will not need to worry about EQ as much. It still helps to boost at around 2.5 KHz to compensate for the high frequency loss, but boosting too much will make music sound thin and tinny.

9. *Normalization.* Normalization is a process included in most audio recording software whereby the computer calculates exactly how much it can turn up the volume of a file without distortion. Because we always want to feed the encoder the loudest files possible, this is a very handy function. This is why you can afford to be fairly conservative with your recording input levels, and then let your program's normalization function take care of the rest. Normalization should be the last thing you do. If you normalize your file and then add some EQ, you will end up with distortion.

Appendix D

Web Site Evaluation

1. Executive Summary

The evaluation techniques described in this document can be used to assess the effectiveness of any Web site. The specific methodologies used for an evaluation depend on what is already known about the site and its users, and the resources available for the evaluation. The methodologies can be summarized as follows, according to the sequence in which they are likely to be used and what is learned from each:

- Background information
  - Document analysis
  - Literature review and Web site reviews
- Web site information
  - Site mapping
  - Webmaster and staff questionnaires
- Usability and accessibility issues
  - Heuristic review/expert panel
  - Usability testing
- User information
  - Web server log analysis
  - E-mail content analysis
- Customer service
  - Customer satisfaction questionnaire
  - Customer satisfaction focus group

The first steps are collecting background information and information about the characteristics of the site to be evaluated through document analysis, literature reviews, site mapping, and Webmaster questionnaires. To look at customer satisfaction, usability, and accessibility issues and conduct focus groups, more specialized skills and knowledge are required. Each of these methodologies is more labor-intensive than the more automated tasks, but each provides high quality information and the evaluator has considerable control over the type of information collected.

The overall evaluation design focuses on the experience of the user and is organized around performance measures that can be used in preparing responses to federal legislation and Executive Orders. Together, the evaluation methodologies are complementary in their focus on specific performance measures — extensiveness, customer service, effectiveness, and impact — that can be used to assess the Web site.

2. Investigative Methodologies

Document Analysis

To the extent that they are available, the identification and review of existing documents can help the Web site evaluator understand several key items: the purpose and original conceptualization of the site; the stakeholders that should be interviewed or surveyed; the documents that have been cleared for publication on the site (and which may or may not have been published); and the target audiences of the site. Documentation of a Web development effort is likely to be in the form of e-mail messages, minutes from Web committee meetings, and handwritten notes in individual committee members' files.

Site Mapping

A graphical representation of the document structure of a Web site provides an excellent overview of the site content and the relationships among the documents.

Web Master and Staff Survey

Data collected directly from staff involved in Web site administration can provide a picture of the performance of Web technology and the Web development process, and the resources expended. QRC developed a multi-segmented questionnaire with skip patterns that allows selective responses from individuals who have specialized knowledge about various aspects of Web site development and administration. The data collection instrument consists of questions in six sections:

- Contact information
- Web server hardware and operating system software
- Web server software
- Networking or connectivity to the Web server
- Publication of static Web content, such as "pure" HTML pages
- Publication of dynamic Web content, such as multimedia, CGI-scripted, or database- or program-generated pages

As the first step of the Webmaster and staff survey, individuals identified by the Web site evaluator during the document review and analysis or from interviews are e-mailed an invitation to participate. The invitation should clearly state the purpose of the evaluation and the questionnaire, how responses will be treated with respect to confidentiality, and the release and due dates of the survey.

Expert Critique

Heuristic usability evaluations (also called "expert reviews" or "usability audits") are an efficient method of assessing a Web site for usability. This methodology provides for one or more usability professionals who are familiar with industry best practices in user interface design to evaluate an application or an entire Web site based on recognized rules of thumb. The objective is to identify possible difficulties that site users may have with the current interface and to recommend design improvements.

Heuristic evaluation of a Web site by a small group of experts can provide the first indication of areas for improvement and indicate what is likely to be most effective on the site.

It is important to distinguish between heuristic evaluations of a Web site user interface and other types of design reviews. Heuristic evaluations focus on established design rules. Typically, the emphasis is not on comprehensively examining the functionality of the site. More often the review is conducted in the context of typical user tasks or "use cases." The emphasis is on providing feedback to the site's developers on the extent that the "look and feel" seems consistent with industry best practices and is likely to be compatible with the intended users' needs and preferences.

While a review conducted by one usability expert can provide very valuable information about a Web site, a panel of independent experts can offer the combined expertise of individuals with different points of view. Within the past few years, Web usability research has begun to expand beyond classic Human-Computer Interaction (HCI) research. While HCI continues to provide the foundation for usability research, other related disciplines offer insight into areas that directly affect the success of a Web site. These include:

- Information architecture and information design
- Accessibility and assistive technology
- Usability and marketing or branding

Summary of Investigative Methodologies

The investigative methodologies provide background information, structural and functional information about the Web site, and information about usability and accessibility deficiencies. Some approaches are relatively automated (e.g., site mapping), while others vary in their degree of manual involvement.

Document analysis provides background information about the development and purposes of the site. The availability of information will vary, depending on whether the process was systematically documented. The need for the information will vary, depending on the longevity of involvement of the current Webmaster and other Web site development and maintenance staff. The literature and Web site reviews available represent a body of knowledge that is growing, but which may be adequate without any augmentation, depending upon the Web site evaluator's needs and the amount of time elapsed since preparation of this report.

Site mapping and Webmaster questionnaires provide information about the structure and function of the Web site. The need to use these tools depends on the knowledge the Web site evaluator has about the site being evaluated. Current site maps may exist. Likewise, a well-informed Webmaster may have up-to-date information about hardware, software, development and maintenance activities, levels of effort, and other details of the site.

Once the investigative methodologies are employed as needed, the Web site evaluation should collect information from and about the site's users — who they are, the information they are seeking, the questions they are asking, the usability and accessibility challenges they face, and their satisfaction with the Web site. These are the user-centered methodologies.

3. User-Centered Methodologies

Usability Tests

Unlike the expert critique, usability tests are conducted using representative Web site users. Users are systematically observed as they perform realistic tasks like searching for information or otherwise utilizing the functionality of the site. The tests are typically conducted by a human factors engineer or other usability professional using a script of test scenarios developed from information obtained during the heuristic review. Such tests produce high quality data and can reveal the extent to which a Web site or application meets users' needs, and the extent to which it can be readily used and learned. The test is often conducted in a laboratory setting with audio-video equipment to record and measure performance; however, such equipment is now available in portable units that can be taken into most workplaces or field settings. Typical measures that are utilized include:

- The incidence of various usability problems (derived from observations of performance or user comments)
- The time required to accomplish specific tasks or subtasks
- The nature and incidence of various user errors or failures to accomplish tasks
- Subjective ratings of user satisfaction along various design dimensions

A typical process for conducting a usability test would include the following steps:

Planning the Test. The Test Administrator becomes acquainted with the Web site, and through a heuristic review identifies specific usability issues. With the assistance of the Web site developer or Webmaster, the Test Administrator defines the test objectives and clarifies the performance measures to be used. The Test Administrator then develops the experimental design, and determines the number and characteristics of participants required for the test and the appropriate configuration of recording equipment to be used (if any).

Preparing the Test. The necessary equipment, both that which the participant will use and any observational recording equipment to be utilized, is set up, the materials to be used are readied, and the participants are recruited and scheduled. Test participants are typically offered an honorarium. The materials needed typically include task scenarios (i.e., the tasks to be accomplished by the test participants), notes for briefing and debriefing the participants, and any questionnaires to be used to gather demographic information from participants or quantify their perceptions of the site. Often a coding scheme is devised to facilitate the collection of observational data with regard to specific behaviors, events, or expected participant comments.

Data Collection. Test participants are typically observed individually for approximately 1.5 hours as they attempt to accomplish the predefined tasks. The sessions are usually videotaped; a real-time, scan-converted image of the users' computer screens can be particularly informative. Depending upon the purposes of the test and the usability challenges that are anticipated, the Test Administrator may observe relatively unobtrusively or may carry on a running dialog with the test participant to obtain user feedback on various design issues. Of interest may be the participants' performance, how they go about accomplishing the tasks, and their comments as they proceed. The data collected can consist of notes, documentation of the time taken to accomplish various tasks, such as a search for specific information, and participant questionnaire responses. A data logging software package may be used to facilitate the collection of time-stamped observational notes.

Analysis. Depending upon the objectives of the evaluation, the analysis phase may involve compiling and categorizing the usability problems observed, transferring the data logs to a database package or spreadsheet in order to better summarize the coded observations, or calculating summary statistics on the subjective ratings data collected. Audio and video recordings of the test sessions can be reviewed as needed. Typically, an attempt is made to categorize the severity of the usability problems that emerged, taking into account the effect on user task performance, incidence, and frequency of occurrence of each problem.

Reporting. The usability test objectives, methods, results, and any design recommendations are documented in a written report. Design change recommendations for improving the Web site are offered as needed. Often the suggested design changes involve screen design or informational architecture. However, some problems can also be addressed in online help or user documentation, by briefing help desk personnel (i.e., call center technical support), or in user education programs. If sufficient cost estimates and return on investment data are available, a cost-benefit analysis of alternative means for dealing with design deficiencies may be helpful in deciding how to ameliorate the usability problems observed.

Usability testing includes users' overall impression of the site's home page and an assessment of navigation, including both the "search" option and following the structure of the site. Test procedures are adapted as needed to the special circumstances of accessibility-challenged test participants. After each task, test participants are asked to rate, on a scale of 1 to 9, the ease or difficulty of navigation, and the ease or difficulty of understanding the content of the material they found.

Transaction Log Analysis

Analysis of Web server transaction logs provides comprehensive information about Web server traffic. Typically conducted as an automated procedure with log analyzer software, all activity of the Web server is logged, including data such as the IP address or domain of the individual requesting a Web page from the server, the date and time the request was made, the filename of the page accessed, and the number of bytes of data served.

E-mail Content Analysis

E-mail messages containing comments, questions, and feedback on a Web site provide valuable insights into the kinds of informational needs users have and the types of problems they encounter with the site. Content analysis is a method used to categorize and analyze textual information, such as e-mail messages. Content analysis is a technique used to classify sets of words (textual or verbal) that relies on the judgment of an analyst or group of analysts who seek to find patterns in the data. Rigor is introduced into the methodology through the measurement and emphasis on reliability and the replicability of observations and subsequent interpretations.

The main issue to consider when conducting an e-mail content analysis is the derivation of a content analytic coding scheme. This should include developing the categories, creating the dimensions needed to understand the nature of a particular message (i.e., question), and assigning the coding rules to be used for each e-mail message.

Customer Satisfaction Focus Groups

The flexible environment of a focus group provides subjective feedback and adds a dimension of research that is not available from other sources. Focus groups are also an excellent source of information on why people make certain decisions, how they arrive at decisions, and how they might respond in proposed situations.

Conducting customer satisfaction focus groups online obtains the same information as face-to-face focus groups, and produces other benefits. Anyone in the world with a computer, Web browser, and Internet access can participate, moderate, or administer. State, regional, and national boundaries are eliminated; in a typical focus group, participation would be limited to an immediate local area. Comments are often more thoughtful and useful, and a transcript is automatically produced, eliminating many hours of labor needed to transcribe recorded conversations. Online focus group participants must obviously have a basic level of computer literacy, but this is appropriate because our topic is dealing with a Web site and online health information sources.

A typical process for conducting an online customer satisfaction focus group would include the following steps:

Recruitment. The moderator works with the client to determine the user population from which to recruit the online focus group members. Text for a recruitment screener (i.e., a Web page) is developed, and the Webmaster places a link to the screener on the Web site. The responses are monitored, and a follow-up e-mail is sent to qualified and interested individuals. A test log-in site is set up, and potential participants then attempt to log in. Finally, a reminder e-mail is sent the day before the focus group is scheduled to those participants who have successfully completed the test login.

Preparation. The moderator develops a guide, online presentation materials, and an online feedback survey for the focus group. Within one week of the focus group, a walk-through is conducted with the administrator, the moderator, and a few "dummy" participants. This ensures that the system is functioning, and provides a chance to review the materials and procedures one last time. Also during this time, test log-ins may be conducted by anyone wanting to observe the online focus group "silently."

Implementing the online focus group. A Web-integrated, real-time chat solution is used to conduct online focus groups. This software allows individuals and groups of users across the world to talk to each other in virtual space using the Internet. Prior to the start of the online focus group, an introductory slide is placed on the site for participants to read as they log in. The moderator welcomes participants and observers, and specifies the ground rules. At the assigned time, the online focus group begins with group members introducing themselves. The online focus group is conducted in the same manner as a face-to-face focus group (i.e., the discussion is moderated, and everyone is given a chance to provide input to the questions). Following the online focus group, a complete transcript is produced and edited. An online feedback survey is administered at the conclusion of the focus group session. Survey results are tabulated and a final written analysis is produced.

Customer Satisfaction Questionnaires

The use of online surveys is a cost-effective way to gather Web site customer satisfaction information from a large and geographically dispersed population. A Web-based questionnaire can assess customer satisfaction with the Web site and many of the issues explored in the customer satisfaction focus groups.

Placement of the online survey is likely to be an important determinant of response rate and the types of respondents who participate. A sample selection of questionnaire respondents is non-random (self-selected), regardless of where a questionnaire is positioned on a Web site. Demographic information collected by the survey helps to characterize respondents, but care should be taken in generalizing responses to all Web site visitors.

The questionnaire results can provide information about the variety and characteristics of users participating in the survey, how they learned about the Web site, and how frequently they have used it. Questions can be designed to target user satisfaction with content and design, and to identify valuable new services and features that users may desire. Respondents can also provide information about how the Web site under review compares to other Web-based sources of similar information.

The process for conducting an online customer satisfaction survey includes the following steps:

Development. The survey instrument is developed based on research questions that have been identified. The questions are formatted using a Web-enabled survey software package. Placement of the survey is determined based on level of traffic through the site, as well as the survey objectives.

Implementation. A link inviting participation in the survey is placed on the Web site and responses are monitored daily. Placement of the link may be adjusted based on the number of responses received from a given location. A pilot test period can help determine the best placement. The link and the data collection instrument should remain available until the desired number of responses is obtained. A total of 45 to 50 responses is usually sufficient.

Reporting. After the data collection is complete and the survey is removed from the Web site, data is stored in database records for analysis. Closed-ended questions (e.g., scales and pick lists) are tabulated and summarized by category of respondent; open-ended questions are coded and categorized.

Summary of User-Centered Methodologies

The user-centered methodologies provide information from and about Web site users regarding the usability and accessibility of the site, user characteristics and interests, and customer satisfaction with the form and content of the site. As with investigative methodologies, the approaches vary in the extent to which they require the direct participation of the Web site evaluator. Web server log analysis is a relatively automated methodology. Two methodologies, usability testing and online customer satisfaction focus groups, require specialized knowledge, skills, and equipment. The customer satisfaction questionnaire should use a well-constructed and pre-tested instrument.

Usability testing reveals the extent to which the Web site meets the users' needs and expectations, and the extent to which it can be readily used. It can also be used to assess the accessibility of the Web site to disabled or accessibility-challenged users. Individuals recruited to participate in usability testing should be selected from among members of the Web site's intended audience.

Web server log and e-mail content analyses provide information about Web site users. Analysis of the server transaction logs provides information about the domain of the user and the most popular pages and access times. E-mail content analysis categorizes and summarizes messages from users to Webmasters or other individuals who are responsible for site content. Content analysis was pilot tested using questions submitted by users via e-mail. The methodology can also be used to compile information about users' comments as well as staff responses to users' comments and questions.

Customer satisfaction surveys are used to collect information from a large and geographically dispersed user population. The customer satisfaction questionnaire collects subjective information in a primarily close-ended format for easier analysis and reporting. The customer satisfaction focus group collects similar information in a format designed to obtain more qualitative data, which allows for real-time probing for additional information when required. When conducted online, customer satisfaction focus groups also collect information from a geographically dispersed user population.

4. Performance Measurement

The investigative and user-centered methodologies provide a practical suite of tools and approaches that are complementary in their focus on specific performance measures that can be used to assess the effectiveness of a Web site. There is some overlap in the constructs that are measured by each methodology; multiple methodologies contribute to understanding and measuring a single performance metric, and a single methodology can contribute to several performance measurements. The overall evaluation design focuses on the experience of the user and is organized around four performance measures.

Extensiveness

This performance measure includes the extensiveness of the services and information provided and the users reached. The following methodologies can be used to understand and evaluate this performance measure:

- Document analysis — to identify and define the intended audience
- Site mapping — to illustrate Web site size, content, and organization
- Webmaster and staff questionnaires — to understand services provided and resources used
- Transaction log analysis — to identify domains of Web site users
- E-mail content analysis — to characterize Web site users based on the information they are seeking
- Customer satisfaction questionnaires — to characterize Web site users and where they are seeking specific types of information

Customer Service

This performance measure includes responsiveness or level of customer service, the intuitive provision of content, and user satisfaction with the design and content. The following methodologies can be used to understand and evaluate this performance measure:

- Webmaster and staff questionnaires — to determine use of resources, responsiveness to users, efforts to design and assess accessibility and/or usability, and how content is managed
- Expert review/expert panel — to assess usability of content
- Usability tests — to determine probable incidence and type of usability problems encountered by users
- Transaction log analysis — to determine responsiveness of Web server to users and use of search engine
- E-mail content analysis — to identify areas for improvement on basis of comments and questions
- Customer satisfaction focus groups — to assess user satisfaction with content and design; comparison with other similar sites
- Customer satisfaction questionnaires — to assess user satisfaction with content and design; comparison with other similar sites; to identify need for new services or content

Effectiveness

This performance measure includes an assessment of how well the Web site is meeting its mission and objectives. This assessment can include an evaluation of the availability of the site to accessibility-challenged users, whether users can find what they are looking for, and how the site compares to other sites with similar missions. The following methodologies can be used to understand and evaluate this performance measure:

- Document analysis — to identify individuals responsible for content and service; to identify purpose of Web site
- Literature and Web site reviews — to collect information on current standards and other similar sites
- Webmaster and staff questionnaires — to identify efforts to assess accessibility and usability, how content is managed, and resources used to serve content
- Expert critique/expert panel — to assess usability and accessibility of site to determine whether objectives and mission can be achieved
- Usability tests — to assess the extent to which the Web site meets users' expectations and is available to accessibility-challenged individuals
- Transaction log analysis — to identify "most popular" Web pages
- Email content analysis — to assess how well content and design match user needs, based on comments and questions received
- Customer satisfaction focus groups — to assess the extent to which users are finding the information they need and how the Web site compares with other sources of information
- Customer satisfaction questionnaires — to assess the extent to which users are finding the information they need and how the Web site compares with other sources of information

Impact

This performance measure assesses the impact or benefit to the user, including comparisons to other sources of health information and effects on attitudes or behavior. This is the most qualitative and most difficult performance measure to assess. The following methodologies can be used to understand and evaluate this performance measure:

- Expert critique/expert panel — to assess the usability and accessibility of the Web site, both of which affect the benefit to users
- E-mail content analysis — to identify anecdotal evidence of benefit and possible effect on users
- Customer satisfaction focus groups — to identify and assess information and services that benefit Web site users and compare benefit with other similar sites

- Customer satisfaction questionnaires — to identify and assess information and services that benefit Web site users and compare benefit with other similar sites

5. Conclusion

The Evaluation and Performance Measures Toolkit described in this document can be used to assess the effectiveness of any Web site. The specific methodologies used for an evaluation depend on what is already known about the site and its users, and the resources available for the evaluation. The methodologies can be summarized as follows, according to the sequence in which they are likely to be used and what is learned from each:

- Background information
  - Document analysis
  - Literature review and Web site reviews
- Information about the Web site
  - Site mapping
  - Webmaster and staff questionnaires
- Usability and accessibility issues
  - Heuristic review/expert panel
  - Usability testing
- Information about the users
  - Web server log analysis
  - E-mail content analysis
- Customer service
  - Customer satisfaction questionnaire
  - Customer satisfaction focus group

The first steps are collecting background information and information about the characteristics of the site to be evaluated through document analysis, literature reviews, site mapping, and Webmaster questionnaires. These tasks require research, analytic skills, and technical skills that are likely to be present on Web development staffs. The site mapping and transaction log analysis methodologies are relatively automated, while the preliminary research, document analysis, and questionnaires require more effort.

To look at usability and accessibility issues and conduct focus groups, more specialized skills and knowledge are required. This is also true for performing a content analysis of the communication with Web site users. Each of these methodologies is more labor-intensive than the automated tasks, but each should provide high quality information and the evaluator has considerable control over the type of information collected.

The customer satisfaction survey is somewhat less specialized in the skills required, since model questionnaires may be available — including the one pilot tested in this project — and posting a survey on a Web site is not technically difficult.

The overall evaluation design focuses on the experience of the user and is organized around performance measures that can be used in preparing responses to federal legislation and executive orders. Together, the evaluation methodologies are complementary in their focus on specific performance measures — extensiveness, customer service, effectiveness, and impact — that can be used to assess a Web site.

References

Excerpted from the Web Site Evaluation Design/Planning and Methodology for NIH. Retrieved May 6, 2006, from:
irm.cit.nih.gov/itmra/Webeval.doc

Appendix E

Heuristic Guidelines for Expert Critique of a Web Site

Heuristic usability evaluations (also called "expert reviews" or "usability audits") are an efficient method of assessing a Web site for usability. This methodology provides for one or more usability professionals who are familiar with industry best practices in user interface design to evaluate an application based on recognized "rules of thumb." The objective is to identify possible difficulties that users of the site may have with the current user interface and to recommend design improvements.

Heuristic Evaluations, Compliance Reviews, and Verification/Validation Evaluations

It is important to distinguish heuristic evaluations of a Web site user interface from other types of design reviews. Heuristic evaluations focus on established design rules of thumb. Typically, the emphasis is not on comprehensively examining the functionality of the site. More often, the review is conducted in the context of typical user tasks or "use cases," with an emphasis on providing feedback to the site's developers on the extent to which the "look and feel" seems consistent with industry best practices and is likely to be compatible with the intended users' needs and preferences.

Heuristic usability reviews can be contrasted with evaluations that are conducted for the purposes of assuring compliance with a chosen design style or for verification and validation of site functionality. Development teams should formulate a user interface style guide for a particular Web site to ensure the implementation of a consistent look and feel. Style compliance reviews focus on checking for such consistency, usually with the goal of systematically evaluating the entire site. Verification and validation reviews of Web sites focus on whether the interface works as intended. The validation review may examine the extent to which the interface meets users' needs and may utilize the same types of "use cases" that would be used for a heuristic evaluation. However, verification and validation reviews typically focus on site functionality, whereas heuristic evaluations focus on look and feel in the context of user tasks.

Personnel

How Many Reviewers? Heuristic evaluations are typically conducted by one or a small number of reviewers. Studies that have examined the number of usability problems identified in a user interface as a function of the number of reviewers, e.g., Nielsen (1994), have shown the advantages of involving more than one reviewer. It is difficult for any one reviewer, no matter how knowledgeable, to anticipate the full range of usability issues that a system's users may encounter. On the other hand, there are diminishing returns as additional reviewers are added. Typically, the most egregious problems are identified by most or all reviewers. Having three to five reviewers examine an interface is advisable, but meaningful reviews can be accomplished with fewer.

Qualifications of Reviewers? Because heuristic evaluations focus on the user interface design and likely user concerns, it is best if they are conducted by reviewers who are knowledgeable about industry best practices and current thinking in designing for ease of use. Design rules of thumb are subject to some interpretation, so this places a premium on the heuristic reviewer's experience and knowledge of best practices. Having completed such evaluations productively in the past is probably a better predictor of competence than any particular academic credentials. There are two professional certification programs for human factors professionals, but the field of human factors and ergonomics is broad enough that an individual having these credentials can not be guaranteed to possess current knowledge in computer-human interface technology and practices. There are many competent usability engineers who have not sought this certification. There is no particular academic discipline that "owns" usability or user interface design. Usability professionals often come to that specialty from backgrounds in experimental or cognitive psychology, industrial engineering, human factors engineering, or computer science. Heuristic evaluations are best accomplished by individuals other than those who created the interface that is under review. Prior domain knowledge about the content of the Web site is helpful, although not critical. It is useful for the reviewer to consider the business goals of the Web site, the nature of the competition, and the constraints under which the organization responsible for the Web site is operating. It is critical, however, that the reviewer examine the Web site from the perspective of a user who may not have prior domain knowledge about the Web site. Thus empathy is an important qualification for a heuristic reviewer.

Time Required to Conduct the Evaluation

Most heuristic reviews can be accomplished within days rather than hours or weeks. The time required for a heuristic evaluation of a Web site varies with the size of the site, its complexity, the purpose of the review, the nature of the usability issues that arise in the review, and the competence of the reviewers. The time required includes not only visual inspection of the site, but also understanding of the design objectives, the range of users that it is intended to accommodate, and typical user tasks (i.e., "use cases"). There is also time involved in documenting usability concerns and, if required, formulating design change recommendations. The stage of development of the Web site is another consideration. A cursory review of an early stage prototype for the purpose of assuring the developers that they are on the right track can be done more quickly than a more comprehensive review of a fully developed site for the purpose of assuring consistency in the implementation of certain design approaches.

When to Evaluate a Design?

Conducting usability evaluations early and often throughout the development process greatly facilitates user-centered design. Because heuristic evaluations can often be conducted relatively quickly, they provide a cost-effective way in which to iteratively evaluate an interface design as it proceeds through development. Heuristic evaluations can be conducted on very early stage prototypes, including paper mock-ups, as well as later stage electronic prototypes, with or without all of the "back-end" functionality implemented. Usability problems discovered early in the design process can usually be fixed more cost effectively than if the same problems are discovered later.

Design Rules of Thumb

There are several conceptualizations of usability design heuristics and best practices that are widely used. These are not mutually exclusive and, in fact, cover many of the same aspects of user interface design. The most pervasive is a set of user interface design principles that were elucidated by Nielsen (1994), based on a principal components analysis of the usability problems found in a number of studies of various user interfaces. These design principles are summarized as follows:

- *Visibility of system status.* The system should always keep users informed about what is going on, through appropriate feedback within reasonable time.
- *Match between system and real world.* The system should speak the users' language, with words, phrases, and concepts familiar to the user, rather than system-oriented terms. Follow real-world conventions, making information appear in a natural and logical order.
- *User control and freedom.* Users often choose system functions by mistake and will need a clearly marked "emergency exit" to leave the unwanted state without having to go through an extended dialogue. Support undo and redo.
- *Consistency and standards.* Users should not have to wonder whether different words, situations, or actions mean the same thing. Follow platform conventions.
- *Error prevention.* Even better than a good error message is a careful design [that] prevents a problem from occurring in the first place.
- *Recognition rather than recall.* Make objects, actions, and options visible. The user should not have to remember information from one part of the dialogue to another. Instructions for use of the system should be visible or easily retrievable whenever appropriate.
- *Flexibility and efficiency of use.* Accelerators — unseen by the novice user — may often speed up the interaction for the expert user to such an extent that the system can cater to both inexperienced and experienced users. Allow users to tailor frequent actions.
- *Aesthetic and minimalist design.* Dialogues should not contain information that is irrelevant or rarely needed. Every extra unit of information in a dialogue competes with the relevant units of information and diminishes their relative visibility.
- Help users recognize, diagnose, and recover from errors. Error messages should be expressed in plain language (no codes), precisely indicate the problem, and constructively suggest a solution.
- *Help and documentation.* The ideal system can be used without documentation, but it may often be necessary to provide help and documentation. Any such information should be easy to search,

focused on the user's task, list concrete steps to be carried out, and not be too large.

A second set of usability principles were proposed by Constantine (1994):

- *Structure Principle.* Organize the user interface purposefully, in meaningful and useful ways that put related things together and separate unrelated things based on clear, consistent models that are apparent and recognizable to others.
- *Simplicity Principle.* Make simple, common tasks simple to do, communicating simply in the user's own language and providing good shortcuts that are meaningfully related to longer procedures.
- *Visibility Principle.* Keep all needed options and materials for a given task visible without distracting the user with extraneous or redundant information.
- *Feedback Principle.* Keep users informed of actions or interpretations, changes of state or condition, and errors or exceptions using clear, concise, and unambiguous language familiar to users.
- *Tolerance Principle.* Be flexible and tolerant, reducing the cost of mistakes and misuse by allowing undoing and redoing while preventing errors wherever possible by tolerating varied inputs and sequences and by interpreting all reasonable actions reasonably.
- *Reuse Principle.* Reduce the need for users to rethink and remember by reusing internal and external components and behaviors, maintaining consistency with purpose rather than merely arbitrary consistency.

Conducting the Evaluation

Planning for a heuristic evaluation involves acquainting the reviewers with the Web site or application, specifying usability objectives, identifying the characteristics of typical users, and delineating "use cases," i.e., typical task scenarios in which the site is used. The reviewer should take full advantage of any known usability problems. Information on problems that may have surfaced from help desk type inquiries, user e-mail comments, or professional critiques by the media or industry reviewers should be incorporated into the preparation for the evaluation.

Characteristics of the Intended Users. The usability criteria against which a site is evaluated depend in part on the characteristics of its intended users. User characteristics that should be taken into account include education, domain knowledge, technological sophistication, computer literacy, and specific experience in using the Web. Also important are the types of computer platforms and Internet connectivity that users are likely to be utilizing to access the site. A Web site that is designed for scientists or medical personnel might be held to somewhat different standards than a site that is expected to be accessed by the public. While in many respects good design is good design, one might anticipate the use of certain terminology or information architecture if one can assume a particular level of user domain knowledge.

Typical Tasks. Because heuristic evaluation of a user interface is more user-centered than comprehensive, the review is usually best accomplished in the context of typical user tasks. A task analysis of the site's intended usage as well as identification of tasks that are the most frequently executed or are the most important to users will identify tasks that should be emphasized. The tasks that would be derived from such an exercise are likely to coincide with the major elements of the site's functionality. In formulating user tasks, one should consider the likely perspective of the typical user, including motivation for accessing the site, initial knowledge and assumptions, likely expectations and preferences, and their "mental model" of how the site should work. It may also be helpful to conceptualize the likely experience that the site offers to first-time users versus repeat visitors.

Examining the Site. After gathering background information on site objectives, user characteristics, and user tasks, the reviewer can proceed with a systematic examination of the site. If more than one reviewer is involved, each should work independently. The site should be accessed with computer platforms and Internet connectivity that are representative of a range of typical users. It is advisable for a reviewer to make two passes: the first to become acquainted with the overall flow of the application and the second to focus more specifically on individual elements of dialog or the look and feel (see e.g., Nielsen, 1994). Possible problems should be documented with reference to specific Web pages or on-screen design elements. It is also advisable to note the pervasiveness of each problem.

Documenting the Results

Specific statements of usability problems and design solution(s) are most helpful to developers. Usability problems noted in writing during the review can be grouped and content analyzed; observations made by different reviewers should be combined in order to determine the degree of consensus or to elucidate alternative positions. It is sometimes of interest to assign a level of severity to the usability problems revealed. One scheme (Nielsen, 1994) for assigning severity codes is to consider (1) the frequency with which users will encounter each problem (what proportion of users will encounter it and how often a given user will experience it in a single session), (2) the impact of the problem (the ease with which the user may overcome the problem), and (3) the persistence of the problem (the likelihood of encountering the problem in multiple sessions). Another scheme is to categorize severity in terms of problems that prevent task completion, those that hinder but do not prevent task completion, and those that present a nuisance or variance from what users might expect but do not significantly hinder task performance. Recognizing that it is easier to critique than to design, it is advisable for reviewers to provide design solutions, or to suggest alternatives, along with a delineation of the problems.

Usability Checklist

The following checkpoints represent a list of items a human factors engineer or other usability professional might use to analyze a Web site. They are derived from Jakob Nielsen's "Ten Usability Heuristics1," his Alertbox2 column, and *Designing Usability: The Practice of Simplicity.*

Checkpoint	Yes	No	NA
1. **Visibility of system status:** The system should always keep users informed about what is going on, through appropriate feedback within reasonable time.			
1.1 Structure helps users navigate. Without structural links, pages are orphaned in cyberspace. Provide users with a path to higher levels of navigation and content.			
1.2 Accommodate and support user-controlled navigation. Do not force users through set paths. Make alternate paths easy to follow, consistent, and logical.			

1 Nielsen, Jakob. "Ten Usability Heuristics." http://www.useit.com/papers/heuristic/heuristic_list.html
2 http://www.useit.com/alertbox/

Checkpoint		Yes	No	NA
2.	**Match between system and the real world:** The system should speak the users' language, with words, phrases, and concepts familiar to the user, rather than system-oriented terms. Follow real-world conventions, making information appear in a natural and logical order.			
2.1	Avoid using technical, scientific or legal language. On main pages of the site, create content that can be understood by a general audience.			
2.2	When creating your site's navigation, do not simply copy your organization's structure. Create a navigation design and options that reflect user tasks on your site.			
3.	**User control and freedom:** Users often choose system functions by mistake and will need a clearly marked "emergency exit" to leave the unwanted state without having to go through an extended dialogue. Support undo and redo.			
3.1	Instead of cramming everything about a product or topic into a single page, use hypertext to structure the content space into a starting, overview page and several secondary pages that each focus on a specific topic. Help users avoid wasting time on subtopics that don't concern them.			
3.2	Don't disabled the Back button on a browser by opening a new window or using an immediate redirect. The Back button is the second-most used navigation feature (after following hypertext links). Users know that they can try anything on the Web and then click on the Back to return to familiar territory.			
3.3	People rarely read Web pages word by word; instead, they scan the page, picking out individual words and sentences. Use lists, headings, and other HTML formatting tools to help users find the information that suits their needs.			
3.4	Credibility is important for Web users. It is unclear who is behind information on the Web, and users need to know whether a page's content can be trusted. High-quality graphics, good writing, and use of outbound hypertext links can increase credibility.			

Checkpoint		Yes	No	NA
3.5	If your users have analog modems, warn them of the download size for any file over 50 kilobytes.			
4.	**Consistency and standards:** Users should not have to wonder whether different words, situations, or actions mean the same thing. Follow platform conventions.			
4.1	Do the same as everybody else. If most big Web sites do something in a certain way, then follow along. Users will expect things to work the same way on your site.			
4.2	Avoid using HTML that does not comply with standards[a] or causing the user's browser to engage in a nonstandard behavior.			
5.	**Error prevention:** Even better than a good error message is a careful design which prevents a problem from occurring in the first place.			
5.1	Use link titles to provide users with a preview of where each link will take them, before they have clicked on it. Help them avoid waiting for unnecessary page downloads.			
5.2	Avoid linkrot by keeping pages up indefinitely once they have been put on the Web. Other sites may link to your page. Users may have bookmarked the page because they want to go directly to a relevant part of your site. Search engines are slow in updating their databases, so they too will lead users astray if you remove pages.			
5.3	Avoid using a new technology for one to two years after it is first introduced in non-beta version. If your users have not adopted the new technology, they will not be able to access content that uses that technology.			
6.	**Recognition rather than recall:** Make objects, actions, and options visible. The user should not have to remember information from one part of the dialogue to another. Instructions for use of the system should be visible or easily retrievable whenever appropriate.			
6.1	Provide search if the site has more than 100 pages.			

Checkpoint		Yes	No	NA
6.2	Write straightforward and simple headlines and page titles that clearly explain what the page is about and that will make sense when read out-of-context in a search engine results listing.			
6.3	Structure the page to facilitate scanning; for example, use grouping and subheadings to break content into smaller "chunks."			
6.4	Page titles, headlines, and subject lines needs to clear and succinct. You only get 40–60 characters to explain your content. Unless the title or subject makes it absolutely clear what the page or email is about, users will never open it.			
7.	**Flexibility and efficiency of use:** Accelerators — unseen by the novice user — may often speed up the interaction for the expert user such that the system can cater to both inexperienced and experienced users. Allow users to tailor frequent actions.			
8.	**Aesthetic and minimalist design:** Dialogues should not contain information that is irrelevant or rarely needed. Every extra unit of information in a dialogue competes with the relevant units of information and diminishes their relative visibility.			
8.1	When designing for the Web, download speed must be the overriding criterion. To keep page sizes small, graphics should be kept to a minimum, and multimedia effects should be used only when they can add to a user's understanding of the information. Keep it simple.			
8.2	Split long pages of text into multiple pages, connected with hyperlinks. Each "chunk" of content should cover a specific topic. No more, no less.			
8.3	Avoid creating huge scrolling pages of text; as they move down the page, users will no longer be able to see navigation options.			
9.	**Help users recognize, diagnose, and recover from errors:** Error messages should be expressed in plain language (no codes), precisely indicate the problem, and constructively suggest a solution.			

Checkpoint	Yes	No	NA
10. **Help and documentation:** Any Help or documentation should be easy to search, focused on the user's task, list concrete steps to be carried out, and not be too large.			
10.1 When writing documentation, provide multiple examples to help the user contextualize their problem.			
11. **Design for accessibility:** Our analysis of accessibility is based on the World Wide Web Consortium's (W3C) guidelines.			

ª   See http://www.w3.org/MarkUp/ for more information on HTML standards.

References

Constantine, L.L. (1994). Collaborative Usability Inspections for Software. *Software Development '94 Proceedings*, San Francisco: Miller Freeman.

Nielsen, J. (1994). Heuristic Evaluation. In J. Nielsen and R.L. Mack (Eds.), *Usability Inspection Methods*, New York: John Wiley & Sons, Inc., pp. 25–62.

Notes

Excerpted from the Web Site Evaluation Design/Planning and Methodology for NIH. Retrieved May 6, 2006, from: irm.cit.nih.gov/itmra/Webeval.doc

Appendix F

The X Audit

Why do systems need to be audited? Take a look at Table F1. There are a lot of issues — and possible liability — there, from the hacker who changes your Web site to executables that create havoc on a customer's client; from customer service agents who provide anything but to E-commerce sites that take orders for nonexistent merchandise.

Organizing Your Audit

While it is recommended that you hire an external consulting firm to perform this critical effort, your EDP auditing department, with adequate training, would be a sufficient alternative. The reason this author much prefers an external auditor is that a "neutral third party" is usually more objective because they are neither stakeholders nor are they friendly with stakeholders. There is nothing like an unbiased opinion.

At a minimum, the auditor should obtain the following documentation:

1. *A diagram of the application system.* An X system is not unlike any other computer system. It has processes (e.g., process credit card) and entities (e.g., airline ticket) and shows the flow of data between the entities via the processes. Figure F1 shows a typical data flow diagram.
2. *A network diagram.* Most modern computer systems are developed using one of several traditional network architectures (i.e., two-tier, three-tier, etc.). Add the required IP (Internet Protocol) connectivity for X systems and you have quite a sophisticated environment. The

Table F1   Reasons for Auditing

Response time/availability
Accessibility
Ergonomics
Logistics
Customer service
Security (passwords, penetration, intrusion)
Privacy
Navigability
Fulfillment
Liability
Copyright infringement
Illegal usage
Defective software

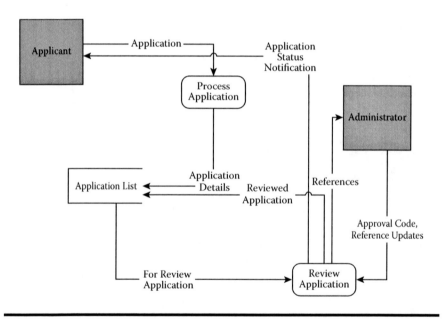

Figure F1   A data flow diagram.

auditor will need a roadmap to this environment to be able to determine if there are any connectivity issues. Figure F2 demonstrates what a simple network diagram should look like.

3. *Staff hierarchy diagram.* A complete list, preferably a diagram, that shows direct reports along with phone numbers and e-mail addresses is required.

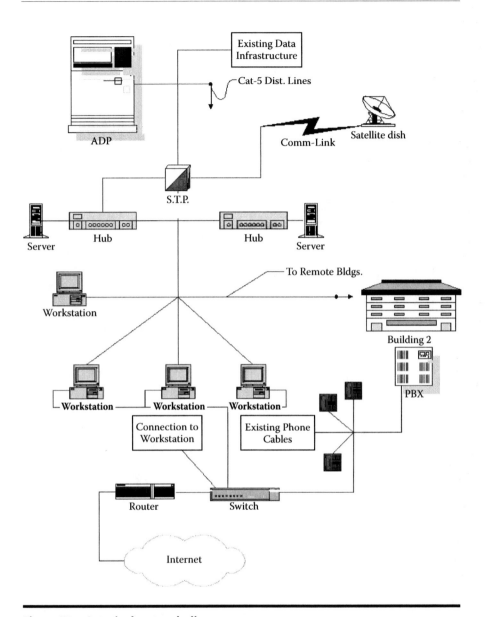

Figure F2   A typical network diagram.

One would think that a modern organization would have these three items readily available. Think again. (In my own experience, few of the organizations that I audit possess all three of these required items...few possess even two.)

If these are not available to the auditor, my recommendation is to start the audit effort with a series of brainstorming sessions where, at least, the two diagrams are created. Even if diagrams are available, one or more brainstorming sessions is still advisable. This provides the auditors a "walk through" where system and network architects can be questioned directly. This invariably speeds up the audit process.

Once the preliminary way has been completed (i.e., understanding the system), the auditor can proceed to go through his or her paces in a logical, methodical manner. The following sections, presented as a series of checklists, represent areas of the audit that can actually be performed in any order.

The checklists are actually a series of questions or areas to be studied. The responses to these questions form the data collected for input to the final audit report. The final audit report will contain problems found, issues overlooked, as well as recommendations for improvement.

For example, the auditor might find that the company has done inadequate security testing. The recommendation here might be to bring in a "white hat" to perform both penetration as well as intrusion testing. Alternatively, the audit might uncover a deficiency in the fulfillment processes the company follows to ship products purchased to the customer. Again, the audit report will make recommendations for improvement.

1.0 Systemic Audit

It is surprising that many companies spend millions of dollars on advertising budgets to draw more "eyeballs" to their Web sites but never factor in whether or not the projected additional load can be supported by the current system configuration. This is particularly true in the case of an X system where one or more executables will be downloaded to the client.

A systemic audit looks at such things as response time, network architecture, and linkages.

1.1 *Response time.* Measurables in this section include actual response time versus projected response time. Despite advances in supplying high-bandwidth connections to consumers, many PCs are connected to the Web with slow-speed connections. This means that sites that are highly graphical or use add-ons such as Macromedia Flash will appear slower to download.

Given the wide variety of modem-types, auditors should test the response time of the site using different scenarios such as:
- Using a DSL or cable modem connection
- Using a 56 kb connection
- At random times during the day, particularly 9 a.m. (start of workday) and 4 p.m. (kids home from school)

Web sites such as netmechanic.com, a subscription service, can assist in this endeavor by checking for slow response time directly from their Web sites.

1.2 *Broken links.* One of the top five irritants that Web surfers report is clicking on a link and getting a "nonexistent page" error message. This is often the result of poor system maintenance, where Web programmers move the actual page but neglect to modify the link to that page. Unfortunately, this is a frequent occurrence. One of a number of tools, including netmechanic.com, can assist in tracking down these broken links.

1.3 *Database audit.* Originally, the Web was a simple place. It consisted of mostly text and there was nary a database in sight. Today, the Web is filled to the brim with databases. The addition of databases makes the audit process even more complex. Because programming code is used to query, and perhaps even calculate, against that database, it is imperative that random checks be performed in an effort to pinpoint database query and calculation errors.

Essentially, auditing database access is similar to the traditional IT (information technology) QA (quality assurance) process. One or more scripts must be written that will take that database through its paces. For example, if a database program calculates insurance rates based on a zip code, then that calculation should be duplicated either manually or in a different parallel automated fashion to ensure that the result is correct. The same can be said for information that visitors to the site enter via a form. Is the information being entered the same that is being sent to the database?

1.4 *Network audit.* The network itself, including node servers, should be tested to see if it is effectively configured to provide optimum response. It is not uncommon to find the Web development group separated from the traditional IT development group. This means that one frequently finds network configurations architected inappropriately for the task at hand. For example, a site attracting tens of thousands of hits a day would do well to run a multitude of Web servers rather than just one.

Most organizations use one or more ISPs (Internet service providers) to host their sites. The auditor should carefully gauge the level of service provided by these ISPs as well.

1.5 *Download transparency.* Many X executables will be automatically downloaded to the end user's client. How transparently and how quickly are the two measures of importance here. Because X is still in its infancy, there are really no peer-oriented benchmarks to guide us here.

2.0 Security and Quality

There is no one topic that is discussed more in the press than Internet security. From "love bug" viruses to wily hackers breaking into Western Union, security is an important component of any audit. It is worthwhile to keep in mind that the auditor is not a security auditor, nor should he be. His role is to do a top-level assessment of the security of the E-business and, if warranted, recommend the services of a security firm well-versed in penetration and intrusion testing.

The entire issue of security is wrapped within the more comprehensive issue of quality. This section addresses both issues.

2.1 Review the security plan. All organizations must possess a security plan — in writing. If they do not have this, then they are severely deficient. The plan, at a minimum, should address:

2.1.1 *Authentication.* Is the person who he says he is?

2.1.2 *Authorization.* What users have what privileges? That is, who can do what?

2.1.3 *Information integrity.* Can the end user maliciously modify the information or the executables?

2.1.4 *Detection.* Once a problem is identified, how is it handled?

2.2 *Passwords.* Passwords are the first shield of protection against malicious attacks. Questions to ask in this section include:

2.2.1 Is anonymous log-in permitted? Under what conditions?

2.2.2 Is a password scanner periodically used to determine if passwords used can be hacked?

2.2.3 How often are passwords changed?

2.2.4 How often are administrative accounts used to log on to systems? Passwords are difficult to remember. This means that, to quickly gain entrance to systems, administrative and programming systems people often create easy-to-remember passwords such as admin. These are the first passwords used by hackers to try to gain entrance into a system.

2.3 *Staff background.* Administrative network staff must have a security background as well as a technical background. Those wishing to train their staff would do well to look into the Security Skills Certification Program provided by www.sans.org.

2.4 *Connectivity.* Today's organization may have many external connections (i.e., partners, EDI, etc.). For each company connected to, the auditor should examine:

2.4.1 *The data being passed between organizations.* Is what the company sent being received correctly?

2.4.2 *The security of the connection.* How is the data being transmitted? Is it required to be secure? Is encryption being used?

2.4.3 *If encryption is indeed being used,* it must be determined whether an appropriate algorithm is being deployed.

2.5 *The product base.* All organizations invest and then use a great deal of third-party software. As publicized by the press, much of this software, particularly browsers and e-mail packages and also word processing packages, contain security holes that, left unpatched, put the organization at risk. Therefore, for each software package being used:

2.5.1 Check for publicized security holes.

2.5.2 Check for availability of software patches. Always upgrade to the latest version of software and apply the latest patches.

2.5.3 Check to see if patches have been successfully applied.

2.5.4 Check security software for security holes. Security software, such as a firewall, can contain security holes just like any other type of software. Check for updates.

2.6 *Executable development.* When developing executables in-house, it is important to ensure that your own staff does not leave gaping holes through which malicious outsiders can gain entrance to your computers — or your client's computer. There are a variety of programming "loopholes," so to speak, that open wide the door to hackers:

2.6.1 In programming parlance, a "GET" sends data from the browser (client) to the server. For example, look at the query string below:

http://www.site.com/process_card.asp?cardnumber=
123456789

All HTTP (Hypertext Transport Protocol) requests get logged in to the server log as straight text, as shown below:

2000-09-15 00:12:30 - W3SVC1 GET/process_card.asp
cardnumber=123456789 200 0 623 360 570
80 HTTP/1.1 Mozilla/4.0+(compatible;+5.01;+Windows+NT)

Not only is the credit card number clearly visible in the log but it might also be stored in the browser's history file exposing this sensitive information to someone else using the same machine later on. Security organizations recommend the utilization of the POST method rather than the GET method for this reason.

2.6.2 Are the programmers using "hidden" fields to pass sensitive information? An example of this is relying on hidden form fields used with shopping carts. The hidden fields are sometimes used to send the item price when the customer submits the form. It is rather easy for a malicious user to save the Web page to his or her own PC, change the hidden field to reflect any price he or she wants, and then submit it.

2.6.3 One way to combat the problem discussed in 2.6.2 is to use a hash methodology. A hash is a function that processes a variable-length input and produces a fixed-length output. Because it is difficult to reverse the process, the sensitive data transmitted in this matter is secure. The auditor is required to assess the utilization of this methodology given any problems he or she might find in assessing 2.6.2.

2.6.4 Is sensitive data being stored in ASP or JSP pages? An early version of Microsoft's Internet Information Server (IIS) contains a number of security flaws that, under certain circumstances, allow the source of an ASP or JSP page to be displayed rather than executed. That is, the source code is visible to anyone browsing that particular Web site. If sensitive data, such as passwords, is being stored in the code, then this sensitive data will be displayed as well. The rule here is to not hardcode any security credentials into the page itself.

2.6.5 Are application-specific accounts with rights identified early in the development cycle? There are two types of security. One is referred to as "declarative" and takes place when access control is set from outset the application program. "Programmatic" security occurs when the program itself checks the rights of the person accessing the system. When developing code for executables or software that runs on a Web server, it is imperative that the rights issued are addressed early on in the development cycle. Questions to ask include:

- How many groups will be accessing the data?
- Will each group have the same rights?
- Will you need to distinguish between different users within a group?
- Will some pages permit anonymous access while others enforce authentication?

2.6.6 How are you dealing with cross-site scripting? When sites accept user-provided data (e.g., registration information, bulletin boards), which is then used to build dynamic pages (i.e., pages created on the spur of the moment), the potential for security problems increases 100-fold. No longer is the Web content created entirely by the Web designers — some of it now comes from other users. The risk comes from the existence of a number of ways in which text can be entered to simulate code. This code can then be executed as any other code written by the Web designers — except that it was written by a malicious user instead.

Both JavaScript and HTML can be manipulated to contain malicious code. Some forms of X port the code and then compile that code on the end user's client, leaving open the possibility of code manipulation. The malicious code can perform a number of activities such as redirecting users to other sites, modifying cookies, etc. More information on this topic can be obtained from the CERT Web site at http://www.cert.org/advisories/CA-2000-02.html and http://www.cert.org/tech_tips/malicious_code_mitigation.html.

2.6.7 Have you checked wizard-generated/sample code? Often, programmers "reuse" sample code they find on the Web or make use of generated code from Web development tools. Often, the sample or generated code contains hardcoded credentials to access databases, directories, etc. The auditor will want to make sure that this is not the case in the code being audited.

2.6.8 Are code reviews being performed? There is nothing worse than the lone programmer. Many of the problems discussed in the sections above can be negated if the code all programmers write is subject to peer review. Code reviews, a mainstay of traditional, quality-oriented programming methodology, are rarely done in today's fast-paced E-business environment. This is one of the reasons there are so many security break-ins.

2.6.9 Web server review. To run programs on the Web, many organizations use the CGI (common gateway interface) to enable programs (i.e., scripts) to run on their servers. CGI is not only a gateway for your programming code (i.e., via data collections forms). It is also a gateway for hackers to gain access to your systems. Vulnerable CGI programs present an attractive target to intruders because they are easy to locate and usually operate with the privileges and power of the Web server software itself. The following questions must be asked of developers using CGI:

- Are CGI interpreters located in bin directories? This should not be the case because you are providing the hacker with all the capabilities he needs to insert malicious code and then run it directly from your server.
- Is CGI support configured when not needed?

- Are you using Remote Procedure Calls (RPCs)? Remote Procedure Calls allow programs on one computer to execute programs on a second computer. There is significant evidence to show that the majority of distributed denial-of-service attacks launched during 1999 and early 2000 were executed by systems that had RPC vulnerabilities. It is recommended wherever possible to turn off or remove these services on machines directly accessible from the Internet. If this is not possible, then at least ensure that the latest patches to the software are installed, because these mitigate some of the known security holes.

2.7 *Testing.* Pre-PC testing was a slow and meticulous process. Today's faster pace means that inadequate testing is being performed by most organizations. In addition, many organizations forego security testing entirely. In this section of the audit we determine whether adequate security is being performed.

    2.7.1 Has penetration testing been done? Penetration testing is used to assess the type and extent of security-related vulnerabilities in systems and networks, test network security perimeters, and empirically verify the resistance of applications to misuse and exploitation. While it is possible that system administrators are sophisticated enough to be able to utilize the toolsets available to scan the systems for vulnerabilities, a whole host of "white-hat" hacker security consulting firms has sprung up over the past several years and it is these folks that are recommended.

    2.7.2 Has intrusion testing been done? There are a whole host of software tools available on the market today that "monitor" systems and report on possible intrusions. These are referred to as intrusion detection systems (IDSs). In this section of the audit we determine whether an IDS is being used and how effectively it is used.

    2.7.3 Is there a QA (Quality Assurance) function? While QA departments have been a traditional part of the IT function for decades, many newer pure-play Internet companies seem to ignore this function. In this section the auditor determines if the QA function is present. If it is present, then it will be reviewed.

2.8 *Reporting.* Logging of all log-ins, attempted intrusions, etc., must be maintained for a reasonable period of time. In this section, the auditor determines if these logs are maintained and for how long.

2.9 *Backup.* In the event of failure, it is usual that the last backup be used to restore the system. In this section, the auditor determines the frequency of backups as well as the reasonableness of this schedule.

3.0 Ergonomics

At this stage, the auditor becomes involved in more abstract issues. To achieve this end will require the auditor to meet, not only with the system developers, but also with the end users. At times, these end users will be current customers of the system, or potential customers of the system. To this end, it might be necessary to develop surveys form focus groups.

The goal here is nothing less than determining a "thumbs-up" or "thumbs-down" on the ergonomics of the system.

3.1 *Navigability.* Navigation means the determination of whether or not the site makes sense in terms of browsing it, or how easy it is to navigate the downloaded executable. Keep in mind that executables are mini-software programs, so all the tried-and-true tenets of "ease of use" we learned in Software Engineering 101 should be applied equally to an executable as they are to a traditional software program.

3.1.1 How easy is it to find something on this site? If looking for a specific product, how many pages does one have to surf through to find it?

3.1.2 Is there a search engine? If so, review for correctness and completeness. Many sites do not have search engines (in this instance, we are talking about a search engine to search the site only, rather than the Internet). If the site exhibits depth (i.e., many pages), it becomes rather difficult to navigate around it to find that for which you are looking. If a search engine is available, the auditor must check to see if what is being searched for can be correctly found.

3.1.3 Is there a sitemap? If so, review for correctness and completeness. While not required and not often found, site maps are one of the most useful site navigation tools. If available, the auditor determines the correctness of this tool.

3.1.4 Are back and forward (or other) buttons provided? What tools are provided the end user for moving backward and forward within the site? Are the browser's Back/Forward buttons the only navigation tools — or did the Web designers provide fully functional toolbars? If so, do these toolbars work on all pages? We have found that, of those firms audited, 10 percent of the pages pointed to by the toolbars cannot be found.

3.1.5 Are frames used? If so, do toolbars and other navigation tools still work?

3.1.6 When executables are in use, the auditor should ask whether or not the end user understands that some software has just been downloaded to his or her PC and that he or she has given permission. Where are these executables stored? If an executable is iteratively downloaded, does it overlay the original copy, or are duplicates created? Is it possible for the end user to create his own executable to replace the one downloaded and, thus, create false transactions on the server?

3.2 *Usability.* In the end, it comes down to one question really: How usable is the Web site and/or executable? In this section we ask:

3.2.1 How easy is it to use this site or executable? While the auditor might have an opinion that might well be valid, in this section we resort to surveys and focus groups to determine the answer.

3.2.2 How useful is this site/executable?

3.2.3 Does the executable come with instructions (e.g., Help, and "Contact Us" for assistance)?

3.3 *Content.* In this section we assess the value of the information contained within the site as compared to competitive sites.

3.3.1 Is content updated regularly?

3.3.2 Is content relevant?

3.3.3 Do visitors consider content worthwhile? The auditor will use survey techniques to determine the answer to this question.

3.3.4 How does content compare with competitors? The auditor will use survey techniques to determine the answer to this question.

3.4 *Search engine.* While the use of search engines has declined in popularity as a way to find a site, it is still an important marketing vehicle on the Web. In this section the auditor determines where the site places when performing a search using the top ten search engines.

4.0 Customer Service

The Web is a doorway to the company's business. However, it is just one part of the business. Tangential services must also be audited. Customer service is one of the biggest problem areas for Net firms. There have been many well-publicized instances of shoddy customer service. It is in the company's best interests, therefore, to assess customer service within the firm vis-à-vis its Web presence.

4.1 *Accessibility.* How easy is it for your customers to reach you?
    4.1.1 Review e-mail response. How long does it take you to respond to a customer e-mail?
    4.1.2 Review telephone response. How long does a customer have to wait on hold before a person answers his query?
4.2 *E-commerce.* If your site doubles as an E-commerce site (i.e., you sell goods or services from your site), then you need to assess the quality of this customer experience. Keep in mind that in an X world, some of the shopping cart functionality might take place on the client through use of an executable.
    4.2.1 Check shopping experience. Using a "mystery shopper" approach, the auditor will endeavor to make routine purchases using the Web site to determine:
        4.2.1.1 Is the shopping cart correct (i.e., are the goods you purchased in the shopping cart)?
        4.2.1.2 Does the E-commerce software calculate taxes properly?
        4.2.1.3 Does the E-commerce software calculate shipping charges properly?
    4.2.2 Check the fulfillment experience:
        4.2.2.1 Is a confirmation e-mail sent to the purchaser?
        4.2.2.2 Is the return policy carefully explained?
        4.2.2.3 How quickly does the company refund money on returns?
4.3 *Privacy.* At a minimum, the auditor must review the company's privacy policy statement. The auditor should then review the data flow to determine if the privacy policy is being adhered to.

5.0 Legality

The digital age makes it easy to perform illegal and potentially litigious acts. From a corporate perspective, this can be anything from a Web designer illegally copying a copyrighted piece of art to employees downloading pornography.

5.1 *Copyright.*
    5.1.1 Check the content ownership of text on your site or any text copied into an executable. It is quite easy to copy text

from one site to another. Ensure that your copy is completely original or that you have the correct permissions to reprint the data.

    5.1.2 In the same way, check image ownership.

5.2 *Illegal usage.* There have been a number of court cases where employees claimed harassment when other employees within the organization downloaded or e-mailed pornographic materials. The company is responsible for the actions of its employees and therefore it is highly recommended that the company do the following:

    5.2.1 Create a policy memo detailing what can and cannot be done on the Internet (include e-mail). Make sure all employees sign and return this memo. Use tools such as those on surfcontrol.com to monitor employee Net usage.

    5.2.2 Determine whether any e-mail monitoring software is used and determine its effectiveness.

5.3 *Liability.* Web site publishers and software vendors currently use disclaimers and licensing agreements to protect themselves from any liability issues. It is important that these be even more diligently utilized when executables are launched from a Web site or IP address. Questions to ask include:

    5.3.1 Has the disclaimer and licensing agreement been approved by Legal?

    5.3.2 Does the executable itself contain a disclaimer or licensing agreement?

    5.3.3 Organizations can mount a strong defense against liability issues if they can prove that they utilized robust software engineering and QA techniques when developing the code. Is there adequate documentation that tracks the methodologies used during systems development of these executables? Is there an audit trail that tracks the development of each executable — from planning to testing?

    5.3.4 How are bugs being tracked? Is there a procedure for handling problems? How are software bugs resolved, and how quickly? How are end users notified that a new executable has been loaded to the Web site?

Conclusion

As one can see from this checklist, the audit is extensive and quite thorough. It is recommended that it be performed at least once a year. If the Web site and its associated executables are modified continually, then the audit should also be done more frequently.

Appendix G

Computer Use Policy

In consideration of being authorized by _____ (hereinafter referred to as "Company") to use and access Company computer and communications facilities and resources (hereinafter referred to as "Company facilities and resources"), I agree to comply with the conditions set forth in paragraphs (a) through (j) below:

(a) Use of and access to Company facilities and resources is provided only for Company business. I will use or access Company facilities and resources only in ways that are cost-effective and in the Company's best interest. I will not attempt to use or access resources or data that I have not been authorized to use or access.

(b) When a user ID is assigned to me, I will change the password so that it is not easily guessed. I will not share, write down, electronically store (without strong encryption), or otherwise disclose the password, authentication code, or any other device associated with any user ID assigned to me. I will take precautions to ensure that no other person makes use of any Company facilities and resources with any of my user IDs.

(c) All data stored on or originating from, and all communications transmitted or received using, Company facilities and resources are considered the property of the Company. Such data and communications are subject to monitoring or review by authorized personnel designated by Company Management. The term "private" as referred to in operating systems, application software, or electronic mail does not refer to personal privacy of an individual's data or mail. I also acknowledge that my use of or access to Company facilities and resources may be monitored at any time to ensure that such use or access is in compliance with these conditions.

(d) Company information in any form shall be safeguarded. I will not copy, or distribute to others, any Company sensitive information except as authorized. I will not upload, publish, transmit or otherwise disclose any such information concerning the Company, its operations and activities, on or through non-Company networks without prior approval of authorized Company Management.

(e) I will respect and observe the customs, traditions, and laws of the _____ and other countries where _____ has computer assets. I will not use Company facilities and resources to access or attempt to access any computer data or computer site, or send or knowingly receive any electronic transmission that contains political, religious, pornographic, indecent, abusive, defamatory, threatening, illegal, or culturally offensive materials. I will report any such material with the source of the site name of such material to the concerned organization.

(f) I will not use Company facilities and resources for unauthorized access to, interference with, or disruption of any software, data, hardware, or system available through Company facilities and resources. I will use standard Company procedures to check all downloaded files for viruses or destructive code prior to using the files on Company facilities and resources.

(g) I will not copy or download any material or any portion thereof protected by copyright without proper authorization from the copyright owner.

(h) I will not connect or use any channel of communication not authorized in compliance with Company policy and guidelines. For any situation in which I am uncertain of what behavior is expected of me in regard to using or accessing company facilities and resources, I will contact the concerned organization.

(i) I will not utilize unauthorized Internet access connections.

(j) I acknowledge that any violations of the above paragraphs (a) through (i) may result in disciplinary action, including loss of access to Company facilities and resources, termination of my employment, my contract, or my employer's contract, legal action or other measures, as appropriate.

ACKNOWLEDGMENT

I acknowledge that I have read and understood the _____ Computer Use Policy as set of forth above and I shall abide by it while using or accessing company Computer and Communication facilities and resources.

Employee Name   Signature   Date

_____   _____   _____

Appendix H

Web Site Terms and Conditions

The following Web site Terms and Conditions Agreement (the "Agreement") governs your use of the Web site(s) accessible at universal resource locators x.com, x1.com, x2.com, and x3.com (collectively the "Service"), which are operated by _____. Your acceptance of the Agreement provides you with a limited and temporary license and permission to use the software and other resources of the Service, which license and permission are freely revocable at any time, with or without cause, and with or without notice, by the _____, as described more fully below. Please print a copy of this document for your records. To retain an electronic copy of this Agreement, you may save it into any word processing program.

1. Copyright Rights

All copyright rights in the text, images, photographs, graphics, user interface, and other content provided on the Service, and the selection, coordination, and arrangement of such content, are owned by the _____, as applicable among us, or their third-party licensors, to the full extent provided under the United States Copyright laws and all international copyright laws. Under applicable copyright laws, you are prohibited from copying, reproducing, modifying, distributing, displaying, performing, or transmitting any of the contents of the Service for any purposes. Nothing stated or implied on the Service confers on you any license or right under any copyright of the _____, or any third party.

The Service and the information contained in reference herein are for informational purposes only. Any reproduction, copying, or redistribution for commercial purposes of any materials or design elements of the Service is strictly prohibited, without the prior written consent of the _____. Systematic retrieval of data or other content from this Service to create or compile, directly or indirectly, a collection, compilation, database, or directory without written permission from the _____ is prohibited.

2. Trade and Service Mark Rights

All rights in the product names, company names, trade names, logos, product packaging, and designs of all the _____ or third-party products or services, whether or not appearing in large print or with the trademark symbol, belong exclusively to the _____, as applicable, or their respective owners, and are protected from repro-duction, imitation, dilution, or confusing or misleading uses under national and international trademark and copyright laws, as applicable. The use or misuse of these trademarks or any materials, except as permitted herein, is expressly prohibited and nothing stated or implied on this Service confers on you any license or right under any patent, copyright, or trademark of the _____ or any third party.

3. Modification of This Agreement

The _____ reserve the right to amend this Agreement at any time. You are bound by any such revisions and should therefore periodically visit this page to review the then-current Terms and Conditions to which you are bound. Your use of the Service after the posting of modifications to this Agreement will constitute your acceptance of this Agreement, as modified. If, at any time, you do not wish to accept this Agreement, you may not use the Service.

4. Links

This Service may contain links to other services ("Linked Services"). The Linked Services are not under the control of the _____, and the _____ are not responsible for the contents of the Linked Services, including, without limitation, links contained on Linked

Services, or any changes or updates to Linked Services. The _____ provide any Linked Services to you only as a convenience, and the inclusion of any such Linked Services is not an endorsement by the _____ in favor of any company offering Internet services, products, or services on the Linked Services.

Other sites may link without prior permission to the home page of the Service only through a plaintext link. Permission must otherwise be granted by us for any other type of link to the Service. To seek our permission, you may write to _____. Additional Agreement by Linked Services: any third-party Web site that links to the Service: (a) shall not create a frame, browser, or border environment around any of the content of the Service; (b) may link to, but not replicate, Service content; (c) shall not imply that the _____ are endorsing or sponsoring it or its products or services; (d) shall not present false information about the _____ or its products or services; (e) shall not use _____ trademarks without the prior written permission from the _____; and (f) shall not contain content that could be construed as distasteful, offensive, or controversial.

Notwithstanding anything to the contrary contained in this Agreement, we reserve the right to deny or rescind permission to link to the Service from any Web site, and to require termination of any link to the Service, for any reason in our sole and absolute discretion.

5. Obligations

You are required to comply with all applicable laws in connection with your use of the Service, and such further limitations as may be set forth in any written or on-screen notice from the _____. As a condition of your use of the Service, you represent and warrant that you will not use the Service for any purpose that is unlawful or prohibited by this Agreement.

6. Prohibited Uses Generally

Without limiting the foregoing, you agree not to transmit, distribute, post, communicate, or store information or other material on, to, or through the Service that:

(a) Is copyrighted, unless you are the copyright owner or valid licensee to such materials and you have the right to grant the _____ the rights and licenses set forth in Section 8 of this Agreement;

(b) Reveals trade secrets, unless you own them, or you are the valid licensee to such materials and you have the right to grant the _____ the rights and licenses set forth in Section 8 of this Agreement;

(c) Infringes on any other intellectual property rights of others or on the privacy or publicity rights of others;

(d) Is obscene, defamatory, threatening, harassing, abusive, hateful, slanderous, or embarrassing to any other person or entity or in violation of applicable law as determined by the _____ in their sole discretion;

(e) Is sexually explicit;

(f) Constitutes advertisements or solicitations of business, surveys, contests, chain letters, or pyramid schemes; or

(g) Contains viruses, Trojan horses, worms, time bombs, or other computer programming routines or engines that are intended to damage, detrimentally interfere with, surreptitiously intercept, or expropriate any system, data, or information.

You further agree not to:

(a) Use any incomplete, false, or inaccurate biographical information or other information for purposes of registering as a user of the Service, or for purposes of registering for any promotions offered through the Service;

(b) Delete or revise any material or other information of any other user of the Service;

(c) Harvest, collect, or send information about others, including e-mail addresses, without their consent;

(d) Take any action that imposes an unreasonable or disproportionately large load on the Service's infrastructure;

(e) Use any device, software, or routine to interfere or attempt to interfere with the proper working of the Service or any activity being conducted on this site;

(f) Use or attempt to use any engine, software, tool, agent, or other device or mechanism (including without limitation browsers, spiders, robots, avatars, or intelligent agents) to navigate or search the Service to harvest or otherwise collect information from the Service to be used for any commercial purpose;

(g) Allow any other person or entity to use your username or password for posting or viewing comments or sending or receiving materials; or

(h) Attempt to decipher, decompile, disassemble, or reverse-engineer any of the software comprising or in any way making up a part of the Service.

You further agree not to violate or attempt to violate the security of the Service, including, without limitation:

(a) Accessing data not intended for you or logging into a server or account that you are not authorized to access;

(b) Attempting to probe, scan, or test the vulnerability of a system or network or to breach security or authentication measures without proper authorization;

(c) Attempting to interfere with service to any user, host or network, including, without limitation, by way of submitting a virus to, or overloading, "flooding," "spamming," "mailbombing," or "crashing" the Service;

(d) Sending unsolicited e-mail, including promotions and advertising of products or services; or

(e) Forging any TCP/IP packet header or any part of the header information in any e-mail or posting. Violations of system or network security may result in civil or criminal liability.

The _____ may investigate occurrences that may involve such violations and may involve, and cooperate with, law enforcement authorities in prosecuting users who are involved in such violations.

The _____ reserve the right (but do not have the obligation) to review postings on its Service, to remove any postings, and to terminate your ability to post to the Service at any time without notice, in its sole discretion. The _____ also reserve the right to disclose any information necessary to satisfy any applicable law, regulation, legal process, or governmental request, or to edit, refuse to post, or to remove any information or materials, in whole or in part.

7. Conduct

You are responsible for, and assume all liability associated with, any material you make available or transmit through the Service, whether through chat rooms, messages boards, or other forums, including liability for claims of infringement, libel, and slander. You may not post, transmit through, or otherwise make available on or through the Service (i) any material that violates or infringes in any way upon the rights of others, that is unlawful, defamatory, obscene, abusive, profane, vulgar, sexually explicit, racist, threatening, hateful, or otherwise objectionable or that encourages conduct that would constitute a criminal offense, give rise to civil liability, or otherwise violate any law; (ii) without the express written consent of the owner thereof, any copyrighted material; or (iii) without the express prior written consent of the _____ any advertising or any solicitation with respect to products or services (unless posted in an area specifically designated for that purpose). Although the _____ do not and cannot review every message posted on or transmitted through the Service, the _____ shall be under no obligation to permit any material posted or transmitted to remain on the Service, and may remove from, or refuse to display on the Service any material that the _____, in the exercise of their sole discretion, believe violates this Agreement.

8. License Granted

We do not claim ownership of any information or material you transmit, distribute, post, communicate, or store on, to, or through the Service (expressly excluding your user data, which is collected in accordance with the Service Privacy Policy) ("Your Content"). However, by submitting or posting Your Content, to or through the Service, you grant the _____ a worldwide, royalty-free, perpetual, irrevocable, and non-exclusive right (including any moral rights) and license to use, reproduce, modify, adapt, publish, translate, create derivative works from, distribute, perform, and display Your Content anywhere, for any purpose, and in any form, media, or technology now known or later developed. No compensation will be paid with respect to the use of Your Content. The _____ are free to use any ideas, concepts, know-how, or techniques contained in Your Content for any purpose whatsoever, including, but not limited to, developing, manufacturing, and marketing products using Your Content. The _____ are under no obligation to maintain any of Your Content and may remove any of Your Content at any time in its sole discretion.

By posting or submitting Your Content to this Service, you also represent and warrant that you own or otherwise control all of the rights to Your Content, and that use of Your Content by the _____ will not infringe or violate the rights of any third party or violate applicable law.

9. Notice of Copyright Infringement

If you believe that your work has been copied and is accessible on this Service in a way that constitutes copyright infringement, please provide the _____ Copyright Agent with the following information:

(a) Identification of the copyrighted work claimed to have been infringed;
(b) Identification of the allegedly infringing material on the Service that is requested to be removed;

(c) Your name, address, and daytime telephone number, and an e-mail address if available, so that _____ may contact you if necessary;

(d) A statement that you have a good-faith belief that the use of the copyrighted work is not authorized by the copyright owner, its agent, or the law;

(e) A statement that the information in the notification is accurate, and under penalty of perjury, that the signatory is authorized to act on behalf of the owner of an exclusive copyright right that is allegedly infringed; and

(f) An electronic or physical signature of the copyright owner or someone authorized on the owner's behalf to assert infringement of copyright and to submit the statement.

The _____ reserve the right to remove any posted submission which infringes the copyright of any person under the laws of the United States upon receipt of such a statement (or, more specifically, any statement in conformance with 17 U.S.C. § 512(c)(3)). United States law provides significant penalties for submitting such a statement falsely.

10. Registration, Username, Password, Security

(a) Registration. Registration may be required for the use of certain portions of the Service. Your registration shall not impose any duty on us to provide any particular service to you. If the terms of any _____ registration agreement conflict with the terms of this Agreement, the registration agreement shall control.

(b) Your User Identity. Your username and password will be your identity for purposes of interacting with Service and other users through the Service.

(c) User Name, Passwords, and Password Access. You shall keep confidential, shall not disseminate, and shall use solely in accordance with this Agreement, your username and password for the Service. You shall immediately notify the _____ if you learn of or suspect (i) any loss or theft of your username or password, or (ii) any unauthorized use of your username or password or of the Service. In the event of such loss, theft, or unauthorized use, the _____ may impose on you, at the _____'s sole discretion, additional security obligations.

(d) Security Breaches and Revision. If any unauthorized person obtains access to the Service as a result of any act or omission by you, you shall use your best efforts to ascertain the source and manner of acquisition and shall fully and promptly brief the _____.

You shall otherwise cooperate and assist in any investigation relating to any such unauthorized access.

11. Privacy Policy

We are committed to protecting your privacy and security, and have explained in detail the steps we take to do so in the Service Privacy Policy, a copy of which you should review by clicking here. You in turn agree and consent to the terms of the Service Privacy Policy by your use of the Service.

12. Access to the Service

To access the Service, you must have access to the World Wide Web, either directly or through devices that access Web-based content, and pay any service fees associated with such access. In addition, you must use all equipment necessary to make such connection to the World Wide Web, including a computer and modem or other access device.

13. Disclaimer of Warranties

THE SERVICE IS PROVIDED "AS IS." THE _____ MAKE NO REPRESENTATION OR WARRANTY OF ANY KIND WHATSOEVER TO YOU OR ANY OTHER PERSON RELATING IN ANY WAY TO THE SERVICE, INCLUDING ANY PART THEREOF, OR ANY WEB SITE OR OTHER CONTENT OR SERVICE THAT MAY BE ACCESSIBLE DIRECTLY OR INDIRECTLY THROUGH THE SERVICE. THE _____ DISCLAIM TO THE MAXIMUM EXTENT PERMITTED BY LAW, ANY AND ALL SUCH REPRESENTATIONS AND WARRANTIES. WITHOUT LIMITING THE GENERALITY OF THE FOREGOING, THE _____ DISCLAIM TO THE MAXIMUM EXTENT PERMITTED BY LAW ANY AND ALL (i) WARRANTIES OF MERCHANTABILITY OR FITNESS FOR A PARTICULAR PURPOSE, (ii) WARRANTIES AGAINST INFRINGEMENT OF ANY THIRD-PARTY INTELLECTUAL PROPERTY OR PROPRIETARY RIGHTS, (iii) WARRANTIES RELATING TO DELAYS, INTERRUPTIONS, ERRORS, OR OMISSIONS IN THE SERVICE, OR ANY PART THEREOF, (iv) WARRANTIES RELATING TO THE TRANSMISSION OR DELIVERY OF THE SERVICE, (v) WARRANTIES RELATING TO THE ACCURACY OR CORRECTNESS OF DATA, AND (vi) WARRANTIES OTHERWISE RELATING TO PERFORMANCE, NONPERFORMANCE, OR OTHER ACTS OR OMISSIONS BY THE _____ OR ANY THIRD PARTY. FURTHER, AND WITHOUT LIMITING THE GENERALITY OF ANY OF THE FOREGOING, THERE IS

NO WARRANTY THAT THE SERVICE WILL MEET YOUR NEEDS OR REQUIREMENTS OR THE NEEDS OR REQUIREMENTS OF ANY OTHER PERSON.

THE _____ MAKE NO WARRANTIES OR REPRESENTATIONS, EXPRESS OR IMPLIED, THAT THE INFORMATION PROVIDED THROUGH THE SERVICE WILL BE FREE FROM ERROR, OMISSION, INTERRUPTION, DEFECT, OR DELAY IN OPERATION. ANY INFORMATION ON THIS SERVICE IS SUBJECT TO CHANGE WITHOUT NOTICE, AND WE DISCLAIM ALL RESPONSIBILITY FOR THESE CHANGES, INCLUDING, BUT NOT LIMITED TO, CHANGES TO PRICES, DISCOUNTS, AND HOURS OF OPERATION.

14. Limitation of Liability

IN NO EVENT WILL THE _____ OR THEIR AFFILIATES, OR ANY PARTY INVOLVED IN CREATING, PRODUCING, OR DELIVERING THIS SERVICE, OR ON ANY WEB SITE LINKED TO THIS SERVICE, BE LIABLE IN ANY MANNER WHATSOEVER FOR ANY DIRECT, INCIDENTAL, CONSEQUENTIAL, INDIRECT, SPECIAL, OR PUNITIVE DAMAGES ARISING OUT OF YOUR ACCESS, USE, OR INABILITY TO USE THIS SERVICE OR ANY SITE LINKED TO THIS SERVICE, OR IN CONNECTION WITH ANY FAILURE OF PERFORMANCE, ERROR, OMISSION, INTERRUPTION, DEFECT, DELAY IN OPERATION OR TRANSMISSION, COMPUTER VIRUS, OR LINE OR SYSTEM FAILURE. IN NO EVENT SHALL THE _____ OR THEIR AFFILIATES OR ANY THIRD PARTY BE LIABLE TO YOU OR ANY OTHER PERSON FOR CONSEQUENTIAL, INCIDENTAL, SPECIAL, EXEMPLARY, PUNITIVE, OR INDIRECT DAMAGES ARISING UNDER OR IN ANY WAY RELATED TO THE SERVICE, INCLUDING ANY PART THEREOF, OR ANY OTHER CONTENT, (INCLUDING LOST PROFITS, LOSS OF BUSINESS OR DATA, BUSINESS INTERRUPTION, TRADING LOSSES, AND DAMAGES THAT RESULT FROM INACCURACY OF THE INFORMATION OR INCONVENIENCE, DELAY, OR LOSS OF THE USE OF THE SERVICE) EVEN IF THE _____ OR ANY THIRD PARTY HAS BEEN ADVISED OF THE POSSIBILITY OF SUCH DAMAGES OR LOSSES.

THE _____ RESERVE THE RIGHT TO ALTER THE CONTENT OF THIS SERVICE IN ANY WAY, AT ANY TIME, FOR ANY REASON, WITHOUT PRIOR NOTIFICATION, AND WILL NOT BE LIABLE IN ANY WAY FOR POSSIBLE CONSEQUENCES OF SUCH CHANGES. THESE LIMITATIONS APPLY WHETHER THE ALLEGED LIABILITY IS BASED ON CONTRACT, TORT, NEGLIGENCE, STRICT LIABILITY, OR ANY OTHER

BASIS, EVEN IF THE _____ HAVE BEEN ADVISED OF THE POSSIBILITY OF SUCH DAMAGE. BECAUSE SOME JURISDICTIONS DO NOT ALLOW THE EXCLUSION OR LIMITATION OF INCIDENTAL OR CONSEQUENTIAL DAMAGES, THE _____'S LIABILITY IN SUCH JURISDICTIONS SHALL BE LIMITED TO THE EXTENT PERMITTED BY LAW.

IN NO EVENT SHALL THE _____'S TOTAL LIABILITY TO YOU FOR ALL DAMAGES, LOSSES, OR CAUSES OF ACTION ARISING UNDER THIS AGREEMENT EXCEED ONE HUNDRED DOLLARS ($100.00).

15. Indemnification

Upon a request by the _____, you agree to indemnify and hold harmless the _____ and their respective subsidiaries, affiliates, directors, officers, agents, licensors, co-branders, or other partners and employees from and against all liabilities, claims, and expenses, including reasonable attorneys' fees, made by any third party due to or arising out of content you submit, post to, or transmit through this Service, your use of the Service, your violation of this Agreement, or your violation of any rights of another.

16. Choice of Law and Forum

This Agreement shall be governed by and construed in accordance with the laws of the State of _____, excluding its conflict of law rules. You expressly consent and agree to submit to the exclusive jurisdiction and venue of the United States District Court for the _____ or, for matters not susceptible to adjudication in the federal courts, the courts of the _____ located in _____, in all disputes arising out of or relating to the use of this Service.

17. United States Jurisdiction

The Service is operated in the United States of America. We do not represent that content or materials presented on the Service are appropriate or available for use in other locations. If you access the Service from a jurisdiction other than the United States, you agree that you do so on your own initiative, and are responsible for compliance with local laws, if and to the extent local laws are applicable to your use of the Service.

18. Severability and Integration

Unless otherwise specified herein, this Agreement constitutes the entire agreement between you and the _____ and governs your use of this Service, superseding any prior or contemporaneous communications and proposals (whether oral, written, or electronic) between you and the _____. If any portion of this Agreement is held invalid or unenforceable, that portion shall be construed in a manner consistent with applicable law to reflect, as nearly as possible, the original intention of the parties, and the remaining portions shall remain in full force and effect. This Agreement may be modified only by our posting on the Service changes to this Agreement, or by a subsequent writing signed by the _____.

19. No Waiver

The failure of the _____ to enforce any provisions of this Agreement or respond to a breach by you or other parties shall not in any way waive its right to enforce subsequently any terms or conditions of this Agreement or to act with respect to similar breaches.

20. No Professional Advice

Any information supplied by any employee or agent of the _____, whether by telephone, e-mail, letter, facsimile, or other form of communication, is intended solely as general guidance on the use of the Service, and does not constitute legal, tax, accounting, or other professional advice. Individual situations and state laws vary and users are encouraged to obtain appropriate advice from qualified professionals in the applicable jurisdictions. The _____ make no representations or warranties concerning any course of action taken by any person following or otherwise using the information offered or provided within or through the Service, and the _____ will not be liable for any direct, indirect, consequential, special, exemplary, or other damages that may result, including but not limited to economic loss, injury, illness, or death.

21. Miscellaneous

You agree that no joint venture, partnership, employment, or agency relationship exists between you and the _____ as a result of this Agreement or your use of this Service. Nothing contained in this

Agreement is in derogation of the _____'s right to comply with governmental, court, and law enforcement requests or requirements relating to your use of this Service or information provided to or gathered by the _____ with respect to such use. A printed version of this Agreement and of any notice given in electronic form shall be admissible in judicial or administrative proceedings based upon or relating to this Agreement to the same extent and subject to the same conditions as other business documents and records originally generated and maintained in printed form.

22. Termination

_____ reserve the right, in its sole discretion, to terminate this Agreement and your access to all or part of this Service, with or without notice and with or without cause. Termination of your access to this Service means the revocation of the limited and temporary license and permission to use the software and other resources of the Service granted to you under this Agreement by the _____. The provisions of this Agreement will survive the termination of your access to the Service and of this Agreement.

23. Notices

The _____ may give notices to users of the Service, at the _____'s option, by posting a message on the Service, by electronic or conventional mail, or by any other means by which users obtain actual knowledge thereof. Notices by users to the _____ must be given by electronic or conventional mail. Notices to the _____ by electronic mail must be sent to _____. Notices to the _____ by conventional mail must be sent to _____. Notices by a user to the _____ will not change the terms of this Agreement unless the change is expressly accepted in writing by an authorized officer of the _____.

24. Violations

Please report any violations of this Agreement to _____.

Appendix I

Executable Software Terms and Conditions

Thank you for using _____! This page contains the terms and conditions ("Terms and Conditions") for _____. By download-ing _____, you agree to this agreement either for yourself or on behalf of your employer or another entity and agree to be bound by its terms and conditions. If you are accepting on behalf of your employer or another entity, you represent and warrant that you have full legal authority to bind your employer or such entity to these terms and con-ditions. If you do not have the legal authority to bind, please press the "I do not accept" button below.

Personal or Internal Business Use Only

_____ is made available to you for your personal or internal business use in compliance with all applicable laws, rules and regulations. If you want to make commercial use of _____, including but not limited to selling or distributing _____ for payment, you must enter into an agreement with _____ or obtain _____ written permission in advance. If you are asked to register, you must provide complete and accurate identification, contact, and other information required as part of the registration process. _____ reserves the right to refuse or discontinue participa-tion to any applicant at any time in its sole discretion.

Prohibited Actions

Except for distributions for internal business and personal use to your employees or contractors in compliance with these Terms and Conditions, you may not distribute _____ or any services or software associated with or derived from it, modify, copy, license, or create derivative works from _____, unless you obtain _____ written permission in advance. If you wish to do any of the above, please contact us by visiting _____.

Distribution

Once you have obtained _____ permission, you may make copies of _____ and distribute such copies to others provided that any such recipient has had an opportunity to review and agree to be bound by these Terms and Conditions. If others to whom you would like to distribute _____ do not have this opportunity to review and agree to these Terms and Conditions but you would still like to distribute copies to them, you may do so provided that you have the legal right to bind each of those third parties to these Terms and Conditions. If you do not have this right and the recipients do not have an opportunity to review and agree to these Terms and Conditions, you may not distribute _____ to them. If you have any questions regarding the terms of distribution, please contact us by visiting _____.

Automatic Updates

_____ may communicate with _____ servers (unless you are using _____ for internal business use and your settings prevent this communication) to check for available updates to the software, such as bug fixes, patches, enhanced functions, missing plug-ins and new versions (collectively, "Updates"). During this process, _____ sends _____ a request for the latest version information. By installing _____ (unless you are using _____ for internal business use and your settings prevent this communication), you hereby agree to automatically request and receive Updates from _____ servers.

Information Practices

Protecting users' privacy is very important to us. As a condition of downloading and using _____, you agree to the terms of the _____ Privacy Policy [link], which may be updated from time to time, as expressed in the most recent version that exists at the time of your use. Information collected by _____ may be stored and processed in the United States or any other country in which _____ or its agents maintain facilities. By using _____, you consent to any such transfer of information outside of your country.

Intellectual Property

You acknowledge that _____or third parties own all right, title, and interest in and to _____, portions thereof, or software or content provided through or in conjunction with _____, including without limitation all Intellectual Property Rights. "Intellectual Property Rights" means any and all rights existing from time to time under patent law, copyright law, trade secret law, trademark law, unfair competition law, and any and all other proprietary rights, and any and all applications, renewals, extensions and restorations thereof, now or hereafter in force and effect worldwide. You agree not to (and agree not to allow third parties to) modify, adapt, translate, prepare derivative works from, decompile, reverse engineer, disassemble or otherwise attempt to derive source code from _____, or to extract significant portions of _____'s files for use in other applications. You also agree to (and agree not to allow third parties to) not remove, obscure, or alter _____ or any third party's copyright notice, trademarks, or other proprietary rights notices affixed to or contained within or accessed in conjunction with or through _____.

Feedback

If you have comments on _____ or ideas on how to improve it, please visit _____. Please note that by doing so, you also grant _____ and third parties permission to use and incorporate your ideas or comments into _____ (or third-party software or content) without further compensation or approval.

Changes to Terms and Conditions

_____ reserves the right to modify these Terms and Conditions from time to time in its sole discretion, without notice or liability to you. You agree to be bound by these Terms and Conditions, as modified. Please review the most current version of the Terms and Conditions from time to time, located at _____ (or such successor URL as _____ may provide), so that you will be apprised of any changes.

Disclaimer of Warranties

_____and any third party who makes its software or content available in conjunction with or through _____ disclaim any responsibility for any harm resulting from your use (or use by your employees, agents or contractors) of _____ or any third-party software or content accessed in conjunction with or through _____. _____ AND ANY THIRD-PARTY SOFTWARE AND CONTENT MADE AVAILABLE IN CONJUNCTION WITH OR THROUGH _____ ARE PROVIDED "AS IS," WITH NO WARRANTIES WHATSOEVER. _____ AND SUCH THIRD PARTIES EXPRESSLY DISCLAIM TO THE FULLEST EXTENT PERMITTED BY LAW ALL EXPRESS, IMPLIED, AND STATUTORY WARRANTIES, INCLUDING, WITHOUT LIMITATION, THE WARRANTIES OF MERCHANT-ABILITY, FITNESS FOR A PARTICULAR PURPOSE, AND NON-INFRINGE-MENT OF PROPRIETARY RIGHTS. _____ AND ANY THIRD PARTY WHO MAKES ITS SOFTWARE OR CONTENT AVAILABLE IN CONJUNCTION WITH OR THROUGH _____ DISCLAIM ANY WARRANTIES REGARDING THE SECURITY, RELIABILITY, TIMELI-NESS, AND PERFORMANCE OF _____ AND SUCH THIRD-PARTY SOFTWARE OR CONTENT. YOU UNDERSTAND AND AGREE THAT YOU DOWNLOAD AND USE _____ AND ALL THIRD-PARTY SOFTWARE OR CONTENT MADE AVAILABLE IN CON-JUNCTION WITH OR THROUGH _____ AT YOUR OWN DISCRETION, AND RISK AND THAT YOU WILL BE SOLELY RESPONSIBLE FOR ANY DAMAGES TO YOUR COMPUTER SYSTEM OR LOSS OF DATA THAT RESULTS FROM THE DOWNLOAD OR USE OF _____ AND SUCH THIRD-PARTY SOFTWARE AND CONTENT. SOME STATES OR OTHER JURISDICTIONS DO NOT ALLOW THE EXCLUSION OF IMPLIED WARRANTIES, SO THE ABOVE EXCLUSIONS MAY NOT APPLY TO YOU. YOU MAY ALSO HAVE OTHER RIGHTS THAT VARY FROM STATE TO STATE AND JURISDICTION TO JURISDICTION.

Limitation of Liability

UNDER NO CIRCUMSTANCES SHALL _____ OR ANY THIRD PARTY WHO MAKES ITS SOFTWARE OR CONTENT AVAILABLE IN CONJUNCTION WITH OR THROUGH _____ BE LIABLE TO ANY USER ON ACCOUNT OF THAT USER'S USE OR MISUSE OF _____ OR SUCH THIRD-PARTY SOFTWARE OR CONTENT. SUCH LIMITATION OF LIABILITY SHALL APPLY TO PREVENT RECOVERY OF DIRECT, INDIRECT, INCIDENTAL, CONSEQUENTIAL, SPECIAL, EXEMPLARY, AND PUNITIVE DAMAGES WHETHER SUCH CLAIM IS BASED ON WARRANTY, CONTRACT, TORT (INCLUDING NEGLIGENCE), OR OTHERWISE, (EVEN IF _____ AND/OR A THIRD-PARTY SOFTWARE OR CONTENT PROVIDER HAVE BEEN ADVISED OF THE POSSIBILITY OF SUCH DAMAGES). SUCH LIMITATION OF LIABILITY SHALL APPLY WHETHER THE DAMAGES ARISE FROM USE OR MISUSE OF AND RELIANCE ON _____ AND ALL THIRD-PARTY SOFTWARE OR CONTENT MADE AVAILABLE IN CONJUNCTION WITH OR THROUGH _____, FROM INABILITY TO USE _____ AND ALL THIRD-PARTY SOFTWARE OR CONTENT MADE AVAILABLE IN CONJUNCTION WITH OR THROUGH _____, OR FROM THE INTERRUPTION, SUSPENSION, OR TERMINATION OF _____ AND ALL THIRD-PARTY SOFTWARE AND CONTENT MADE AVAILABLE IN CONJUNCTION WITH OR THROUGH _____ (INCLUDING SUCH DAMAGES INCURRED BY THIRD PARTIES). SUCH LIMITATION SHALL APPLY NOTWITHSTANDING A FAILURE OF ESSENTIAL PURPOSE OF ANY LIMITED REMEDY AND TO THE FULLEST EXTENT PERMITTED BY LAW. SOME STATES OR OTHER JURISDICTIONS DO NOT ALLOW THE EXCLUSION OR LIMITATION OF LIABILITY FOR INCIDENTAL OR CONSEQUENTIAL DAMAGES, SO THE ABOVE LIMITATIONS AND EXCLUSIONS MAY NOT APPLY TO YOU.

Miscellaneous Provisions

These Terms and Conditions will be governed by and construed in accordance with the laws of the State of _____, without giving effect to the conflict of laws provisions of _____ or your actual state or country of residence. If for any reason a court of competent jurisdiction finds any provision or portion of these Terms and Conditions to be unenforceable, the remainder of these Terms and Conditions will continue in full force and effect. These Terms and Conditions constitute the entire agreement between the parties with respect to the subject matter hereof and supersede and replace all prior or contemporaneous under-standings or agreements, written or oral, regarding such subject matter. Any waiver of any provision of these Terms and Conditions will be effective only if in writing and signed by _____ or a third party who make its software and/or content available in conjunction with or through _____.

Appendix J

Sample Privacy Policy

Thank you for visiting our Web site. This privacy policy tells you how we use personal information collected at this site. Please read this privacy policy before using the site or submitting any personal information. By using the site, you are accepting the practices described in this privacy policy. These practices may be changed, but any changes will be posted and changes will only apply to activities and information on a going forward, not retroactive basis. You are encouraged to review the privacy policy whenever you visit the site to make sure that you understand how any personal information you provide will be used.

Note: the privacy practices set forth in this privacy policy are for this Web site only. If you link to other Web sites, please review the privacy policies posted at those sites.

Collection of Information

We collect personally identifiable information, such as names, postal addresses, e-mail addresses, etc., when voluntarily submitted by our visitors. The information you provide is used to fulfill your specific request. This information is only used to fulfill your specific request, unless you give us permission to use it in another manner, for example, to add you to one of our mailing lists.

Cookie/Tracking Technology

The Site may use cookie and tracking technology depending on the features offered. Cookie and tracking technology are useful for gathering information such as browser type and operating system, tracking the number of visitors to the Site, and understanding how visitors use the Site. Cookies can also help customize the Site for visitors. Personal information cannot be collected via cookies and other tracking technology. However, if you previously provided personally identifiable information, cookies may be tied to such information. Aggregate cookie and tracking information may be shared with third parties.

Distribution of Information

We may share information with governmental agencies or other companies assisting us in fraud prevention or investigation. We may do so when (1) permitted or required by law; or, (2) trying to protect against or prevent actual or potential fraud or unauthorized transactions; or, (3) investigating fraud which has already taken place. The information is not provided to these companies for marketing purposes.

Commitment to Data Security

Your personally identifiable information is kept secure. Only authorized employees, agents, and contractors (who have agreed to keep information secure and confidential) have access to this information. All e-mails and newsletters from this site allow you to opt out of further mailings.

Privacy Contact Information

If you have any questions, concerns, or comments about our privacy policy, you may contact us using the information below:

By e-mail:
By Phone:

We reserve the right to make changes to this policy. Any changes to this policy will be posted.

Index

UNIVERSITY OF WOLVERHAMPTON
LEARNING & INFORMATION SERVICES